Ho
Pea
2019

with
World Peace Directory

66th Edition   ISSN 0957-0136

Published and distributed by

JOHN BIRD
Ground Floor Flat
56 Leathwaite Road
London SW11 6RS - UK
Tel: + 44 (0)20 7228 55??

HOUSMANS BOOKSHOP
5 Caledonian Road, Kings Cross, London N1 9DX, UK
(tel +44-20-7837 4473; email diary@housmans.com)

ISBN 978 0 85283 280 6

Editorial co-ordination — Albert Beale
Cover design & month illustrations — Phil Wrigglesworth
Dates & quotations compilation — Bill Hetherington
Historical research — Bill Hetherington
Lay-out & production — Chris Booth, graphics.coop

Directory from Housmans Peace Resource Project,
editor Albert Beale (www.housmans.info)

Copyright © 2018 Housmans Bookshop Ltd

Printed by iPrint (UK) Ltd, Leicestershire

Personal Notes

Name

Address

Telephone

JOHN BIRD
Ground Floor Flat
56 Leathwaite Road
London SW11 6RS - UK
Tel: +44 (0)20 7228 5576

EXPLANATORY NOTES

National public holidays in the UK, Republic of Ireland, Canada and the USA are noted by the abbreviation HOL, followed by abbreviations for relevant countries: ENG – England, NI – Northern Ireland, SCOT – Scotland, W – Wales; UK – United Kingdom (ie all the preceding four); IRE – Republic of Ireland; CAN – Canada; US – United States. We regret that we are not able to show holidays in other countries.

Dates of moon phases, solstices and equinoxes are for GMT; users in other time zones will find that the local date is different in some cases.

ORDERING INFORMATION

Copies of the Diary may be ordered from:
Housmans, 5 Caledonian Road, Kings Cross, London N1 9DX, UK
(tel +44-20-7837 4473; email orders@housmans.com)

Introduction

Welcome to the 66th edition of the *Housmans Peace Diary*, intended – as always since its inception – as both a resource and an inspiration for campaigners around the world.

The feature in this edition celebrates the 60th anniversary of the opening of a settled home for *Peace News*, Housmans Bookshop and the *Peace Diary* in central London. Since 1959, Peace House – as it came to be known – has also provided a base for a range of other radical organisations and causes, not only peace organisations but many other groups striving to improve the world; and many in the building have also been involved during this period in the struggles of the community around them. We tell some of their stories here.

Other anniversaries include several centenaries arising from the 1918 Armistice ending the fighting of the First World War – including the Versailles Treaty formally ending the war for the main belligerents, the planning of the League of Nations as an attempt to inhibit future wars, and the centenaries of both the Women's International League for Peace and Freedom and the International Fellowship of Reconciliation.

We also note the 80th anniversary of the final events leading to the Second World War, thereby demonstrating the tragic futility of the vaunted "War to End War", the 70th anniversary of the last known executions of conscientious objectors in Europe, the 60th anniversary of the inauguration of the European Court of Human Rights, the 50th anniversary of the recrudescence of "the troubles" in Northern Ireland, the 40th anniversary of the second wave of the British nuclear disarmament movement, the 30th anniversary of the dismantling of the Berlin Wall and the end of the Cold War, and the 20th anniversary of the final and complete abolition of the death penalty in Britain.

The *Diary* and its Directory are both non-profit services to fellow activists, depending on much voluntary labour. We welcome promotional help – leaflets are available from: **Housmans Diary Group, 5 Caledonian Road, Kings Cross, London N1 9DX, UK (fax +44-20-7278 0444; email diary@housmans.com)**. We are grateful to all who have helped in many ways over the past year.

HOUSMANS DIARY GROUP

60 years at 5 Caledonian Road

The late 1950s was a busy time for the peace movement in many parts of the world. In 1956 the Suez crisis, arising from Egypt's nationalisation of the Suez Canal, led to an Israeli/British/French invasion, aborted by US and other diplomatic intervention. Simultaneously, the Soviet Union suppressed the Hungarian uprising against oppressive government (as it had suppressed an uprising in Berlin in 1953 and would again in Czechoslovakia in 1968).

In Britain, the pacifist Peace Pledge Union (PPU) and other groups had barely recovered from activity against the Suez and Hungarian confrontations when, in April 1957, the government formally committed the country to reliance on nuclear weapons as a major component of "defence". (Phased abolition of military conscription of men, which had continued since imposition in May 1939, was a complementary compensation.)

The renewed nuclear threat (which for many had been a background issue since the actual use of two atomic bombs in 1945) led to the formation in Britain that same year of the Direct Action Committee Against Nuclear War (DAC). The following year, the more lobbying-oriented Campaign for Nuclear Disarmament (CND) was launched. The early slogan "Ban the Bomb" represented the dominant issue of the peace movement over the next few years. *Peace News* played a part in developments, as the then *PN* office hosted DAC, under whose auspices Gerald Holtom first produced his design for what became the nuclear disarmament symbol – subsequently generalised by some as "the Peace Sign" – which quickly gained worldwide recognition.

It was entirely fortuitous that, at this time, a new physical resource for the peace movement was established. In August 1958, Tom Willis, a young Anglican curate working in a poor parish in Hull, inherited £10,000. Embarrassed by such riches – his stipend amounted to

Opening ceremony of the original Housmans Bookshop in Shaftesbury Avenue, 26 October 1945. Laurence Housman is fifth from the left.
Photo: Peace News Trustees

£7 10s weekly – he decided to give it away, half to one worthy cause and the remainder divided among other objects. He asked Harry Mister, a member of the pioneering groups of both *Peace News* in 1936 and Housmans Bookshop in 1945, and still involved in both, what he would do with £5000. Harry – prescient as always in such matters – said he would buy a building as a permanent base for both enterprises, to provide long-term security, rather than spend the money on campaigning.

Peace News had been launched in June 1936 by a pacifist group in north London. From the ninth issue it was adopted by the recently established Peace Pledge Union as its regular interface with the public. *PN* operated from rented offices at 3 Blackstock Road, Finsbury Park, north London, remaining there when the PPU purchased it own offices in Bloomsbury, central London, in 1939 using the proceeds of a memorial fund for its founder, Dick Sheppard.

Housmans Bookshop has its origins in a temporary shop run by the PPU in 1936 in Ludgate Hill, in the City of London, and then from 1943 at the PPU offices. In October 1945 it became Housmans Bookshop, named in honour of pacifist author and PPU Sponsor Laurence Housman, when it was opened by him at 124 Shaftesbury Avenue, in central London, with the aim of finally having a permanent physical presence as a bookshop.

The rent was initially low because of the bomb damage to the building. But when the rent was increased after three years, the shop was unable to sustain itself and retrenched to being a small mail order business – still registered as Housmans Bookshop – operating from the *Peace News* office.

Coming together

This was the context of Harry Mister's suggestion of using the £5000 gift to buy a building for *PN* and Housmans. Ownership would permanently avoid prohibitive rental increases, and a shared building would reduce overheads. An appropriate building was found at the southern end of Caledonian Road ("the Cally"), a long and historic road heading north out of central London.

It was an 1870s five-storey (including basement) terraced building, just one block from Kings Cross station, with St Pancras and Euston stations also nearby, providing numerous bus, tube and train connections to other parts of London and the country. The ground floor shop had been a cafe (much of the glass-panelled ceiling remains to this day); before that (from the 19th century to a time between the two world wars) it had served the community by housing the local Post Office.

The cost was actually £5700, and Tom agreed to meet the whole, diverting £700 of the £5000 designated for other causes. Repairs and refurbishment were needed, with much of the basic cleaning and decoration undertaken by volunteers from the PPU's enthusiastic Pacifist Youth Action Group. Among their number was a youthful Ian Dixon, a conscientious objector (as were other male members), who – more than 40 years later – returned to No 5 to become Chair of Peace News Trustees (PNT), the formal owners of the building, bringing his decades of experience managing buildings professionally.

Although purchased in 1958, the building was not ready for regular occupation until 17 July 1959, when *Peace News* moved in, the bookshop opening in November.

Two ceremonies were held. On Friday 20 November the new Housmans Bookshop was opened, not this time by Laurence Housman, who had died earlier that year – "the Grand Old Man of pacifism" (according to *PN*), and "an incorrigible rebel" (according to War Resisters' International, of which he was sometime President) – but by Dora Dawtry, the shop manager. Present were Tom Willis, Vera Brittain (Chair of Peace News Ltd), Hugh Brock (*PN* Editor), Harry Mister and others. The following day, coinciding with the *Peace News* Christmas Bazaar held nearby, the *Peace News* office was declared open by Tom Willis unveiling a commemorative plaque – which is now on the wall behind the counter of Housmans. The meeting room – then in the front basement – was packed with people associated with the paper, and representatives of organisations served by the paper bringing greetings, including Sybil Morrison (PPU), Fenner Brockway (Central Board for Conscientious Objectors), and Max Parker (from the Fellowship of Reconciliation).

In those days, the Kings Cross area, though a bit down-at-heel in the way of many inner city sites alongside major transport interchanges, had many small businesses, and a few major ones as well. One was the headquarters of Bravingtons, the 19th century company specialising in jewellery, clocks and watches, on the south side of the same block as No 5; the block is still known to locals as the Bravingtons Block, decades after the shop closed. From the rear windows of No 5 there was the regular sight of smoke rising from steam locomotives running through a cutting under the middle of the block, hauling suburban trains from the Kings Cross lines onwards into the City of London.

At one stage, the building's architectural consultant was Sunand Prasad, son of Devi Prasad. (Devi had worked with Mohandas Gandhi, and was later General Secretary, then Chair, of War Resisters' International.) Born at Sevagram, site of Gandhi's ashram, Sunand is now a prestigious architect, who served for a period as president of the Royal Institute of British Architects.

The building has had much support over the years from people prominent (or who were to become prominent) in various areas of life. Some self-assembly furniture was only put together after help from the designer of the plane which held the world record for human-powered flight for some years – the person concerned also being the nephew of famous WW1 conscientious objector (and long-time campaigner) Fenner Brockway.

A building of this type naturally thrives on its political interconnectedness and its history – as does the Peace Diary of course. It feels appropriate, for example, that the Diary's cover designer a few years ago was – surely uniquely – born at one of the country's peace camps in the 1980s; and that the desk used by the present editor of the Diary is the one used by the editor of (the then beleaguered) *Peace News* during the Second World War.

Re-structuring

Within two years of the purchase of the building, in the name of Peace News Ltd, the formal connection between *Peace News* and PPU was broken by mutual agreement (the issue was the balance of coverage of nuclear disarmament campaigns as against wider rejection of all forms of warfare). Because of its close involvement with *PN*, Housmans remained linked to the paper. But despite the *PN* set-up's formal break with the PPU in 1961, PPU people have continued to this day to play a part in *PN*, Housmans and the building.

In 1972, the 1961 re-configuration was consolidated by a legal restructuring. A new entity, Peace News Trustees Ltd, took over from Peace News Ltd as owner of the building; two subsidiary companies, Peace News Ltd and Housmans Bookshop Ltd, were established to look after the day-to-day running of the two businesses. All are private not-for-profit companies with a commitment to the abolition of war and building a pacifist society by nonviolent means, continuing the ethos of the original Peace News company.

The role of the trustees – all of whom have always been pacifists committed to the renunciation of war – was (and is) to manage the building, and to be a "back-stop"

The Caledonian Road shop as it appeared in the 1960s. The post box which was later destroyed by an IRA bomb can still be seen.

Photo: Peace News Trustees

to ensure that the two subsidiary companies remain viable and maintain their original political purposes. The purposes being producing a pacifist publication, in the case of the publishing company, and promoting and selling relevant literature, in the case of the shop company. Relevant, for the shop, never meant just pacifist literature, or even just directly peace-related material. In line with the pacifist approach of trying to solve problems which can lead to war, as well as directly resisting any war that's threatened, the shop has promoted the widest range of progressive material that would address the world's problems and injustices. The idea is to help ameliorate some of the pressures which lead non-pacifists to think that fighting might be needed.

The ethos of the building has also included a sense of rootedness in the community in which it finds itself, supporting local initiatives and campaigns, with the shop stocking a certain amount of less political material of use to its neighbours. For most of the shop's time this has included common stationery items; it still includes things such as seasonal greetings cards, amongst the books, magazines and pamphlets which make up the bulk of the sales.

Onwards and upwards – and downwards

When setting up 5 Caledonian Road in 1959, massive wooden letters spelling PEACE NEWS were attached to the fascia above the first floor windows across the width of the building. They were a local landmark for decades until the ravages of weather made them dangerous and the ones which weren't already falling down had to be removed.

The development of the building has involved fending off attacks, as well as making positive changes. In the 1980s, property "developers" started buying up the area. Having bought the properties on each side of No 5, and the one behind, they pointed out that they had the building surrounded, and it was in the way of their scheme to knock down half the block to build a new office tower. There wasn't exactly a meeting of minds: the developers thinking that the only matter of interest to a building owner was the price; whilst Peace News Trustees took the view that the existing Kings Cross community (of which the building was a part) didn't want to see the existing homes and shops and pubs razed to the ground to build swish offices. And that was where the trustees' loyalty lay – the offers were rejected.

In the 1990s, with the new Channel Tunnel rail connection opening using a route through south London into Waterloo Station, a decision was made to augment or replace this with a faster, dedicated line into a north

London terminus. The official preference was not for the obvious choice of putting the new infrastructure on the swathes of derelict former railway land behind St Pancras and Kings Cross stations, since that would take away some of the disused public land which could otherwise be repurposed for private profit. Rather, the idea was to make an *additional* area derelict, and build the new station there. This area included No 5's block. Hence many in the building spent years involved with a local community campaign to resist such nonsense, including fighting off a parliamentary bill, until better sense prevailed and the new connection and station was built on the derelict lands after all.

The successful defence of the area led to both further problems and further opportunities. With the development of the main railway lands finally on the horizon, areas round the periphery became a magnet for property companies. Much of the ownership was further consolidated, and premises left empty. It was possible to walk from Kings Cross station to Housmans and to go past almost no premises which were open, apart from the odd burger bar. The bookshop's passing trade was decimated, the state of the area frightened off people unfamiliar with it, and for a while the shop's income took a nosedive.

But on this occasion, official policy was in tune with the preferences of those still remaining at the bottom of Cally Road – namely, the retention of small businesses (and some residential space too). And in order that the existing businesses didn't drag down the tone of the soon-to-be-revamped area, grants were available to some existing companies to tidy themselves up, providing they could raise matching funds themselves. An appeal was fronted by local MP (and Culture Secretary in the 1997 Labour government) Chris Smith, a friend of the building partly because of his status as the first "out" gay MP, and the building's history of hosting the offices of gay organisations. The appeal raised enough to release the official funds and a rebuilt shop-front (which retained the original historic pattern) resulted.

Later developments to the building – which had anyway been extended from its original state by earlier occupiers in several phases over the generations – included making functional use of a lean-to on the back roof; adding an extra room in the basement, carved out of the back yard; and a cleverly inserted mezzanine area on a landing as a bike park.

Then followed an expansion for which we do have the neighbouring property owners to thank. Putting a mansard roof on top of the existing top floor had previously been impossible for structural reasons, and because of design concerns on a terrace of historic buildings. But after a neighbouring building added a new flank wall, to allow build-out at the back and to add an extra floor of their own, No 5 was allowed to add a level too; and by linking to next door's new wall there was no risk of anything collapsing...

Most recently, in 2015, the front basement was refurbished, and expanded out into the previously disused vaults under the street (space which was always owned by the building). In Victorian times there would have been coal-holes in the pavement for deliveries of coal into the basement, but the area had been abandoned and boarded up well before the PN Group moved in. Now, re-opened, secured against damp (and with the aid of some expensive work to prop up the building in the process), an arched area, partly lit by pavement lights long set in the pavement, is an attractive feature in the expanded bookshop.

Comings and goings

Although an office for *Peace News* had been half of the original reason for buying the building in 1958, in 1974 the paper's office migrated to Nottingham (travelling by narrowboat from the canal basin a short distance up Caledonian Road). This was to take advantage of a house inherited by a well-wisher, who wanted to put it to good use, but also because most of the then staff felt that such a venture might exemplify the communitarian ethos of the paper – and might also strike a (nonviolent) blow against metrocentricity. But 15 years later, the advantages of a move back to London outweighed the disadvantages, and *PN* joined War Resisters' International (WRI) in accommodation in south London, before both moved into 5 Caledonian Road in 1994. In fact, *PN* had never wholly left, retaining a small office for a London link person on the staff during the Nottingham period.

In the era of the first Gulf War and emerging new regimes in eastern Europe, and the vicious civil wars in the Balkans, the closeness to WRI helped *PN*'s coverage of international nonviolent initiatives. The connection to WRI, and the paper's continued financial precariousness, led *PN* to agree to a period of formal "cohabitation" with WRI. From 2000 to 2005, *PN* was effectively the quarterly magazine of WRI, somewhat similarly to being the paper of the PPU from 1936 to 1961.

Meanwhile a smaller volunteer-run complementary monthly paper, *Nonviolent Action*, was published during the cohabitation period, with networking news for peace activists in Britain. Irrespective of the changes to the nature of the *PN*-WRI relationship, WRI's head office has continued in the building to this day.

War Resisters' International was founded in 1921 – out of the same political milieu which later led to *Peace News* (and the PPU) – as a means of linking pacifist and conscientious objector movements around the world. Many of these movements were inspired by those who had struggled against WW1 (of the European belligerents, Britain was the only one to recognise conscientious objection to compulsory military service, and that in an unsatisfactory way). *PN* and Housmans are affiliated to WRI, as is the PPU.

The broken rifle, symbol of the WRI

By an odd coincidence, the WRI had rented office space above the shop next door at 3 Caledonian Road for a period in the 1960s and early 1970s.

One *PN*-related project of that era took advantage of the *PN*-WRI proximity. Operation Omega, established by indefatigable *PN* staffer Roger Moody in 1971, combined nonviolent political activism with aid in the context of the Pakistan-Bangladesh conflict. One organisation supplied some desk space, the other a phone line (passed between buildings via the first floor windows).

What enabled the WRI and *PN* to move into Peace House – as 5 Cally came to be known – in 1994 was the departure of one of the then long-term occupiers, Gay Switchboard. There has always been a policy that space in the building not directly needed for the activities of the PNT Group should be let to organisations involved in issues related to or compatible with PNT's own aims and ethos. Gay Liberation Front had an early home in the basement at the start of the 1970s, at a time when the stigma of previous illegality had not yet dissipated (partial decriminalisation of male homosexuality in Britain had only happened in 1967), and accommodation was not easy for such a group to find. When London Lesbian and Gay Switchboard was established in 1974 as a 24-hour advice and support telephone service for gays and lesbians – the only one in the world outside the west coast of the USA – they were also welcomed into the building.

Switchboard expanded, taking up increasing space in the building, eventually using two floors. By 1994 they had become sufficiently recognised and established to be able to buy their own building, hence leading to the *PN* office "coming home".

Another of the most significant and long-running groups that started life in the building is the Campaign Against Arms Trade. CAAT was founded in 1974 to enable a number of peace campaigns and other organisations – which all shared a concern about the merchants of death, but (individually) had insufficient resources to do much on the issue – to pool their efforts. It has subsequently developed to become an organisation in its own right, in the meantime moving out of Peace House to larger space in another building PNT used to own.

Trials and tribulations

CAAT's period in the building will forever be remembered for its connection with the solid old Victorian pillar box that used to stand almost directly outside the shop, on account of its days as the local Post Office. The date was Monday 25 November 1974; CAAT had been launched, with one part-timer worker, the previous month. These were the days of stencils cut on a typewriter, the smell of correction fluid, and hand-cranked cylindrical duplicators. These were also the days of IRA bombing campaigns in London and elsewhere.

**► CAMPAIGN
► AGAINST
► ARMS
► TRADE**

The very first CAAT Newsletter had just been lovingly produced and stuffed into envelopes, which were all stamped and placed in the pillar box outside at around 5.30pm ready for the evening collection. An IRA unit was also posting things that night, targeting post boxes at stations. They found the post boxes at Victoria station and at Piccadilly Circus underground station, but it seems they couldn't find the box on Kings Cross station (which, it's true, was rather hidden away in a corner). So they found the nearest post box… in the next street along…

About 20 minutes after the newsletter for anti-arms trade campaigners was posted, the pillar box exploded. The heavy, round, iron top flew up almost vertically, and came down a few feet away causing a deep dent in the roof of the car of Harry Mister, then the shop manager. The charred remains of the CAAT mailing could be seen blowing in the gutter. Two passers-by were injured, neither seriously.

In 1978 the building was a deliberate bomb target, being one of four radical addresses targeted by a far-right group. The member of Housmans staff who opened the package sustained only minor injuries.

Over the last 60 years there have also been less physical assaults on the building and its denizens. And the building has often provided a base for defence campaigns for other activists under attack.

One notorious case was that of the British Withdrawal from Northern Ireland Campaign (BWNIC), founded in 1973, and launched with a full-page statement in *Peace News* signed by a large number of people. One campaign activity was producing a leaflet for people in the military. This advised soldiers who might be thinking – as BWNIC did – that sending more weapons into Northern Ireland wasn't the best way to solve the problem, that there were ways (some were legal) to try to quit the army. The leaflet didn't urge any one course of action, and pointed out the risks and penalties involved in some of the options.

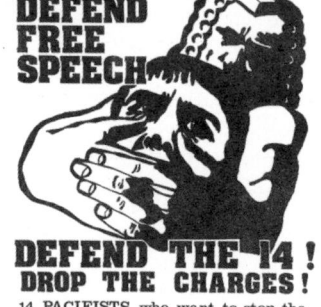

In 1974, pacifist campaigner Pat Arrowsmith, veteran of direct action campaigns and several times imprisoned, was prosecuted and convicted under the 1934 Incitement to Disaffection Act for her role in distributing the leaflets; she was sentenced to 18 months' imprisonment. Placed in an open prison, she walked out and went to 5 Caledonian Road where she let it be known that she was available for re-arrest; she was duly collected. (This is not, of course, the only time that police have turned up at the building "on business".)

> **DEFEND FREE SPEECH**
>
> **DEFEND THE 14! DROP THE CHARGES!**
>
> 14 PACIFISTS, who want to stop the war in Ireland, have been charged with conspiracy and face possible life imprisonment.
>
> DO YOU CARE? IF SO CONTACT
>
> The British Withdrawal From Northern Ireland Campaign Defence Group • 01 837 9794 •
> Box 69 %197 Kings Cross Rd. London W.C.1

Poster in support of the BWNIC 14

Rather than being the intended deterrent, Pat's imprisonment led to intensification of the leafleting at military bases around the country. This provoked the arrest of 14 further BWNIC members – including a member of *PN* staff, a former staff member, and a director of the PN company. This time the charge was of *conspiring* to contravene the Incitement Act – an easier charge to prove than the substantive offence, and one which also carried higher penalties. *PN* led the way in the defence of the 14 – including reprinting the "offending" leaflet, possession of which was allegedly illegal. After 10 weeks in the Old Bailey, the 14 won unanimous Not Guilty verdicts on all 31 counts – after a retirement, mercifully, of only 90 minutes by a jury which obviously knew repressive overkill when they saw it. (Some of them even came to the party to celebrate the acquittal.) All other pending charges under the Act were dropped; that law has never been used since.

The other most significant political trial of that era involving 5 Cally Road was the ABC [from the initials of the accused] Official Secrets case, and the associated Colonel B affair; the interlocking cases spanned 1977–79. Two journalists and a former soldier were arrested and charged – following a phone tap – after meeting to discuss SIGINT (Signals Intelligence). Information well-known to Britain's "enemies" was deemed too secret to be revealed to the public. One of the military witnesses due to give evidence as to the gravity of the harm that *might* be caused if information of that sort *were* to be revealed (not that it had been) appeared at a – normally boring and routine – preliminary hearing to give evidence to demonstrate his credentials to be an expert witness. He was so secret himself that he was allowed to be known in court just as Colonel B.

But to prove his credentials he had to give details of his military background. The sole journalist bothering to sit through this technical hearing was *PN*'s dogged court reporter, who was then able – on the basis of what was said in court, together with published military records – to name Col B as Col H A Johnstone. Hugh (as he was), the expert on secrecy who'd blown his own cover, went on to star in *Peace News*. And thus history was made, with the name appearing on walls all over the country, a constitutional crisis when the colonel was named in parliament, and all the *PN* staff appearing before the Lord Chief Justice charged with criminal contempt.

After a combined defence campaign operating at No 5, AB&C were ultimately convicted of only minor charges and not imprisoned; and *PN*'s conviction for contempt of court was subsequently overturned by the House of Lords Judicial Committee ("the Law Lords"), forerunner of the Supreme Court.

In 1995, for the first time in its history, *Peace News* was sued for libel – by a company called COPEX – because of the (true) accusation that COPEX organised trade fairs for suppliers of "security" and torture equipment. Other peace organisations who were being sued were thinking of withdrawing the torture accusation and apologising. But *PN* decided, despite the risk, to face down the company, and finally won.

Housmans faced a serious legal and financial threat in the 1990s and 2000s. Right-wing activists took advantage of the fact that British libel law allows action to be taken not just against authors, publishers, and so on, but against shops stocking allegedly offensive material. Radical bookshops around the country were being threatened for stocking *Searchlight*, an anti-fascist magazine carrying articles about named right-wingers. An attempt was made to amend the 1996 Defamation Act – a piece of tidying-up legislation then going through parliament – to provide better protection for shops (and libraries) in this situation. Two new clauses were drafted by a member of the Housmans board, and a couple of helpful MPs (one being a certain Jeremy Corbyn) formally tabled them, and spoke to them, in the Commons. But the then Tory government wouldn't accept the amendments.

After instances of the magazine being withdrawn from sale, and shops paying small-ish sums to have threatened cases dropped without going to court, two shops – Housmans and Bookmarks, another London shop – decided that resistance was in order and stood their ground in the face of the next set of writs. Housmans ended up in the High Court, where a jury found the libel nominally proved, but showed their contempt for the bringing of the case by awarding damages of £14, the value of the shop's percentage of the cover price of the seven copies that had been sold of the relevant issue. The person bringing the case was ordered to pay the shop's legal costs. When he was unable to do so, the shop narrowly avoided insolvency by raising a five-figure sum in donations to pay its legal bills. And the writs stopped coming.

Reaching out

The Housmans Peace Diary was another initiative of Harry Mister, co-founder of both *PN* and Housmans. The first (1954) edition was a commercial pocket diary with a small directory of mainly British peace organisations added; since 1984 it has been a complete publication in its own right, with more international listings, thematic material, anniversaries, quotations, and special peace-related days given the same prominence as bank holidays. Although the directory long ago spawned a more detailed on-line equivalent, an edited version of the fuller information is still included in the diary each year.

The worldwide distribution of Peace Diaries has made the Housmans name internationally known around the peace movement; and overseas visitors continue to visit the shop to search out rare items they might not otherwise find.

What's wrong with McDonald's?

Everything they don't want you to know.

Cover of the leaflet which led to the McLibel case

In recent years, the shop has hosted talks, events, book launches, and similar, as a way of enticing more people into contact with the literature it has to offer; and encouraging use of the building's meeting room by outside groups has built connections too. This has gone along with a reinforcement of the shop's role in coverage of alternative cultural, as well as alternative political, material – a synthesis which used to be commoner in *PN* in earlier times.

The building – inside and out – has appeared occasionally in films and TV programmes, including with explicit connection being made with its politics.

PN has also been responsible for outreach into the world, though in less physical ways. There have been several times in its history where its political role was pivotal, sometimes in its influence, more frequently in its role as a rallying point and support for those committed to nonviolent struggle. Often a lifeline, it sometimes became a mouthpiece for the sort of (elsewhere unpopular) movements that the building has housed or otherwise hosted, such as the direct action wing of the nuclear disarmament movement.

Awareness of *PN* in "the outside world" has been highest when it has hit the headlines, such as when it won the Granada TV "Scoop of the Year" award in 1974, for disclosing secret plans for a strike-busting "army". But awareness – and appreciation – within the peace movement has often been at its height at times such as the Falklands War, when the paper filled a lonely but essential role of a sort that had not been seen since its issues during the Second World War.

They also serve who sit in our offices

The range of organisations and campaigns which have shared the building with the shop and the *PN* staff over the years matches the breadth of issues represented in the shop's stock.

Human rights and anti-racism; sexual politics and sexual freedom and self-definition; the environment and climate change; war resistance and many varieties of peace campaigning; struggles against state power, corporate power and nuclear power; support for free speech and opposition to fundamentalism; liberation, development and anti-Zionism; public transport, cycling and planning; anti-Olympics activism – all these issues, and many more, have been worked on and struggled over by denizens of the building. Such groups sometimes had to be squeezed in, reflecting the often crowded boxes of pamphlets to be found in corners of the shop.

Notable peace campaigns on the building's roll of honour include London Region CND, Support (which worked with exiles from the USA who were resisting involvement in the Vietnam War), ForcesWatch, Network for Peace, the Catholic peace organisation Pax Christi – where Bruce Kent (later leader of CND) was to be found in his early days in the peace movement, and Peace Brigades International (organisers of nonviolent accompaniment for those at risk in repressive countries).

Some less welcome visitors to the building have been spies – both police and corporate. And one particular tenant brought more than its fair share of both. The London Greenpeace Group (which predated the British wing of the separate international Greenpeace network) is best known for publishing a leaflet critical of the McDonald's burger chain, leading to the notorious McLibel legal case. Two of the group defended themselves in the longest ever British libel trial – subsequently described as the biggest PR own goal in corporate history. During the main part of the case, in the 1990s, the presence of 7 McDonald's spies at various meetings was disclosed. Subsequently, the group has outed two undercover police spies who took part in the group; there may be more to come.

On 27 October 2017, 5 Cally was proud to be the first building to have a new type of blue plaque unveiled; these plaques are to mark places where undercover political police are known to have infiltrated campaigning and protest groups. It seems certain that, as part of the campaign around the current Public Inquiry into Undercover Policing, much more news of such activities at No 5 will be prised out – which will be a sign that the building has been doing the right things all these years.

The intention is that Peace House should continue for further decades to play its part in the local community, and in wider struggles for a better world – in particular, by continuing to house a range of groups working in the cause of peace and nonviolent revolution.

Plaque marking police surveillance, as awarded to 5 Caledonian Road

DEC-JAN

The first enemy of mankind today is the uncontrolled machine... It is destroying the human person and the foundation of good living everywhere.

Wilfred Wellock, *Peace News*

WEEK 1

MON
31

TUE
1

NEW YEAR'S DAY
(HOL UK/IRE/CAN/US)
WORLD PEACE DAY

1989 - 2 Ploughshares activists attack airplanes destined for Turkey, Woensdrecht airbase, Netherlands

WED
2

(HOL SCOT)

1879 - Wilfred Wellock, pacifist activist, born, Britain

THU
3
1969 - Police use water cannon to disperse civil rights demonstrators, Derry, Northern Ireland

FRI
4
1969 - UN Convention on Elimination of Racial Discrimination comes into force

SAT
5
1929 - Inter-American Treaty of Arbitration signed, Washington DC, USA

SUN
6
1969 - Call-up of "B Specials" (paramilitary police) authorised, Northern Ireland

JANUARY

When we pay our army and navy estimates, let us set down – so much for killing, so much for maiming, so much for making widows and orphans... We shall by this means know what we have paid our money for.

Anna Laetitia Barbauld (1743–1825)

WEEK 2

MON

7

1979 - Khmer Rouge regime ousted, Cambodia

TUE

8

1989 - Intention to destroy chemical weapons announced by USSR

WED

9

1799 - Income tax introduced to pay for war, Britain

THU
10
1989 - Parliament agrees alternative service for conscientious objectors to military service, E Germany

FRI
11
1989 - Geneva Protocol against chemical weapons reaffirmed by 149 states

SAT
12
1979 - Military conscription extended to 50/59-year-olds, Rhodesia

SUN
13
1928 - Army abolishes lance as war weapon, Britain

JANUARY

In this country a stage has been reached where little more can be done effectively to limit the liability to suffer the death penalty... the real issue is whether capital punishment should be retained or abolished.

Report of Royal Commission on Capital Punishment, 1953.
[Its terms of reference did not permit formal recommendation of abolition, but the report was widely interpreted as implicitly advocating abolition.]

WEEK 3

MON

14

1979 - Human rights demonstration, Beijing, China

TUE

MARTIN LUTHER KING DAY

15

1989 - 80 arrested in demonstration for freedom of expression and meeting, Leipzig, E Germany

WED

16

1969 - Jan Palach immolates himself in protest against Soviet invasion, Prague, Czechoslovakia

THU
17
1989 - USSR announces intention to withdraw some tactical nuclear weapons from Europe

FRI
18
1919 - Post-WWI Peace Conference opens, Versailles, France

SAT
19
1969 - Death of Victor Yates, pacifist parliamentarian, Britain

SUN
20
1949 - Royal Commission on Capital Punishment appointed, Britain

JANUARY

Contrary to popular opinion, I indicated that wars and revolutions were not disappearing, but would grow in the twentieth century to an absolutely unprecedented height, giving place to various kinds of despotism.

Pitirim A Sorokin

WEEK 4

MON
21

1889 - Pitirim Sorokin, founder, Institute for Creative Altruism, born

○ MLK DAY OBSERVED (HOL US)

TUE
22

1939 - Atom split, Cambridge University, Britain

WED
23

1809 - Baker massacre of Blackfeet, USA

THU
24
1969 - Martial law imposed, Spain

FRI
25
1919 - Peace Conference endorses project of a League of Nations, Versailles, France

SAT
26
1979 - Islamic revolutionary violence, Tehran, Iran

HOLOCAUST MEMORIAL DAY

SUN
27
1999 - Death penalty completely and permanently abolished, Britain

JAN-FEB

There must be, not a balance of power, but a community of power, not organised rivalries but an organised common peace.

President Woodrow Wilson (USA), presenting League of Nations concept, Versailles, 1919

WEEK 5

MON
28

1999 - 1000 clergy urge linking of aid to Israel & Palestine to human rights compliance, USA

TUE
29

1919 - International Federation of League of Nations Associations established, Geneva, Switzerland

WED
30

1979 - Referendum of "white" electorate approves franchising "blacks", Rhodesia

THU
31
1929 - Josef Stalin shows dictatorship by expelling rival, Leon Trotsky, USSR

FRI
1
1979 - *Peace News* criminal contempt conviction overturned by House of Lords, London, Britain

SAT
2
1989 - USSR Army evacuates from Kabul, Afghanistan

SUN
3
1919 - First international meeting to plan a League of Nations, Paris, France

FEBRUARY

The glorification of militarism in history, literature and music, the space devoted to the exploits of generals and admirals, the background of national pride in these achievements, foster in the youthful mind an entirely wrong impression of the attributes of war. The combative instinct is encouraged. At an early age toy soldiers and battleships, always a leading attraction, assist in forming a bias in favour of war.

David Davies, *The Problem of the Twentieth Century*, 1930

WEEK 6

MON

4

1899 - US troops begin civil war by firing on Filipino irregulars, Philippines

TUE

YUAN TAN
(CHINESE NEW YEAR 4717)

5

1994 - 68 killed in Serbian mortar attack on market place, Sarajevo, Bosnia-Herzegovina

WED

6

1919 - In conscious rejection of Berlin militarism, constitutional assembly convenes at "cultural capital" Weimar, Germany

THU
7
1799 - Napoleon Bonaparte establishes dictatorship as First Consul, France

FRI
8
1949 - Republic declines invitation to join NATO, Ireland

SAT
9
1929 - Litvinov Protocol for renunciation of war agreed by Estonia, Latvia, Poland, Romania, USSR

SUN
10
1939 - Japanese troops occupy Hainan Island, China

FEBRUARY

The High Contracting Parties
In order to promote international co-operation and to achieve peace and security,
By the acceptance of obligations not to resort to war...
Agree to this Covenant of the League of Nations.

Preamble to the Covenant of the League of Nations, presented to the Peace Conference, Versailles, 14 February 1919

WEEK 7

MON
11
1979 - Government cedes to Islamic theocracy, Iran

TUE
12
1979 - 59 killed in SWAPO shooting down of airliner, Rhodesia

WED
13
1989 - 5 Presidents' peace accord ends Contra intervention, Nicaragua

THU

14

1919 - League of Nations Covenant presented to Peace Conference, Versailles, France

FRI

15

1989 - Last USSR troops, occupiers since December 1979, flown from Afghanistan

SAT

16

1989 - 2 Ploughshares activists disarm shipment to India from Uddevalle, Sweden

SUN

17

1979 - China invades Vietnam

FEBRUARY

If the masses in all lands would refuse to manufacture arms, there would be no war.
George Lansbury, *My Quest for Peace*, 1938

WEEK 8

MON

18

PRESIDENTS' DAY
(HOL US)

1999 - 2 Plowshares activists gaoled for 3 & 2 years for disarming nuclear missile silo, Denver, Colorado, USA

TUE

19

1959 - Independent dual-community Cyprus guaranteed by UK, Greece & Turkey, London, Britain

WED

20

1989 - 57 publicly declare total resistance to military conscription, Spain

THU
21
1859 - George Lansbury, pacifist parliamentarian, born, Britain

FRI
22
1958 - USA supplies 60 Thor missiles to UK

SAT
23
1959 - European Court of Human Rights inaugurated, Strasbourg, France

SUN
24
1979 - Teenage boys killed in bomb attack, Armagh, Northern Ireland

FEB - MAR

We have got to face the only possible outcome of our Socialist faith: I mean the question of non-resistance to armed force. Don't let us deceive ourselves. The sacredness of human life is the mainspring of all our propaganda.
Clifford Allen, *Is Germany Right and Britain Wrong?*, 1914

WEEK 9

MON
25
1919 - Some released conscientious objectors return government pay for non-combatant services, USA

TUE
26
1989 - Hundreds demonstrate against imprisonment of total resisters to military conscription, Spain

WED
27
1929 - Litvinov Protocol for renunciation of war signed by Turkey

THU
28
1989 - Movement to Stop All Nuclear Testing founded, Nevada, USA and Semipalatinsk, USSR

NUCLEAR-FREE PACIFIC DAY

FRI
1
1999 - International Landmine Treaty comes into force

SAT
2
1989 - Government flies troop reinforcements for civil order, Caracas, Venezuela

SUN
3
1939 - Death of Clifford Allen, British No-Conscription activist, Switzerland

MARCH

I do hereby pledge myself never to enlist or enter into any army or navy, or to yield any voluntary support or sanction to the prosecution of any war, by whomsoever, for whatsoever proposed, declared or waged.

Part of "teetotal peace pledge" composed by Elihu Burritt, July 1846, to be undertaken by members of the League of Universal Brotherhood

WEEK 10

MON
4
1969 - Union of Concerned Scientists founded

TUE
5
1979 - Intention to withdraw troops from Vietnam announced by China

WED
6
ASH WEDNESDAY

1879 - Death of Elihu Burritt, nonviolent activist, USA

THU

7

1989 - Ozone Protection Treaty signed, Montreal, Canada

INT'L WOMEN'S DAY

FRI

8

1989 - City Council demands release of local resisters to military conscription, Pamplona, Spain

---

SAT

9

1989 - UN Human Rights Commission passes first resolution against anti-semitism, Geneva, Switzerland

---

SUN

10

1987 - UN Human Rights Commission recognises conscientious objection to military service as human right

MARCH

*In our approach to life, be it pragmatic or otherwise,
the ultimate truth that confronts us squarely and
unmistakably is the desire for peace, security and happiness.*
XIV Dalai Lama, *The Vegetarian Way*, 1967

WEEK 11

MON

11

1949 - Cease-fire between Israel and Transjordan signed, Rhodes, Greece

TUE

12

1919 - Fight the Famine Council holds protest rally against blockade of Central Powers, London, Britain

WED

13

1949 - Intended full economic union (BENELUX) announced by Belgium, Netherlands, Luxembourg

THU
14
1979 - 5 nuclear power stations shut because of design faults, USA

FRI
15
1939 - Germany forcibly annexes Bohemia & Moravia from Czechoslovakia

SAT
16
1939 - Slovakia unilaterally declared a "protectorate" by Germany

ST PATRICK'S DAY
(HOL NI/IRE)

SUN
17
1959 - After uprising, Dalai Lama flees to India from Tibet

MARCH

We stand for the inviolable rights of conscience in the affairs of life. We ask for liberty to serve, and if necessary to suffer, for the community and its well-being. As long as the Government denies us this right we can only take with cheerfulness and unmistakeable determination whatever penalties are imposed upon us. We want no concessions.

Manifesto of Absolutist COs at Wakefield Prison, September 1918, signed by their Advisory Committee

WEEK 12

MON
18
1939 - National Peace Council reports million signatures to petition for peace conference rather than war, UK

TUE
19
1989 - 4500 join Women Walk Home nonviolent crossing of Green Line, Cyprus

WED
20
EQUINOX

1959 - First national meeting of anti-nuclear war groups, New Zealand

THU
21
1939 - Germany occupies Memel, Lithuania

SAKA
(INDIAN NEW YEAR 1941)

FRI
22
1989 - UN Hazardous Waste Treaty signed

SAT
23
1919 - Benito Mussolini founds found Fascist movement, Milan, Italy

SUN
24
1879 - Walter Ayles, pacifist parliamentarian, born, Britain

MARCH

The angel of death has been abroad throughout the land; you may almost hear the beating of his wings.

John Bright, House of Commons, 13 February 1855, on the effects of the Crimean War

WEEK 13

MON
25
1949 - Execution reported of John Tsourakis as conscientious objector, Greece

TUE
26
1999 - First nuclear waste arrives at WIPP, Carlsbad, New Mexico, USA

WED
27
1889 - Death of John Bright, parliamentarian for peace, Rochdale, Britain

THU
28
1939 - Adolf Hitler denounces 1934 Polish-German non-aggression treaty, Berlin, Germany

FRI
29
1899 - Letter of thanks to supporters of national disarmament from Tsar Nicholas II, Russia

SAT
30
1919 - Hartal (closure of shops) in protest against Rowlatt Bills begins, New Delhi, India

BST BEGINS

SUN
31
1939 - UK & France pledge support to Poland if independence is threatened by Germany

APRIL

Satyagraha was a term I coined because I did not like the term "passive resistance"... I have also called it love force or soul force... the mighty power of truth to be set against the evil of falsehood.

Mohandas Karamchand Gandhi

WEEK 14

MON

1

1939 - Civil War ends in dictatorship of Francisco Franco, Spain

TUE

2

1979 - Mass graves of 2000 Khmer Rouge regime victims found, Cambodia

WED

3

1949 - "Pax not Pacts" rally against NATO, Trafalgar Square, London, Britain

THU
4
1949 - North Atlantic Treaty signed, Washington DC, USA

FRI
5
1979 - Pol Pot leaves for voluntary exile from Cambodia

SAT
6
1919 - Gandhi calls day of Hartal to start countrywide satyagraha campaign, India

SUN
7
1939 - Italian army occupies Albania

APRIL

I grew up with the idea that democracy is not something that you believe in, or a place to hang your hat, but it is something you do. You participate. If you stop doing it, democracy crumbles and falls apart.

Abbie Hoffman, defence statement in response to charge of occupying a Massachusetts University building in protest against CIA recruitment; acquitted, 15 April 1957

WEEK 15

MON

8

1979 - Foundation ceremony for Peace Pagoda, Milton Keynes, Britain

TUE

9

1999 - Peace groups call for end of bombing and resumption of peace process, Belgrade, Yugoslavia

WED

10

1959 - 1000 workers strike 1 hour against nuclear weapons, Stevenage, Britain

THU
11
1919 - International Labour Organisation established

FRI
12
1989 - Death of Abbie Hoffman, peace activist, USA

SAT
13
1919 - Massacre by British army of 379 nonviolent demonstrators, Amritsar, India

SUN
14
1999 - Ballistic missile test-fired, Jhelum, Pakistan

APRIL

It is honourable to die for one's country, but more honourable to die for righteousness and peace.
Max Josef Metzger

WEEK 16

WAR TAX RESISTANCE DAY (US)

MON
15

1949 - "Challenge of conscription" conference for schoolboys opens, Reading, Berkshire

TUE
16

1939 - Soviet invitation to defence pact rejected by UK

WED
17

1944 - Max Josef Metzger, pacifist priest, hanged, Brandenburg, Germany

THU
18
1689 - George Jeffreys, judge of the "Bloody Assizes" (300 hanged), dies in custody, Tower of London, Britain

○
GOOD FRIDAY
(HOL UK/CAN)

FRI
19
1839 - Neutrality of Belgium assured by Treaty of London, Britain

SAT
20
1969 - UK government agrees to make Army units available for guard duty, Northern Ireland

EASTER DAY

SUN
21
1999 - Navy officer sentenced 30 months suspended for conscientiously refusing part in NATO action against Serbia, Greece

APRIL

He had grown up in a country run by politicians who sent the pilots to man the bombers to kill the babies to make the world safe for children to grow up in.

Ursula Le Guin, *The Lathe of Heaven*

WEEK 17

MON
EASTER MONDAY
(HOL ENG/W/NI/IRE/CAN)

22

1944 - 200 blacks establish desegregation of restaurant by sit-in, Washington DC, USA

TUE

23

1909 - 30,000 Armenians massacred by fanatics over previous week, Turkey

WED

24

1994 - Dhammayietra III to Siem Reap leaves Battambang, Cambodia

ANZAC DAY (AUS)

THU
25

1994 - First World Conference on Sustainable Development of Small Island States opens, Barbados

◐

FRI
26

1994 - First non-racial Parliamentary election, S Africa

SAT
27

1939 - Re-introduction of military conscription approved in principle by Parliament, Britain

SUN
28

1979 - 284 arrested at blockade of nuclear power plant, Rocky Flats, Colorado, USA

APR-MAY

Kids know, better than grownups, what we do is more important than what we say.
Pete Seeger

WEEK 18

MON

29

1978 - 10,000 protest against nuclear power plant expansion, Windscale, Cumbria, Britain

TUE

30

1994 - Buddhist monk & nun killed as Dhammayietra IV caught in crossfire, Ping Pouey, Cambodia

WED

1

1909 - Army forms Military League to influence government, Greece

THU
2
1989 - Dismantling of Iron Curtain - frontier fence with Austria - begins, Hungary

FRI
3
1919 - Pete Seeger, peace singer, born, New York, USA

SAT
4
1989 - 30,000 students march for democracy to Tiananmen Square, Beijing, China

SUN
5
1919 - League of Red Cross Societies founded

MAY

A German woman gives her hand to a French woman, and says in the name of the German delegation that we hope we women can build a bridge from Germany to France, and from France to Germany, and that in the future we may be able to make good the wrong doings of men.

Lida Gustava Heymann, greeting Jeanne Melin on arrival at the founding conference of WILPF, Zurich, May 1919

WEEK 19

MON
MAY DAY OBSERVED
(HOL UK/IRE)

6

1919 - German South-West Africa assigned by League of Nations as mandate to S Africa

TUE

7

1999 - 3 killed in NATO bombing of Chinese Embassy, Belgrade, Yugoslavia

WED

8

1939 - Withdrawal from League of Nations by Spain

THU
9
1889 - Clifford Allen, socialist antimilitarist, born, Britain

FRI
10
1999 - Appeal for Peace Conference opens, The Hague, Netherlands

SAT
11
1989 - US sends additional 2000 combat troops to Panama

SUN
12
1919 - Inaugural Conference of Women's International League for Peace & Freedom opens, Zurich, Switzerland

MAY

CHRISTIAN AID WEEK, 12–18 MAY

Christian Aid is the aid and development wing of the Council of Churches in Britain, The week focuses on the need for helping the self-development and achievement of justice of people suffering poverty, famine and war in many parts of the world.
Contact: Christian Aid, 35–41 Lower Marsh, London SE1 7RL, Britain; tel +44-20-7620 4444; www.christianaid.org.uk

WEEK 20

MON
13
1989 - Greens gain balance of power in House of Assembly, Tasmania, Australia

TUE
14
1949 - UN Security Council invites India, Pakistan & S Africa to discuss treatment of Indian races in S Africa

WED
15
INT'L CONSCIENTIOUS OBJECTORS' DAY

1989 - S African war resisters burn call-up papers outside Embassy, London, Britain

THU
16
1828 - Death of Jonathan Dymond, peace activist, Britain

FRI
17
1919 - Women's International League for Peace and Freedom formally established, Zurich, Switzerland

○

SAT
18
1899 - First intergovernmental peace conference opens, The Hague, Netherlands

SUN
19
1918 - 44 killed in German air raid on London, Britain

MAY

Our country is the world, our countrymen are all mankind.

William Lloyd Garrison, peace activist and slavery abolitionist, Motto of his newspaper, *The Liberator*

WEEK 21

MON

20

1989 - To quell pro-democracy movement, martial law ordered, Beijing, China

TUE

21

1944 - Plebiscite votes to cancel union with Denmark, Iceland

WED

22

1939 - Alliance formed by Italy and Germany

THU
23
1929 - Samdech Son Maha Ghosananda, Buddhist pacifist, born, Cambodia

INT'L WOMEN'S DAY FOR DISARMAMENT

FRI
24
1879 - Death of William Lloyd Garrison, nonviolent activist, New York, USA

SAT
25
1939 - Anglo-Polish Treaty signed, London, Britain

SUN
26
1949 - Apartheid adopted as formal state policy, S Africa

MAY-JUN

Resist much. Obey little.
Walt Whitman

WEEK 22

MEMORIAL DAY (US)
(HOL UK/US)

MON
27

1939 -
Reintroduction of
military conscription
comes into force,
Britain

TUE
28

1958 - Ammon
Hennacy ends
40-day anti-nuclear
test fast, USA

WED
29

1968 - Poor People's
Campaign begins,
Washington DC,
USA

THU
30
1989 - Million defying martial law occupy Tiananmen Square, Beijing, China

FRI
31
1819 - Walt Whitman, poet of democracy and peace, born, USA

SAT
1
1919 - Ernest Rutherford publishes findings on splitting the atom, Cambridge, Britain

SUN
2
1979 - March from Aldermaston arrives at Faslane Polaris Base, Scotland

JUNE

There is no hope for an eradication of war but by an absolute and total abandonment of it.

Jonathan Dymond, *The Pacific Principles of the New Testament*

WEEK 23

MON
● (HOL IRE)

3

1989 - "People's Army", with tanks, moves towards Tiananmen Square, Beijing, China

TUE

INT'L DAY FOR CHILDREN AS VICTIMS OF WAR

4

1989 - Massacre of 2000 students demonstrating for human rights, Tiananmen Square, Beijing, China

WED

5

1949 - *Peacemaker* first published, USA

THU
6
1919 - Finland declares war on Bolshevik Russia

FRI
7
1979 - First direct elections to European Parliament

SAT
8
1999 - NATO bombing campaign ceases, Serbia

SUN
9
1969 - Native Americans occupy Alcatraz Island, California, USA

JUNE

I can feel the sufferings of millions and yet, if I look into the heavens I think it will come right, that this cruelty, too, will end, and that peace and tranquillity will return again.

Anne Frank, *Diary*, 1942–44, Amsterdam

WEEK 24

MON
10
1918 - Protest against terms of Versailles Peace Conference by Austria

TUE
11
1994 - Prairie Peace Park opened, Nebraska, USA

WED
12
1929 - Anne Frank, diarist & Holocaust victim, born, Frankfurt, Germany

THU
13
1944 - First German V1 flying bomb launched against Britain

FRI
14
1949 - Provision to Greece of nuclear information and ballistic missiles agreed by USA

SAT
15
1989 - USSR President Mikhail Gorbachev comments that Berlin Wall could one day disappear, W Germany

SUN
16
1989 - Five executed leaders of 1956 uprising are ceremonially re-interred, Hungary

JUNE

We are committed to suffering that will lead us to freedom - as it has been the lot of all oppressed people from time immemorial. What we are determined not to do is to acquiesce in a status quo that makes us semi-slaves in our own country.

Albert Lutuli, 1899–1967, nonviolent anti-apartheid activist and Nobel Peace laureate

WEEK 25

MON
17
1919 - German delegates, finally invited to Peace Conference, are stoned by crowd, Versailles, Paris, France

TUE
18
1959 - Nonviolent invasion of Thor missile base, Great Dalby, Britain

WED
19
1988 - Military coup d'état, Haiti

THU
20
1919 - Philip Scheidemann resigns as Chancellor rather than sign Versailles Peace Treaty, Germany

SOLSTICE

FRI
21
1939 - Government restricts business activities of Jews in Bohemia/Moravia, incorporated in Germany

SAT
22
1919 - National assembly authorises signature of Versailles Peace Treaty, Weimar, Germany

SUN
23
1978 - 12 missionaries working for conciliation & peace massacred by dissidents, Pentecostal Church, Umtali, Rhodesia

JUNE

So few people realise that war preparedness never leads to peace, but that it is, indeed, the road to universal slaughter.

Emma Goldman

WEEK 26

MON

24

1859 - Thousands lie injured and unattended after defeat of Austria (leading to founding of Red Cross), Solferino, Italy

TUE

25

1969 - Senate resolution calling on President not to commit troops overseas without Congressional approval, USA

WED

INT'L DAY FOR VICTIMS OF TORTURE

26

1959 - Albert Lutuli calls for international boycott of goods from South Africa

THU
27
1869 - Emma Goldman, feminist antimilitarist, born, Kovno, Russia

FRI
28
1919 - Peace Treaty confirming end of WWI signed, Versailles, France

SAT
29
1889 - General World Peace Congress opens, Trocadero, Paris, France

SUN
30
1989 - Court seizes £4000 withheld war taxes from Peace Pledge Union's bank account, Britain

JULY

The Peace Pledge Union is no longer willing to have its money conscripted for war purposes, and seeks to put into action the pledge which its members sign.

Peace Pledge Union, November 1982

NUCLEAR POWER? NO THANKS

WEEK 27

MON
CANADA DAY
(HOL CAN)

1

1879 - Leon Jouhaux, trade unionist and Nobel peace laureate (1951), born, France

TUE

2

1939 - Women's Auxiliary Air Force formed, Britain

WED

3

1988 - US warship kills 290 civilians by shooting down Iranian airplane, Persian Gulf

INDEPENDENCE DAY
(HOL US)

THU
4
1919 - Army demobilised, France

FRI
5
1989 - Col Oliver North given suspended sentence and fined over Iran-Contra scandal, USA

SAT
6
1959 - Committee for Nonviolent Action demonstrates against construction of first missile site, Omaha, Nebraska, USA

SUN
7
1858 - Niels Petersen, teacher and peace activist, born, Denmark

JULY

I am pleased at the [French] Revolution, particularly on this account, that it makes the working classes see their real importance, and those who despise them see it, too.
William Cobbett, 1763–1835

WEEK 28

MON

8

1898 - May Picqueray, antimilitarist anarchist, born, Larzac, France

TUE

9

1979 - Referendum approves world's first nuclear-free constitution, Belau, Micronesia

WED

10

1849 - Peace negotiations between Denmark and Prussia

THU
11
1859 - Peace between Austria and Savoy signed, Villafranca, Lombardy

(HOL NI)

FRI
12
1919 - Resumption of commercial relations with Germany authorised by Britain & France

SAT
13
1878 - "Eastern question" settled by signing of Treaty of Berlin

DAY OF COMMEMORATION (IRE)

SUN
14
1789 - Release of prisoners begins Revolution, Bastille, Paris, France

JULY

To understand is hard. Once one understands, action is easy.
Sun Yat-Sen [Sun Zhong Shan], 1867-1925

WEEK 29

MON
15
2016 - Failed military coup d'état (150 civilians killed) evokes authoritarian governmental backlash, Turkey

TUE
16
1949 - Chinese Nationalist forces withdraw to Formosa

WED
17
1979 - After Sandinista uprising, dictator Anastasio Somoza leaves for voluntary exile, Nicaragua

THU
18
1994 - Cease-fire signed, Rwanda

FRI
19
1919 - Peace celebrations, Britain

SAT
20
1944 - Failure of bomb attempt to kill Adolf Hitler leads to execution of 5000 dissidents, Germany

SUN
21
1938 - Raymond Marcano gaoled 2 years for refusing military reserve service, Lille, France

JULY

We insist that ends we believe to be good can justify means which we know to be abominable; we go on believing, against all the evidence, that those bad means can achieve the good ends we desire.

Aldous Huxley, *Ends and Means*, 1937

WEEK 30

MON
22
1979 - Israel bombs 5 towns, Lebanon

TUE
23
1994 - Military coup d'état, Gambia

WED
24
1979 - Government announces test borings for reception of nuclear waste, Britain

THU
25
1994 - Declaration of end of hostilities by Israel & Jordan signed, Washington DC, USA

FRI
26
1894 - Aldous Huxley, pacifist author, born, Godalming, Britain

SAT
27
1979 - 2500 Ugandans expelled by Kenya

SUN
28
1944 - Austrian Walter Krajnic shot for refusing to kill French hostages, Les Angles, France

JUL - AUG

If only I had known, I should have become a watchmaker.
Albert Einstein, on his contribution to research leading to nuclear weapons (quoted, *New Statesman*, 16 April 1965)

WEEK 31

MON
29
1979 - 4 killed by ETA bombs, Madrid, Spain

TUE
30
1989 - 39,000 march against second-class status for Moldavians, Kishinev, Moldavia, USSR

WED
31
1994 - UN Security Council authorises "all necessary means" to remove military regime, Haiti

THU
1
1944 - Rising begins against German occupation, Warsaw, Poland

FRI
2
1939 - Albert Einstein alerts President Franklin Roosevelt to possibility of atomic bomb, USA

SAT
3
1949 - Statute of Council of Europe comes into force

SUN
4
1919 - During police strike, army used to arrest 300 rioters, Liverpool, Britain

AUGUST

There in the place where our city was destroyed
And we buried the ashes of the ones that we loved,
There the green grass grows and the white waving weeds:
Deadly the harvest of two atom bombs.
Brothers and sisters, we must watch and take care
That the third atom bomb never comes.

Ishigo Astu, *Furuato*
[English by Ewan McCall, as *Native Land*]

WEEK 32

MON

(HOL SCOT/IRE)

5

1979 - Truce between Polisario guerillas and government, Mauritania

TUE

HIROSHIMA DAY

6

1949 - International commemoration of Hiroshima bombing becomes established as Hiroshima Day

WED

☽

7

1959 - Chinese troops invade north east India

THU
8
1949 - First meeting of Council of Europe, Strasbourg, France

NAGASAKI DAY

FRI
9
1989 - 22 arrested in protest at nuclear test site, Nevada, USA

SAT
10
1979 - Members of 4th International Nonviolent March for Demilitarisation demonstrate in Warsaw, Poland

SUN
11
1949 - Israeli-Palestinian Armistice agreed, Rhodes, Greece

AUGUST

What is impressive is that as word follows word the effect is weaker, while with each stroke of the pick the effect is stronger. One gets disgusted with words; one does not get disgusted with creative service.

Pierre Ceresole, explaining the motto, Deeds not Words, of International Voluntary Service for Peace, sometimes known as "pick and shovel peacemakers", which he founded in reaction to WW1.

WEEK 33

MON
12
1949 - Convention on protection of war victims signed, Geneva, Switzerland

TUE
13
1969 - USSR troops cross border, Xinjiang, China

WED
14
1969 - British troops again deployed, Northern Ireland

THU
15
1969 - Reserves mobilised and troops moved near border, Republic of Ireland

FRI
16
1819 - 11 killed in cavalry charge at political reform meeting, St Peter's Fields, Manchester, Britain

SAT
17
1879 - Pierre Ceresole, founder of IVSP, born, Switzerland

SUN
18
1982 - 13 members of 7th International March deported from Spain under military escort after climbing over gate from Gibraltar

AUGUST

Let my people go.
Paul Robeson, 1898-1976

WEEK 34

MON
19
1969 - British Army assumes responsibility for security, Northern Ireland

TUE
20
1619 - First arrival of African slaves, North America

WED
21
1959 - On withdrawal of Iraq, Baghdad Pact becomes Central Treaty Organisation, based Ankara, Turkey

THU
22
1959 -
Demonstration at
Thor missile site,
Polebrook, Norfolk,
Britain

FRI
23
1939 - Neutral
European states call
for peace in face of
impending war, Oslo,
Norway

SAT
24
1949 - North
Atlantic Treaty
comes into force

SUN
25
1939 - Britain and
Poland sign treaty of
mutual assistance,
London, Britain

AUG -SEPT

Our... duty is to restore the oppressed nations to independence. But what independence? I say, internal as well as external. Independence from the usurer and aristocrat within, as well as from the Czar or Emperor without.

Ernest Jones, Chartist, on Poland at the time of the Crimean War, 1854-56

WEEK 35
(HOL E/W/NI)

MON
26
1989 - Last of Vietnamese troops withdrawn from Cambodia

TUE
27
1969 - Bob Eaton gaoled 3 years for refusing selective draft, Philadelphia, USA

WED
28
1944 - Death of Dorothy Evans, feminist pacifist, Britain

THU
29
1994 - Russian troops withdraw from Estonia

FRI
30
1999 - Referendum vote to end illegal Indonesian annexation, East Timor

SAT
31
1939 - Government mobilises fleet, Britain

SUN
1
1939 - Germany invades Poland - beginning of WW2

SEPTEMBER

CAMPAIGN AGAINST ARMS TRADE

I'm certain that if a minority of women in every country would clearly express their convictions, they would find they spoke not for themselves alone but for those men for whom war has been a laceration – an abdication of the spirit.

Jane Addams, Nobel Peace laureate, 1931

WEEK 36

MON
2
LABOUR DAY (HOL CAN/US)

1939 - Full-time military conscription re-introduced, Britain

TUE
3
1939 - Britain and France declare war on Germany

WED
4
1944 - Ceasefire between Finland and USSR

THU
5
1929 - European federal union proposed by Aristide Briand, France

FRI
6
1939 - Exchange of bombing raids by Britain and Germany

SAT
7
1929 - Foundation stone laid of Palais des Nations, Geneva, Switzerland

SUN
8
1994 - Last Russian troops leave Poland

SEPTEMBER

CAMPAIGN AGAINST ARMS TRADE

Nowhere have women been more excluded from decision-making than in the military and foreign affairs. When it comes to the military and questions of nuclear disarmament, the gender gap becomes the gender gulf.

Eleanor Smeal, National Organisation of Women, USA

WEEK 37

MON
9
1969 - Israel attacks Egyptian military bases south of Suez

TUE
10
MUHARRAM
(ISLAMIC NEW YEAR 1441)

1944 - Vichy legislature abolished by provisional government, France

WED
11
1989 - New Forum opposition group created, East Germany

THU
12
1944 - Armistice with UK, USA & USSR signed by Romania

FRI
13
1959 - Nuclear Disarmament Week begins, Britain

SAT
14
1949 - Construction begins of UN Headquarters, New York, USA

SUN
15
1939 - August Dickman, conscientious objector, executed by firing squad, Germany

SEPTEMBER

CAMPAIGN AGAINST ARMS TRADE

For the sake of children everywhere, I appeal to men to stop this war.

Mary Taylor, the placard she carried on her walk from Liverpool to London, September 1939

WEEK 38

MON
16
1939 - Mary Taylor begins walk to London appealing to men to stop the war, Liverpool, Britain

TUE
17
1939 - USSR invades Poland

WED
18
1979 - Vote to abolish corporal punishment in schools, Inner London Education Authority, Britain

THU
19
1939 - British air force begins leaflet raids on Germany

FRI
20
1949 - USSR lifts road & rail blockade, West Berlin

INT"L DAY OF PEACE

SAT
21
1944 - National Peace Council launches national petition for a constructive peace, Britain

◐
INT'L DAY OF PRAYER FOR PEACE

SUN
22
1949 - First atomic bomb test by USSR

SEPTEMBER

CAMPAIGN AGAINST ARMS TRADE

We believe that there is of necessity something in the soul of every human being, and that we have to have profound reverence for it, and if that thing is burning in ourselves we can call it out in others.

Gerald Heard, in public discussion on the cause of peace, December 1936

WEEK 39

MON
EQUINOX

23

1999 - Attack on separatist Republic of Chechnya launched by Russia

TUE

24

1944 - Decree integrates Resistance into Army, France

WED

25

1944 - All remaining males 16-60 conscripted to home defence Volksturm, Germany

INT'L DAY FOR TOTAL
ELIMINATION OF NUCLEAR
WEAPONS

THU
26
1989 - Vietnamese troops withdraw from Cambodia

FRI
27
1919 - British troops withdrawn from Archangel, Russia

●

SAT
28
1919 - Mob lynches black man and burns down courthouse, Omaha, Nebraska, USA

ROSH HASHANAH
(JEWISH NEW YEAR 5780)

SUN
29
1939 - Partition of Poland between Germany & USSR signed, Moscow, USSR

SEPT-OCT

The hellish instruments of war must be smoked out while there is still peace. The trade unions must be compelled not to allow their old resolutions to fade in their files, and they will have to go beyond their old resolutions.

Carl von Ossietzky, *Die Weltbuhne*, 19 February 1929

WEEK 40

MON
30

1939 - Mary Taylor arrives from Liverpool appealing to men to stop the war, London

TUE
1

1989 - 7000 refugees permitted to go to West Germany by East Germany

WED
2

INT'L DAY OF NONVIOLENCE

1869 - Mohandas Gandhi born, India

THU
3
1889 - Carl von Ossietzky, Nobel Peace laureate, born, Germany

FRI
4
1944 - Court martial gaols William Douglas-Home 1 year for refusing to attack civilians, Le Havre, France

SAT
5
1789 - Declaration of the Rights of Man & the Citizen promulgated, France

SUN
6
1889 - Gerald Heard, pacifist author, born, Britain

OCTOBER

To establish a world order based on love, it is incumbent on those who believe in this principle to accept it fully, both for themselves and in their relation to others, and to take the risks involved in doing so in a world which does not as yet accept it.

Part of the Basis of the Fellowship of Reconciliation, 1914, carried forward into the International Fellowship of Reconciliation, 1919

WEEK 41

MON

7

1944 - Conclusion of 4-Power Conference on post-WW2 settlement of Europe, Dumbarton Oaks, USA

TUE

8

1939 - Germany incorporates western Poland into Reich

WED

9

1919 - International Fellowship of Reconciliation founded, Bilthoven, Netherlands

THU
10
1989 - 500,000 demonstrate against regime, East Germany

FRI
11
1989 - Border with East Germany opened, and acceptance of refugees, Poland

SAT
12
1899 - Boers open war on Britain by invading Natal & Cape, South Africa

SUN
13
1999 - Senate rejects Comprehensive Test Ban Treaty, USA

OCTOBER

WEEK OF PRAYER FOR WORLD PEACE 12–19 OCTOBER

The week leading towards UN Day was established in 1974 as an opportunity for people of all faiths to focus on peace throughout the world.

Contact: Week of Prayer for World Peace, c/o 126 Manor Green Road, Epsom, Surrey, KT19 8LN, Britain; tel +44-1628-530309; www.weekofprayerforworldpeace.com

WEEK 42

MON 14

THANKSGIVING (CAN)
COLUMBUS DAY (US)
(HOL CAN/US)

1939 - Women's peace march, Liverpool, Britain

TUE 15

1969 - 2 million participate in first moratorium against Vietnam War, USA

WED 16

1989 - State senate votes against Star Wars, Massachusetts, USA

INT'L DAY FOR ERADICATION OF POVERTY

THU
17
1944 - German troops occupy Buda, Hungary

FRI
18
1989 - In response to popular uprising, Erich Honecker resigns Presidency, East Germany

SAT
19
1989 - UK and Argentina formally end hostilities of 1982 Falklands War, Madrid, Spain

SUN
20
1959 - Inter-American Nuclear Energy Commission holds first meeting, Washington DC, USA

OCTOBER

ONE WORLD WEEK 20–27 OCTOBER

Based on UN Day, One World Week is intended to encourage people to link with international issues through taking up overseas concerns in church, trade union, school, etc.
Contact: One World Week, 35-39 London Street, Reading, Berkshire, RG1 4PS, Britain; tel +44-118-939 4933; www.oneworldweek.org

WEEK 43

MON

21

1959 - Call for restoration of civil & religious liberties in Tibet, UN General Assembly

TUE

22

1949 - Each annual session to be opened with Minute of Silence, UN General Assembly, New York, USA

WED

23

1979 - Vaclav Havel & 5 other dissidents convicted of subversion, Prague, Czechoslovakia

UNITED NATIONS DAY

THU
24
1909 - Agreement to maintain status quo in Balkans signed by Russia & Italy, Racconigi, Italy

FRI
25
1909 - Japan imposes dictatorship in Korea

SAT
26
1945 - Laurence Housman opens Housmans Bookshop, Shaftesbury Avenue, London, Britain

BST ENDS

SUN
27
2017 - Unveiling of "Undercover police spies operated here" plaque, Peace House, London, Britain

OCT-NOV

INTERNATIONAL DISARMAMENT WEEK 24–30 OCTOBER

Called for in the Final Document of the first UN Special Session on Disarmament in 1978, Disarmament Week is a time for pressing on all governments and arms manufacturers the urgent need for disarmament of all kinds of weapons.
Contact: Your nearest national UNA.

WEEK 44

MON
28
1939 - Popular demonstrations against Nazi occupation mark Independence Day, Prague, Czechoslovakia

TUE
29
1919 - First session of International Labour Organisation

WED
30
1989 - Half million march for reform, Leipzig, East Germany

THU
31
1939 - Women's peace march, Holborn, London, Britain

FRI
1
1889 - Philip Noel-Baker, disarmament advocate, born, Britain

SAT
2
1989 - East Germans take refuge in West German Embassy, Prague, Czechoslovakia

SUN
3
1989 - New President, Egon Krenz, purges Politburo hardliners, East Germany

NOVEMBER

Defeatism about the desirability of plans for disarmament and ordered peace has been the most calamitous of all the errors made by democratic governments in modern times.

Philip Noel-Baker, *The Arms Race*, 1958

WEEK 45

MON

4

1989 - Million march for reform, East Berlin, East Germany

TUE

5

1944 - Soviet tanks enter Budapest, Hungary

WED

6

1989 - Half a million march in Leipzig & other cities, East Germany

THU
7
1919 - Allied Supreme Council demands removal of Romanian troops from Hungary

FRI
8
1969 - Egyptian navy shells Israeli positions, Sinai

SAT
9
1989 - Wall opened in response to nonviolent action, Berlin

REMEMBRANCE DAY (UK)
WORLD SCIENCE DAY FOR PEACE & DEVELOPMENT

SUN
10
1959 - Apartheid in South Africa and racial discrimination anywhere condemned by UN General Assembly

NOVEMBER

I am not proud of the fact that my son helped to bomb Vietnam… I would like to go up to each one of them [the Vietnamese people] and hold their hands in mine and say… I am sorry about the bombing of their country, and I am terribly sorry that Jim was part of it.

Virginia Warner, mother of war prisoner, Winter Soldier investigation, January 1971

WEEK 46

MON

11

MARTINMAS
REMEMBRANCE DAY (CAN)
VETERANS' DAY (US)
(HOL CAN/US)

1919 - Armistice/Remembrance Day first observed, Britain

TUE

12

1979 - Peace Forum held by UNESCO, Paris, France

WED

13

1839 - Liberty (first anti-slavery) Party, founded, USA

THU
14
1989 - Government relaxes restrictions on travel to West, Czechoslovakia

FRI
15
1969 - Recitation of list of Vietnam War dead takes 36 hours, White House, Washington, USA

SAT
16
1989 - 6 priests & their housekeeper murdered by death squad, El Salvador

SUN
17
1989 - Mass demonstration leads to downfall of regime, Wenceslas Square, Prague, Czechoslovakia

NOVEMBER

Peace News – For Nonviolent Revolution
Long-time masthead

WEEK 47

MON
18
1929 - Japan begins invasion of Manchuria, China

TUE
19
1919 - Senate refuses to ratify Versailles Treaty, leading to exclusion from League of Nations, Washington DC, USA

WED
UNIVERSAL CHILDREN'S DAY
20
1959 - Housmans Bookshop opened in its new premises, 5 Caledonian Road, London, Britain

THU
21
1959 - 5 Caledonian Road inaugurated as Peace News office & peace resource centre, London, Britain

FRI
22
1963 - Death of Aldous Huxley, pacifist writer, USA

SAT
23
1989 - 300,000 march in Prague, Czechoslovakia

SUN
24
1989 - Fall of Communist regime after nonviolent action, Czechoslovakia

NOV-DEC

The Devil has won for us a... short term victory – on the material plane. On the spiritual plane we can expect nothing but defeat.
Laurence Housman, *Peace News*, 31 August 1945, reflecting on the use of atomic bombs against Japan.

WEEK 48

MON
25

INT'L DAY FOR ELIMINATION OF VIOLENCE AGAINST WOMEN

1974 - Anti-arms trade mailing blown up in post box outside Peace House, London, Britain

TUE
26

1969 - Ballot for military draft established, USA

WED
27

1979 - Trial of total resister CO Jean Fabre sets him free, France

THANKSGIVING
(HOL US)

THU

28

1994 - Referendum
rejects EU
membership, Norway

FRI

29

1959 - 1000 march
to Oxford from
Brize Norton USAF
base, Britain

SAT

30

1939 - USSR invades
Finland

ADVENT SUNDAY
PRISONERS FOR PEACE DAY

SUN

1

1959 - Demilitarised
zone declared for
whole Antarctica

DECEMBER

Unity for survival. No nuclear imperialism. Africa for Africans.

Slogans carried by Sahara Protest Team against French nuclear tests, 1959–60

WEEK 49

MON

2

1989 - Presidents of USA & USSR declare end of Cold War

TUE

3

1919 - 1st regular meeting of International Federation of League of Nations Associations, Paris, France

WED

4

1969 - 15 killed in UVF bombing of bar, Belfast, N Ireland

THU
5
1989 - Plan announced to transfer management of Atomic Weapons Establishment to private contractor, Britain

FRI
6
1959 - Sahara Protest Team against French nuclear tests leaves Accra, Ghana

SAT
7
1988 - President Mikhail Gorbachev announces to UN unilateral reduction of armed forces by 500,000, USSR

SUN
8
1988 - 12 arrested for hammering on cruise missile bunkers, Woensdrecht, Netherlands

DECEMBER

It gets harder for any of us to rest comfortably on a king-sized bed of missiles.

Ellen Goodman, *The Boston Globe*, USA, November 1981

WEEK 50

MON

9

1961 - Simultaneous demonstrations against nuclear weapons by 5,000 people at 3 bases and 4 town centres, Britain

TUE

HUMAN RIGHTS DAY

10

1999 - Médecins Sans Frontières awarded Nobel Peace Prize, Oslo, Norway

WED

11

1899 - Henri Roser, pacifist pastor, born, France

THU
12
1979 - NATO decides to install Pershing II & cruise missiles in western Europe

FRI
13
1989 - President F W de Klerk & Nelson Mandela meet, S Africa

SAT
14
1979 - UN establishes University for Peace, Costa Rica

SUN
15
1959 - 6 gaoled 2 months for organising demonstration at Harrington missile base, Britain

DECEMBER

The campaign is designed not only to give expression to women's revolt against war, but to their demand that the Government should, at the earliest possible moment, use the method of negotiation to secure a lasting peace.

Mary Gamble, *Peace News*, on the Women's Peace Campaign, 1939

WEEK 51

MON
16
1939 - Women's Peace Campaign rally, Central Hall, Westminster, Britain

TUE
17
1989 - Demonstration for civil liberty, Timisoara, Romania

WED
18
1929 - Arndt Pekurinen begins hunger strike for conscientious objector status, Finland

THU
19
1939 - Henri Roser, secretary of IFOR, gaoled 4 years as conscientious objector, France

FRI
20
1989 - USA invades Panama

SAT
21
1969 - 700 supporters visit gaoled war resisters, Allenwood, Pennsylvania, USA

SOLSTICE

SUN
22
1989 - Brandenburg Gate reopened, Berlin

DECEMBER

Every nation sincerely desires peace, and all nations pursue courses which, if persisted in, must make peace impossible.

Norman Angell

GREENPEACE London

WEEK 52

MON
23
1989 - First UN Calendar for Peace published by UNAs of USA & UK

TUE
24
1869 - Henrietta Holst, nonviolent theorist, born, Germany

WED
25
CHRISTMAS DAY
(HOL UK/IRE/CAN/US)

1949 - Second session of World Pacifist Meeting begins, Sevagram, India

● ST STEPHEN'S DAY
(HOL UK/IRE/CAN)

THU
26
1872 - Norman Angell, peace advocate, born, Britain

FRI
27
1979 - USSR invades Afghanistan

HOLY INNOCENTS' DAY

SAT
28
1999 - 300 in Global Youth Meet discuss peace, cultural harmony and human rights, Kathmandu, Nepal

SUN
29
1989 - Vaclav Havel elected President, Czechoslovakia

DEC-JAN

War and preparations for war must be judged in moral perspective, perspective derived from centuries of collective experience and expressed in our great religious traditions. These traditions agree with striking similarity and clarity that we must neither contemplate nor prepare for the killing of innocent persons.

US Fellowship of Reconciliation

WEEK 1 (2020)

MON
30
1944 - Death of Romain Rolland, pacifist writer, France

TUE
31
NEW YEAR'S EVE

1915 - American Fellowship of Reconciliation founded, USA

WED
1
NEW YEAR'S DAY
(HOL UK/IRE/CAN/US)
WORLD PEACE DAY

2020 - Suggested dates (and quotations) for future diaries welcome anytime

(HOL SCOT)

THU
2

◐

FRI
3

SAT
4

SUN
5

Forward Planner 2020

	January		February		March	
Mon						
Tue						
Wed	1	1				
Thu	2					
Fri	3					
Sat	4		1			
Sun	5		2		1	
Mon	6	2	3	6	2	10
Tue	7		4		3	
Wed	8		5		4	
Thu	9		6		5	
Fri	10		7		6	
Sat	11		8		7	
Sun	12		9		8	
Mon	13	3	10	7	9	11
Tue	14		11		10	
Wed	15		12		11	
Thu	16		13		12	
Fri	17		14		13	
Sat	18		15		14	
Sun	19		16		15	
Mon	20	4	17	8	16	12
Tue	21		18		17	
Wed	22		19		18	
Thu	23		20		19	
Fri	24		21		20	
Sat	25		22		21	
Sun	26		23		22	
Mon	27	5	24	9	23	13
Tue	28		25		24	
Wed	29		26		25	
Thu	30		27		26	
Fri	31		28		27	
Sat			29		28	
Sun					29	
Mon					30	14
Tue					31	

Forward Planner 2020

	April		**May**		**June**	
Mon					1	23
Tue					2	
Wed	1				3	
Thu	2				4	
Fri	3		1		5	
Sat	4		2		6	
Sun	5		3		7	
Mon	6	15	4	19	8	24
Tue	7		5		9	
Wed	8		6		10	
Thu	9		7		11	
Fri	10		8		12	
Sat	11		9		13	
Sun	12	Easter	10		14	
Mon	13	16	11	20	15	25
Tue	14		12		16	
Wed	15		13		17	
Thu	16		14		18	
Fri	17		15		19	
Sat	18		16		20	
Sun	19		17		21	
Mon	20	17	18	21	22	26
Tue	21		19		23	
Wed	22		20		24	
Thu	23		21		25	
Fri	24		22		26	
Sat	25		23		27	
Sun	26		24		28	
Mon	27	18	25	22	29	27
Tue	28		26		30	
Wed	29		27			
Thu	30		28			
Fri			29			
Sat			30			
Sun			31			

Forward Planner 2020

	July		August		September	
Mon						
Tue					1	
Wed	1				2	
Thu	2				3	
Fri	3				4	
Sat	4		1		5	
Sun	5		2		6	
Mon	6	28	3	32	7	37
Tue	7		4		8	
Wed	8		5		9	
Thu	9		6		10	
Fri	10		7		11	
Sat	11		8		12	
Sun	12		9		13	
Mon	13	29	10	33	14	38
Tue	14		11		15	
Wed	15		12		16	
Thu	16		13		17	
Fri	17		14		18	
Sat	18		15		19	
Sun	19		16		20	
Mon	20	30	17		21	39
Tue	21		18	34	22	
Wed	22		19		23	
Thu	23		20		24	
Fri	24		21		25	
Sat	25		22		26	
Sun	26		23		27	
Mon	27	31	24	35	28	40
Tue	28		25		29	
Wed	29		26		30	
Thu	30		27			
Fri	31		28			
Sat			29			
Sun			30			
Mon			31	36		

Forward Planner 2020

	October		November		December	
Mon						
Tue					1	
Wed					2	
Thu	1				3	
Fri	2				4	
Sat	3				5	
Sun	4		1		6	
Mon	5	41	2	45	7	50
Tue	6		3		8	
Wed	7		4		9	
Thu	8		5		10	
Fri	9		6		11	
Sat	10		7		12	
Sun	11		8		13	
Mon	12	42	9	46	14	51
Tue	13		10		15	
Wed	14		11		16	
Thu	15		12		17	
Fri	16		13		18	
Sat	17		14		19	
Sun	18		15		20	
Mon	19	43	16	47	21	52
Tue	20		17		22	
Wed	21		18		23	
Thu	22		19		24	
Fri	23		20		25	
Sat	24		21		26	
Sun	25		22		27	
Mon	26	44	23	48	28	53
Tue	27		24		29	
Wed	28		25		30	
Thu	29		26		31	
Fri	30		27			
Sat	31		28			
Sun			29			
Mon			30	49		

Calendar 2018

JANUARY
- **MON** 1 8 15 22 29
- **TUE** 2 9 16 23 30
- **WED** 3 10 17 24 31
- **THU** 4 11 18 25
- **FRI** 5 12 19 26
- **SAT** 6 13 20 27
- **SUN** 7 14 21 28

FEBRUARY
- **MON** 5 12 19 26
- **TUE** 6 13 20 27
- **WED** 7 14 21 28
- **THU** 1 8 15 22
- **FRI** 2 9 16 23
- **SAT** 3 10 17 24
- **SUN** 4 11 18 25

MARCH
- **MON** 5 12 19 26
- **TUE** 6 13 20 27
- **WED** 7 14 21 28
- **THU** 1 8 15 22 29
- **FRI** 2 9 16 23 30
- **SAT** 3 10 17 24 31
- **SUN** 4 11 18 25

APRIL
- **MON** 2 9 16 23 30
- **TUE** 3 10 17 24
- **WED** 4 11 18 25
- **THU** 5 12 19 26
- **FRI** 6 13 20 27
- **SAT** 7 14 21 28
- **SUN** 1 8 15 22 29

MAY
- **MON** 7 14 21 28
- **TUE** 1 8 15 22 29
- **WED** 2 9 16 23 30
- **THU** 3 10 17 24 31
- **FRI** 4 11 18 25
- **SAT** 5 12 19 26
- **SUN** 6 13 20 27

JUNE
- **MON** 4 11 18 25
- **TUE** 5 12 19 26
- **WED** 6 13 20 27
- **THU** 7 14 21 28
- **FRI** 1 8 15 22 29
- **SAT** 2 9 16 23 30
- **SUN** 3 10 17 24

JULY
- **MON** 2 9 16 23 30
- **TUE** 3 10 17 24 31
- **WED** 4 11 18 25
- **THU** 5 12 19 26
- **FRI** 6 13 20 27
- **SAT** 7 14 21 28
- **SUN** 1 8 15 22 29

AUGUST
- **MON** 6 13 20 27
- **TUE** 7 14 21 28
- **WED** 1 8 15 22 29
- **THU** 2 9 16 23 30
- **FRI** 3 10 17 24 31
- **SAT** 4 11 18 25
- **SUN** 5 12 19 26

SEPTEMBER
- **MON** 3 10 17 24
- **TUE** 4 11 18 25
- **WED** 5 12 19 26
- **THU** 6 13 20 27
- **FRI** 7 14 21 28
- **SAT** 1 8 15 22 29
- **SUN** 2 9 16 23 30

OCTOBER
- **MON** 1 8 15 22 29
- **TUE** 2 9 16 23 30
- **WED** 3 10 17 24 31
- **THU** 4 11 18 25
- **FRI** 5 12 19 26
- **SAT** 6 13 20 27
- **SUN** 7 14 21 28

NOVEMBER
- **MON** 5 12 19 26
- **TUE** 6 13 20 27
- **WED** 7 14 21 28
- **THU** 1 8 15 22 29
- **FRI** 2 9 16 23 30
- **SAT** 3 10 17 24
- **SUN** 4 11 18 25

DECEMBER
- **MON** 3 10 17 24 31
- **TUE** 4 11 18 25
- **WED** 5 12 19 26
- **THU** 6 13 20 27
- **FRI** 7 14 21 28
- **SAT** 1 8 15 22 29
- **SUN** 2 9 16 23 30

Calendar 2019

JANUARY
MON 7 14 21 28
TUE 1 8 15 22 29
WED 2 9 16 23 30
THU 3 10 17 24 31
FRI 4 11 18 25
SAT 5 12 19 26
SUN 6 13 20 27

FEBRUARY
MON 4 11 18 25
TUE 5 12 19 26
WED 6 13 20 27
THU 7 14 21 28
FRI 1 8 15 22
SAT 2 9 16 23
SUN 3 10 17 24

MARCH
MON 4 11 18 25
TUE 5 12 19 26
WED 6 13 20 27
THU 7 14 21 28
FRI 1 8 15 22 29
SAT 2 9 16 23 30
SUN 3 10 17 24 31

APRIL
MON 1 8 15 22 29
TUE 2 9 16 23 30
WED 3 10 17 24
THU 4 11 18 25
FRI 5 12 19 26
SAT 6 13 20 27
SUN 7 14 21 28

MAY
MON 6 13 20 27
TUE 7 14 21 28
WED 1 8 15 22 29
THU 2 9 16 23 30
FRI 3 10 17 24 31
SAT 4 11 18 25
SUN 5 12 19 26

JUNE
MON 3 10 17 24
TUE 4 11 18 25
WED 5 12 19 26
THU 6 13 20 27
FRI 7 14 21 28
SAT 1 8 15 22 29
SUN 2 9 16 23 30

JULY
MON 1 8 15 22 29
TUE 2 9 16 23 30
WED 3 10 17 24 31
THU 4 11 18 25
FRI 5 12 19 26
SAT 6 13 20 27
SUN 7 14 21 28

AUGUST
MON 5 12 19 26
TUE 6 13 20 27
WED 7 14 21 28
THU 1 8 15 22 29
FRI 2 9 16 23 30
SAT 3 10 17 24 31
SUN 4 11 18 25

SEPTEMBER
MON 2 9 16 23 30
TUE 3 10 17 24
WED 4 11 18 25
THU 5 12 19 26
FRI 6 13 20 27
SAT 7 14 21 28
SUN 1 8 15 22 29

OCTOBER
MON 7 14 21 28
TUE 1 8 15 22 29
WED 2 9 16 23 30
THU 3 10 17 24 31
FRI 4 11 18 25
SAT 5 12 19 26
SUN 6 13 20 27

NOVEMBER
MON 4 11 18 25
TUE 5 12 19 26
WED 6 13 20 27
THU 7 14 21 28
FRI 1 8 15 22 29
SAT 2 9 16 23 30
SUN 3 10 17 24

DECEMBER
MON 2 9 16 23 30
TUE 3 10 17 24 31
WED 4 11 18 25
THU 5 12 19 26
FRI 6 13 20 27
SAT 7 14 21 28
SUN 1 8 15 22 29

Calendar 2020

JANUARY
MON 6 13 20 27
TUE 7 14 21 28
WED 1 8 15 22 29
THU 2 9 16 23 30
FRI 3 10 17 24 31
SAT 4 11 18 25
SUN 5 12 19 26

FEBRUARY
MON 3 10 17 24
TUE 4 11 18 25
WED 5 12 19 26
THU 6 13 20 27
FRI 7 14 21 28
SAT 1 8 15 22 29
SUN 2 9 16 23

MARCH
MON 2 9 16 23 30
TUE 3 10 17 24 31
WED 4 11 18 25
THU 5 12 19 26
FRI 6 13 20 27
SAT 7 14 21 28
SUN 1 8 15 22 29

APRIL
MON 6 13 20 27
TUE 7 14 21 28
WED 1 8 15 22 29
THU 2 9 16 23 30
FRI 3 10 17 24
SAT 4 11 18 25
SUN 5 12 19 26

MAY
MON 4 11 18 25
TUE 5 12 19 26
WED 6 13 20 27
THU 7 14 21 28
FRI 1 8 15 22 29
SAT 2 9 16 23 30
SUN 3 10 17 24 31

JUNE
MON 1 8 15 22 29
TUE 2 9 16 23 30
WED 3 10 17 24
THU 4 11 18 25
FRI 5 12 19 26
SAT 6 13 20 27
SUN 7 14 21 28

JULY
MON 6 13 20 27
TUE 7 14 21 28
WED 1 8 15 22 29
THU 2 9 16 23 30
FRI 3 10 17 24 31
SAT 4 11 18 25
SUN 5 12 19 26

AUGUST
MON 3 10 17 24 31
TUE 4 11 18 25
WED 5 12 19 26
THU 6 13 20 27
FRI 7 14 21 28
SAT 1 8 15 22 29
SUN 2 9 16 23 30

SEPTEMBER
MON 7 14 21 28
TUE 1 8 15 22 29
WED 2 9 16 23 30
THU 3 10 17 24
FRI 4 11 18 25
SAT 5 12 19 26
SUN 6 13 20 27

OCTOBER
MON 5 12 19 26
TUE 6 13 20 27
WED 7 14 21 28
THU 1 8 15 22 29
FRI 2 9 16 23 30
SAT 3 10 17 24 31
SUN 4 11 18 25

NOVEMBER
MON 2 9 16 23 30
TUE 3 10 17 24
WED 4 11 18 25
THU 5 12 19 26
FRI 6 13 20 27
SAT 7 14 21 28
SUN 1 8 15 22 29

DECEMBER
MON 7 14 21 28
TUE 1 8 15 22 29
WED 2 9 16 23 30
THU 3 10 17 24 31
FRI 4 11 18 25
SAT 5 12 19 26
SUN 6 13 20 27

HOUSMANS
World Peace Directory
● 2019 ●

This comprehensive and up-to-date Directory is provided for the *Peace Diary* by the **Housmans Peace Resource Project**, and edited by Albert Beale. **To make the best use of it, please read the next two pages.**

There is a difficult balance to be struck between the usefulness, for many people, of the information in this format, and the fact that the full World Peace Database — from which this Directory is derived — is available on-line at **www.housmans.info/wpd**. Your feedback about this is encouraged.

Groups omitted from this printed version tend to be the more localised or specialised groups — and those which are least efficient at responding to communications from the database editor! The complete on-line information is searchable, and it is also possible to obtain your own copy of the full database.

To keep the database up to date, organisations are contacted regularly by post, and also (where possible) by e-mail. But we rely on other input as well: if your group changes any of its contact details, please send the information without waiting to be asked. There is never a wrong time to send information.

Some information, such as changes in telephone numbering systems, is often available in the country concerned long before it can be obtained elsewhere — so please help by sending any such information you know of.

This Directory is copyright © Housmans Peace Resource Project, 2018. Even where non-profit organisations are allowed to re-use sections of the Directory at nominal charge, *permission must be obtained first*.

Disclaimer: Organisations listed are not necessarily responsible for their inclusion, nor for the way they are described, nor for the terminology used to describe their country.

All correspondence about the Directory should be sent to: **Housmans Peace Resource Project, 5 Caledonian Road, London N1, UK (tel +44-20-7278 4474; fax +44-20-7278 0444; e-mail worldpeace@gn.apc.org)**. Information is preferred in writing.

Directory Introduction

This is the 66th Peace Directory to be published with the Housmans Peace Diary. It is intended to help people find contact points for issues which interest them, and also to be a day-to-day reference resource for activists.

What's in the Directory?

The 2019 Directory lists over 1400 national and international organisations, covering the breadth of the peace movement – with the emphasis on grassroots, non-governmental groups – as well as major bodies in related fields such as environmental and human rights campaigning.

This year, around one-third of the groups listed have either had their information amended since last year's Directory, or are newly included this year.

How to find things in the Directory

Check both the national and international listings if necessary. If you can't find exactly what you want, try a less specialised organisation which might include what you're looking for. (And see the previous page for the availability of further information.)

International organisations are listed alphabetically. The national listings are in alphabetical order of English-language country name; the organisations are then arranged alphabetically within each country. Organisations' names (and addresses) are generally in the language of the country concerned.

Whilst aware of political sensitivities, we use commonly accepted postal and administrative divisions of the world to decide what is or isn't a "country". This doesn't mean we support or oppose countries' divisions or mergers – we just want the Directory to be easy to use.

In the national listings we don't repeat the country name at the end of each address, so you will need to add it.

How the entries are set out

The organisation's name is in **bold print**; or, if the name is that of a magazine, in ***bold italics***. Any common abbreviation is shown [in square brackets], in **bold** or ***bold italics*** as appropriate. Most organisations then have codes (in round brackets) giving an indication of their politics and activities (**see Note 1**). The address is shown next. Then we give (in brackets) any telephone number (**see Note 2**), fax number (**see Note 3**), electronic mail address (**see Note 4**), and web site address (**see Note 4**). Magazines published by the organisation are then shown in *italics*. Where the listing is itself a publication, details of frequency etc may be given next (**see Note 5**). There may be brief additional information where necessary.

The **Notes**, including our standard abbreviations, are given opposite.

Notes

1. Codes used to explain something about the listed organisation are as follows. The codes for international bodies in the left-hand column are used to show an official link to tbe body (or to one of its national affiliates in the country concerned). If these are not sufficient, the general codes on the right are used.

   AI Amnesty International
   FE Friends of the Earth International
   FR International Fellowship of Reconciliation
   GP Greenpeace International
   IB International Peace Bureau
   IP International Physicians for the Prevention of Nuclear War
   PC Pax Christi International
   SC Service Civil International
   SE Servas International
   SF Society of Friends (Quakers)
   UN World Federation of United Nations Associations
   WL Women's International League for Peace and Freedom
   WP World Peace Council
   WR War Resisters' International

   AL Alternativist / Anarchist
   AT Arms Trade / Conversion
   CD Citizen Diplomacy / People-to-People
   CR Conflict Resolution / Mediation
   DA Disarmament / Arms Control
   EL Environmental / Ecological
   HR Equality / Minority & Human Rights
   ND Nuclear Disarmament
   PA Anti-Militarist / Pacifist
   PO Positive Action / Lifestyle
   RA Radical Action / Direct Action
   RE Research into Peace, Conflict / Peace Education
   RP Religious Peace Group
   SD Social Defence / Civilian-Based Defence
   TR War Tax Resistance / Peace Tax Campaigning
   TW Development / Liberation / Third World
   WC International Workcamps
   WF World Federalists / World Citizens

2. Telephone numbers are given in standard international format: +[country code]-[area code]-[local number]. The "+" indicates the international access code used in the country you're phoning from. The area code (if there is one) is given without any national trunk prefix digit(s) that are used in the country concerned – for calls *within* the country you must add them if they exist. Exceptionally, a few countries without area codes still require an extra digit (generally 0) at the start of their national number for internal calls; the main culprits are Belgium, France, Switzerland, South Africa and Thailand. Note that for calls between neighbouring countries there are often non-standard codes outside the normal system.

3. The telephone number of a facsimile (telefax) machine is given without repeating codes which are the same as in the preceding ordinary telephone number; "fax" alone means the fax number is identical to the phone number. Because many groups share a fax machine, always start your message by saying clearly which person and organisation it is meant for.

4. The e-mail and web site addresses are given in standard internet format. (The e-mail address is the one with the "@" in it.) The "http://" which, by definition, starts every web address is **not** repeated each time here.

5. Abbreviations used in connection with publications are:

dly daily	***x* yrly** x per year	**ea** each
wkly weekly	**annl** annual	**pa** per annum
ftly fortnightly	**irreg** irregular	**ftm** free to members
mthly monthly	**occl** occasional	**nfp** no fixed price / donation

INTERNATIONAL ORGANISATIONS

Abolition 2000 International Secretariat (ND EL), c/o International Peace Bureau, Marienstr 19-20, 10117 Berlin, Germany (+49-30-1208 4549) (www.abolition2000.org). Global network to eliminate nuclear weapons.

Alliance Against Genocide (HR), c/o Genocide Watch, 3351 N Fairfax Dr - MS4D3, Arlington, VA 22201, USA (+1-202-643 1405) (communications@genocide-watch.org) (www.againstgenocide.org). Formerly International Alliance to End Genocide.

Alternatives to Violence Project International (CR), PO Box 164, Purchase, NY 10577, USA (avp.international). International network of national AVP organisations. AVP groups organise training to aid creative responses to potentially violent situations.

Amnesty International - International Secretariat [AI] (HR RE), Peter Benenson House, 1 Easton St, London WC1X 0DW, Britain (+44-20-7413 5500) (fax 7956 1157) (contactus@amnesty.org) (www.amnesty.org). *Newsletter*, *Annual Report*. East Asia office (Hong Kong) +852-3963 7100; Southern Africa office (Johannesburg) +27-11-283 6000; Middle East and North Africa office (Beirut) +961-1-748751.

Architects & Planners for Justice in Palestine [APJP] (HR), c/o 100 Whitchurch Lane, Edgware, Middx HA8 6QN, Britain (info@apjp.org) (apjp.org).

Asian Human Rights Commission [AHRC] (HR), Unit 1 & 2 - 12/F, Hopeful Factory Centre, 10-16 Wo Shing St, Fotan, NT, Hong Kong (+852-2698 6339) (fax 2698 6367) (communications@ahrc.asia) (www.humanrights.asia). Engage in daily interventions as well as institutional issues.

Association of World Citizens [AWC] (WF CD RE), PO Box 1206, Novato, CA 94948-1206, USA (+1-415-893 1369) (suezipp@worldcitizen.org) (www.worldcitizensunited.org).

Association pour la Prévention de la Torture / Association for the Prevention of Torture [APT] (HR), BP 137, 1211 Genève 19, Switzerland (+41-22 919 2170) (fax 22 919 2180) (apt@apt.ch) (www.apt.ch). Works to improve legal frameworks and detention monitoring, to prevent torture and other ill-treatment.

Bahá'í International Community - Office of Public Information (RP), PO Box 155, 3100101 Haifa, Israel (+972-4-835 8194) (fax 835 3312) (opi@bwc.org) (www.bahai.org). *One Country*. Magazine office: Suite 120, 866 UN Plaza, New York, NY 10017, USA.

Bellona Foundation (EL), Vulkan 11, 0178 Oslo, Norway (+47-2323 4600) (fax 2238 3862) (info@bellona.no) (bellona.org). Other international office in Brussels. Offices also in Russia (Murmansk and St Petersburg).

Carta de la Paz / Letter of Peace (RE), C/Modolell 41, 08021 Barcelona, Spain (+34-93 414 5936) (fax) (secretaria@cartadelapaz.org) (www.letterofpeace.org). *Information Paper*. Petition to UN. South America office, Chile: +56-2-274 7151. Central America and Caribbean, Dominican Republic: +1809-508 6879. North America, Mexico: +52-66-2213 9827. Central Europe, Switzerland: +41-22-860 2304.

Center for Global Nonkilling [CGNK] (RE PA), 3653 Tantalus Dr, Honolulu, HI 96822-5033, USA (+1-808-536 7442) (info@nonkilling.org) (nonkilling.org). To promote change towards the measurable goal of a killing-free world.

Centre for Humanitarian Dialogue [HD Centre] (CR RE), 114 Rue de Lausanne, 1202 Genève, Switzerland (+41-22 908 1130) (fax 22 908 1140) (info@hdcentre.org) (www.hdcentre.org). Independent confidential mediation. Works with political and civil leaders to establish dialogue.

Child Rights Information Network [CRIN] (HR), Suite 152, 88 Lower Marsh, London SE1, Britain (info@crin.org) (www.crin.org). Supports UN Convention on rights of children. Work includes opposing mutilation of children.

Child Soldiers International (RE PA AT), 4th Floor, 9 Marshalsea Rd, Borough, London SE1 1EP, Britain (+44-20-7367 4110) (fax 7367 4129) (info@child-soldiers.org) (www.child-soldiers.org).

Church and Peace (SF FR PC), Mittelstr 4, 34474 Diemlstadt-Wethen, Germany (+49-5694-990 5506) (fax 1532) (IntlOffice@church-and-peace.org) (www.church-and-peace.org). *Theology and Peace / Théologie et Paix / Theologie und Frieden*. European ecumenical network.

Climate Action Network International [CAN] (EL), Khaldeh, Dakdouk Bldg - 3rd floor, Mount Lebanon, Lebanon (+961-1-447192) (fax 448649) (administration@climatenetwork.org) (www.climatenetwork.org). Network of 1300 organisations in 120 countries.

Co-ordinating Committee for International Voluntary Service [CCIVS] (SC TW WC EL HR), UNESCO House, 1 rue Miollis, 75732 Paris Cedex 15, France (+33-14568 4936) (fax 14568 4934) (secretariat@ccivs.org) (www.ccivs.org).

Coalition for the International Criminal Court - UN Office [CICC] (HR), c/o WFM, 708 Third Ave - Suite 1715, New York, NY 10017, USA (+1-212-687 2863) (fax 599 1332) (cicc@coalitionfortheicc.org)

INTERNATIONAL ORGANISATIONS

(www.coalitionfortheicc.org). Also ICC office, Den Haag (+31-70-311 1080) (cicc-hague@coalitionfortheicc.org).

Conscience and Peace Tax International [CPTI] (TR), c/o Conscience, 17 North Square, London NW11, Britain (+44-20-3515 9132) (co.sec@cpti.ws) (www.cpti.ws). *CPTI Bulletin*.

Coordination Internationale pour une Culture de Non-violence et de Paix (RE PO DA), 148 rue du Faubourg Saint Denis, 75010 Paris, France (+33-14036 0660) (secretariat@nvpnetwork.net) (www.nvpnetwork.net). International Network for a Culture of Nonviolence and Peace.

Ecumenical Accompaniment Programme in Palestine and Israel [EAPPI] (RP HR CD CR SF), c/o World Council of Churches (Public Witness section), PO Box 2100, 1211 Genève 2, Switzerland (+41-22 791 6108) (fax 22 791 6122) (eappi@wcc-coe.org) (www.eappi.org). Accompanying Palestinians and Israelis in non-violent actions; advocacy to end occupation. Also: PO Box 741, Jerusalem 91000 (+972-2-626 2458).

European Bureau for Conscientious Objection [EBCO] (WR SC), 35 Rue Van Elewyck, 1050 Bruxelles, Belgium (+32-2 648 5220) (ebco@ebco-beoc.org) (www.ebco-beoc.org).

European Institute of Peace [EIP] (RE), Rue des deux Églises 25, 1000 Bruxelles, Belgium (+32-2 430 7360) (info@eip.org) (www.eip.org). Independent, "augmenting EU's peace agenda".

European Network Against Arms Trade [ENAAT] (AT), Anna Spenglerstr 71, 1054 NH Amsterdam, Netherlands (+31-20-616 4684) (info@stopwapenhandel.org) (www.enaat.org).

Fédération Internationale de l'Action des Chrétiens pour l'Abolition de la Torture [FIACAT] (HR), 27 rue de Maubeuge, 75009 Paris, France (+33-14280 0160) (fax 14280 2089) (fiacat@fiacat.org) (www.fiacat.org).

Fédération Internationale des Ligues des Droits de l'Homme [FIDH] (HR), 17 Passage de la Main d'Or, 75011 Paris, France (+33-14355 2518) (fax 14355 1880) (contact@fidh.org) (www.fidh.org). International Federation of Human Rights Leagues. At EU: +32-2 609 4423. At UN: +1-646-395 7103. At ICC: +31-70-356 0259.

Friends of the Earth International [FoEI] (EL), PO Box 19199, 1000 GD Amsterdam, Netherlands (+31-20-622 1369) (fax 639 2181) (www.foei.org). Europe office in Brussels (+32-2 893 1000) (www.foeeurope.org).

Friends World Committee for Consultation [FWCC] (SF), 173 Euston Rd, London NW1, Britain (+44-20-7663 1199) (world@friendsworldoffice.org) (fwccworld.org). Also 4 regional offices. Africa: PO Box 41946, Nairobi, Kenya; Americas: 1506 Race St, Philadelphia, PA 19102, USA; Asia & West Pacific: PO Box 6063, O'Connor, ACT 2602, Australia; Europe & Middle East: PO Box 1157, Histon CB24 9XQ, Cambs, Britain.

Gesellschaft für Bedrohte Völker - International (HR TW), Postfach 2024, 37010 Göttingen, Germany (+49-551-499060) (fax 58028) (info@gfbv.de) (www.gfbv.de). *Pogrom*. Society for Threatened Peoples. Campaigns against genocide and ethnocide.

Global Action to Prevent War (RE ND DA HR), 866 UN Plaza - Suite 4050, New York, NY 10017, USA (+1-212-818 1815) (fax 818 1857) (coordinator@globalactionpw.org) (www.globalactionpw.org). Transnational civil society and academic network. Legacy of World Order Models Project in 1990s. Aims for "integrated approach to enhancing security and ending war-related violence".

Global Alliance for Ministries and Infrastructures of Peace [GAMIP] (DA), Chemin de la Caracole 68, 1294 Genthod, Genève, Switzerland (+41-22 535 7370) (www.gamip.org). Formerly Global Alliance for Ministries and Departments of Peace.

Global Anabaptist Peace Commission (RP), c/o Mennonite World Conference, 50 Kent Ave - Suite 206, Kitchener, ON, N2G 3R1, Canada (+1-519-571 0060) (fax 226-647 4224) (Kitchener@mwc-cmm.org) (www.mwc-cmm.org/article/about-peace-commission). Previously Global Anabaptist Peace and Justice Network.

Global Campaign Against US/NATO Military Bases (ND CD), c/o Peace and Neutrality Alliance, 17 Castle St, Dalkey, Co Dublin, Ireland, Republic of (contact@noUSNATOBases.org) (nousnatobases.org). Worldwide network.

Global Campaign on Military Spending - Co-ordination Office [GCOMS] (DA AT), c/o Centre Delàs d'Estudis per la Pau, c/ Erasme de Janer 8 - entresol - despatx 9, 08001 Barcelona, Spain (coordination.gcoms@ipb.org) (demilitarize.org). Organise Global Day of Action on Military Spending. A project of the International Peace Bureau.

Global Ecumenical Network for the Abolition of Military Chaplaincies (RP), c/o IDK, Postfach 280312, 13443 Berlin, Germany (global-network@militaerseelsorge-abschaffen.de) (www.globnetabolishmilitarychaplaincy.webnode.com). Opposes co-option of churches by military, financial links between arms industry and churches, and churches' acceptance of warfare.

INTERNATIONAL ORGANISATIONS

Global Initiative to End All Corporal Punishment of Children (HR), c/o APPROACH, Unit W (West) 125 Westminster Business Sq, 1-45 Durham St, London SE11, Britain (info@endcorporalpunishment.org) (www.endcorporalpunishment.org).

Global Network Against Weapons and Nuclear Power in Space (PA EL RA), PO Box 652, Brunswick, ME 04011, USA (+1-207-443 9502) (globalnet@mindspring.com) (www.space4peace.org).

Global Partnership for the Prevention of Armed Conflict [GPPAC] (RE CR), Laan van Meerdervoort 70, 2517 AN Den Haag, Netherlands (+31-70-311 0970) (info@gppac.net) (www.gppac.net).

Global Policy Forum [GPF] (RE DA HR), 866 United Nations Plaza - Ste 4050, New York, NY 10017, USA (+1-646-553 3460) (gpf@globalpolicy.org) (www.globalpolicy.org). Policy watchdog monitoring work of United Nations. Mainly concerned with UN Security Council, food crisis, and economic isues. Promotes accountability and citizen participation in decision-making. Europe office in Bonn, Germany (europe@globalpolicy.org).

Globe International (EL TW), c/o E3G, 47 Great Guildford St, London SE1, Britain (secretariat@globelegislators.org) (www.globelegislators.org). Environmental organisation of parliamentarians. Europe office: (globe-europe.org); Japan office: globejp@osk.3web.ne.jp.

Green Cross International [GCI] (EL TW DA CR HR), 9-11 rue de Varembé, 1202 Genève, Switzerland (+41-22 789 1662) (fax 22 789 1695) (gcinternational@gci.ch) (www.gcint.ch). Focuses on interface between security and sustainability, by working on conflicts arising from environmental degradation and on environmental consequences of warfare.

Greenpeace International (EL), Ottho Heldringstr 5, 1066 AZ Amsterdam, Netherlands (+31-20-718 2000) (fax 718 2002) (info.int@greenpeace.org) (www.greenpeace.org/international).

Housmans Peace Resource Project [HPRP] (CD RE), 5 Caledonian Rd, London N1, Britain (+44-20-7278 4474) (fax 7278 0444) (worldpeace@gn.apc.org) (www.housmans.info). *Housmans World Peace Database & Directory.*

Human Rights Watch [HRW] (HR), Empire State Building - 34th Floor, 350 5th Ave, New York, NY 10118-3299, USA (+1-212-290 4700) (fax 736 1300) (www.hrw.org). EU liaison office in Brussels (+32-2 732 2009) (fax 2 732 0471). Offices also in: Britain, Canada, France, Germany, Netherlands, South Africa.

Institute for Economics and Peace (RE), 205 Pacific Hwy, St Leonards, Sydney, NSW 2065, Australia (+61-2-9901 8500) (info@economicsandpeace.org) (economicsandpeace.org). Office also in USA (+1-646-963 2160).

International Action Network on Small Arms [IANSA] (AT DA), c/o Action on Armed Violence, 2nd and 3rd Floor, 415 High Street, Stratford, London E15, Britain (communication@iansa.org) (www.iansa.org).

International Association of Lawyers Against Nuclear Arms [IALANA] (IB ND AT DA), Marienstr 19/20, 10117 Berlin, Germany (+49-30-2065 4857) (fax 2065 3837) (office@ialana.info) (www.ialana.info). UN office: c/o LCNP, +1-212-818 1861; Pacific office: +64-9-524 8403.

International Association of Lawyers Against Nuclear Arms - UN Office [IALANA] (IB ND AT DA), c/o LCNP, 866 UN Plaza - Suite 4050, New York, NY 10017-1936, USA (+1-212-818 1861) (fax 818 1857) (johnburroughs@lcnp.org) (www.ialana.info). Main office, Germany (+49-30-2065 4857). Pacific office (+64-9-524 8403).

International Campaign for Boycott, Disinvestment and Sanctions Against Israel (HR RA), c/o PACBI, PO Box 1701, Ramallah, West Bank, Palestine (bdsmovement.net).

International Campaign to Abolish Nuclear Weapons [ICAN] (ND), 150 Route de Ferney, 1211 Geneva 2, Switzerland (+41-22 788 2063) (info@icanw.org) (www.icanw.org). Launched by IPPNW and others in 2007. Works towards a nuclear weapons convention. Asia Pacific office, Australia (+61-3-9023 1958).

International Campaign to Ban Landmines - Cluster Munitions Coalition [ICBL - CMC] (AT), 2 Chemin Eugène-Rigot, 1202 Genève, Switzerland (+41-22 920 0325) (fax 22 920 0115) (icbl@icbl.org), www.icblcmc.org). Also www.icbl.org, www.stopclustermunitions.org.

International Campaign to Stop Rape and Gender Violence in Conflict, 1 Nicholas St - Suite 430, Ottawa, ONT - K1N 7B7, Canada (+1-613-569 8400) (fax 691 1419) (info@stoprapeinconflict.org) (www.stoprapeinconflict.org).

International Coalition to Ban Uranium Weapons [ICBUW] (AT DA), Marienstr 19/20, 10117 Berlin, Germany (+49-30-2065 4857) (info@icbuw.org) (www.bandepleteduranium.org).

International Committee for Robot Arms Control [ICRAC] (AT DA), c/o Noel Sharkey, Department of Computer Science, University

INTERNATIONAL ORGANISATIONS

of Sheffield, Western Bank, Sheffield 10, Yorks, Britain (www.icrac.net).
For peaceful use of robotics. Campaigns for regulation of robot weapons.

International Council of Voluntary Agencies / Conseil International des Agences Bénévoles [ICVA] (HR TW), 26-28 ave Giuseppe Motta, 1202 Genève, Switzerland (+41-22 950 9600) (secretariat@icvanetwork.org) (www.icvanetwork.org). Global network of humanitarian NGOs and human rights groups "promoting principled and effective humanitarian action".

International Fellowship of Reconciliation [IFOR] (RP IB), Postbus 1528, 3500 BM Utrecht, Netherlands (+31-30-303 9930) (office@ifor.org) (www.ifor.org).

International Friendship League [IFL] (CD), PO Box 217, Ross-on-Wye HR9 9FD, Britain (info@iflworld.org) (www.iflworld.org).

International Humanist and Ethical Union [IHEU] (HR PO), 39 Moreland St, London EC1, Britain (+44-20-7490 8468) (office-iheu@iheu.org) (www.iheu.org). *International Humanist News.*
In USA: +1-518-632 1040.

International Institute for Peace through Tourism / Institut International pour la Paix par le Tourisme [IIPT] (CD), 685 Cottage Club Rd - Unit 13, Stowe, VT 05672, USA (+1-802-253 8671) (fax 253 2645) (ljd@iipt.org) (www.iipt.org). Committed to making travel and tourism a global peace industry; believe that every traveller is potentially an ambassador for peace.

International Network of Museums for Peace [INMP] (IB RE), c/o Kyoto Museum for World Peace, 56-1 Toji-in Kitamachi, Kita, Kyoto 603-8577, Japan (secretariat@museumsforpeace.org) (www.inmp.net). Worldwide network of peace museums, gardens, and other peace-related sites, centres and institutions, which share the desire to build a culture of peace.

International Peace Bureau [IPB] (AT TW RE ND TR), Marienstr 19-20, 10117 Berlin, Germany (+49-30-1208 4549) (info@ipb-office.berlin) (www.ipb.org). *IPB News.* Main programme: disarmament for development. Work includes Global Campaign on Military Spending. Most broadly-based international peace networking body. Also office in Geneva; and GCOMS co-ordination office in Barcelona.

International Peace Initiative for Syria (CR PA RE), c/o Study Centre for Peace and Conflict Resolution, 7461 Stadtschlaining, Burg, Austria (info@peaceinsyria.org) (www.peaceinsyria.org). Opposes all military solutions. Stresses importance of a ceasefire and de-escalation, and of priority involvement of unarmed civil society in negotiations. Works with World Social Forum.

International Peace Institute [IPI] (RE DA CR), 777 United Nations Plaza, New York, NY 10017-3521, USA (+1-212-687 4300) (fax 983 8246) (ipi@ipinst.org) (www.ipinst.org). Supports multilateral disarmament negotiations. Independent think-tank – "promoting the prevention and settlement of conflict". Offices also in Austria and Bahrain. Originally called International Peace Academy.

International Peace Institute – Middle East Regional Office [IPI] (RE DA CR), 51-52 Harbour House, Bahrain Financial Harbour, Manama, Bahrain (+973-1721 1344) (www.ipinst.org). Main office in USA. Independent think-tank – "promoting the prevention and settlement of conflict".

International Peace Institute – Vienna Office [IPI] (RE DA CR), Freyung 3, 1010 Wien, Austria (+43-1-533 8881) (www.ipinst.org). Main office in USA. Independent think-tank – "promoting the prevention and settlement of conflict".

International Peace Research Association [IPRA] (RE), c/o Risk and Conflict Network, Dept of Media & Communication Design, Northumbria University, Newcastle-upon-Tyne NE1 8ST, Britain (+44-191-227 3567) (www.iprapeace.org).

International Physicians for the Prevention of Nuclear War [IPPNW] (ND RE TW), 339 Pleasant St - Third floor, Malden, MA 02148, USA (+1-617-440 1733) (ippnwbos@ippnw.org) (ippnw.org).

International Secretariat of Nuclear-Free Local Authorities (ND EL), c/o Nuclear-Free Local Authorities Secretariat, Manchester City Council, Town Hall, Manchester M60 3NY, Britain (+44-161-234 3244) (fax 234 3379) (s.morris4@manchester.gov.uk) (www.nuclearpolicy.info).

International Tibet Network (HR), c/o Tibet Society UK, 2 Baltic Place, London N1 5AQ, Britain (mail@tibetnetwork.org) (www.tibetnetwork.org). Formerly International Tibet Support Network. Links 180 groups around the world. Local Tibet support groups can also be found via www.tibet.org.

Interpeace (CR), 7-9 Chemin de Balexert, 1219 Châtelaine, Genève, Switzerland (+41-22 917 8593) (fax 22 917 8039) (info@interpeace.org) (www.interpeace.org).
Set up by UN; now independent peacebuilding group. Supports societies to build lasting peace. Regional offices: Nairobi, Abidjan, Guatemala City, New York, Brussels.

Journal of Resistance Studies (RE RA PO), c/o Irene Publishing, Sparsnäs 1010, 66891

INTERNATIONAL ORGANISATIONS

Ed, Sweden (editor@resistance-journal.org) (resistance-journal.org).

Mayors for Peace (CD ND DA), c/o Hiroshima Peace Culture Foundation, 1-5 Nakajima-cho, Naka-ku, Hiroshima 730-0811, Japan (+81-82-242 7821) (fax 242 7452) (mayorcon@pcf.city.hiroshima.jp) (www.mayorsforpeace.org).
Mayors for Peace Newsletter.

Mediators Beyond Borders International (CR), 1901 North Fort Myer Dr – Ste 405, Arlington, VA 22209, USA (+1-703-528 6552) (fax 528 5776) (info@mediatorsbeyondborders.org) (mediatorsbeyondborders.org).
Office also in Netherlands.

Nansen Dialogue Network [NDN] (CR CD), Bjørntjerne Bjørnsonsgt 2, 2609 Lillehammer, Norway (+47-6126 5400) (fax 6126 5440) (contact@nansen-dialogue.net) (www.nansen-dialogue.net).

No to War – No to NATO / Na i Ryfel! – Na i NATO / Não à Guerra – Não à NATO (RA DA ND), c/o Reiner Braun, IALANA, Marienstr 19-20, 10117 Berlin, Germany (+41-30-2065 4857) (fax 2065 3837) (info@no-to-nato.org) (www.no-to-nato.org).
International network to delegitimise NATO. Co-ordination of groups in many NATO states; organises actions against NATO events.
Also c/o Arielle Denis, Mouvement de la Paix, in France (Arielle.Denis@mvtpaix.org).

Nonviolent Peaceforce [NP] (CR HR), 13 chemin de Levant - Bat A, 01210 Ferney Voltaire, France (+33-967 461948) (headoffice@nonviolentpeaceforce.org) (www.nonviolentpeaceforce.org). Offices in Belgium, and in USA (+1-612-871 0005).

Organisation for the Prohibition of Chemical Weapons [OPCW] (DA), Johan de Wittlaan 32, 2517 JR Den Haag, Netherlands (+31-70-416 3300) (fax 360 3535) (public.affairs@opcw.org) (www.opcw.org).

Organisation Mondiale Contre la Torture / World Organisation Against Torture [OMCT] (HR), CP 21, 1211 Genève 8, Switzerland (+41-22 809 4939) (fax 22 809 4929) (omct@omct.org) (www.omct.org). Co-ordinates SOS-Torture Network. Europe regional office, Belgium (+32-2 218 3719), (omcteurope@omct.org).
Involves 280 organisations in 93 countries, linking local groups in countries where torture exists with activists elsewhere.

Orthodox Peace Fellowship [OPF] (FR), Kanisstr 5, 1811 GJ Alkmaar, Netherlands (+31-72-515 4180) (office@incommunion.org) (incommunion.org). *In Communion*.

Parliamentarians for Nuclear Non-proliferation and Disarmament [PNND] (ND), c/o Prague Vision Institute for Sustainable Security, Lipanská 4, 13000 Praha 3, Czech Republic (+420-773 638867) (alyn@pnnd.org) (pnnd.org).
Europe office, Basel; UN office, New York. Also London office.
Provides parliamentarians with information on nuclear weapons policies; helps them become engaged in nuclear non-proliferation and disarmament.

Pax Christi International (RP IB CD RE CR), Rue du Progrès 323, 1030 Bruxelles, Belgium (+32-2 502 5550) (fax 2 502 4626) (hello@paxchristi.net) (www.paxchristi.net).
Newsletter. Network of autonomous organisations – Catholic.

Peace Brigades International / Brigadas Internacionales de Paz / Brigades de Paix Internationales [PBI] (HR CD CR RE), Village Partenaire, Rue de Fernard Bernier 15, 1060 Bruxelles, Belgium (+32 2 543 4443) (admin@peacebrigades.org) (www.peacebrigades.org).
Projects in Colombia, Guatemala, Mexico, Honduras, Kenya, Indonesia.

Peace Research Institute Oslo / Institutt for Fredsforskning [PRIO] (RE CR), PO Box 9229, Grønland, 0134 Oslo, Norway (+47-2254 7700) (fax 2254 7701) (info@prio.no) (www.prio.no).
Journal of Peace Research; *Security Dialogue*.
Journals from: SAGE Publications, 6 Bonhill St, London EC2, Britain (+44-20-7374 0645).

Peacebuilding Support Office of the United Nations (CR RE), UN Secretariat - 30th Floor, New York, NY 10017, USA (+1-212-963 9999) (www.un.org/en/peacebuilding). Formerly United Nations Peacebuilding Commission.

PEN International (HR), Unit A, Koops Mill Mews, 162-164 Abbey St, London SE1 2AN, Britain (+44-20-7405 0338) (info@pen-international.org) (www.pen-international.org).
Includes Writers in Prison Committee, Writers for Peace Committee.

Privacy International (HR), 62 Britton St, London EC1, Britain (+44-20-3422 4321) (info@privacyinternational.org) (www.privacyinternational.org). For data protection, and control of surveillance.

Pugwash Conferences on Science and World Affairs (ND EL RE TW), 1211 Connecticut Ave NW - Suite 800, Washington, DC 20036, USA (+1-202-478 3440) (pugwashdc@aol.com) (pugwash.org). Offices also in Rome (+39-06-687 8376),

INTERNATIONAL ORGANISATIONS

Geneva (+41-22 907 3667), London (+44-20-7405 6661).

Quaker Council for European Affairs [QCEA] (SF HR PA EL AT), Square Ambiorix 50, 1000 Brussel, Belgium (+32-2 230 4935) (fax 2 230 6370) (office@qcea.org) (www.qcea.org). *Around Europe*.

Quaker UN Office - Geneva [QUNO] (SF HR TW EL CR), 13 Av du Mervelet, 1209 Genève, Switzerland (+41-22 748 4800) (fax 22 748 4819) (quno@quno.ch) (www.quno.ch). *Geneva Reporter*.

Red Antimilitarista de América Latina e Caribe [RAMALC] (WR), c/o ACOOC, Cr 19 - 33A - 26/1, Bogotá, Colombia (ramalc.org). *Rompiendo Filas*.

Registry of World Citizens [WCR] (WF IB WP RE), 66 Bd Vincent Auriol, 75013 Paris, France (+33-14586 0358) (fax 241 784775) (abc@recim.org) (www.recim.org). Formerly World Citizen Registry.

Religions for Peace (RP IB RE CR TW), 777 United Nations Plaza, New York, NY 10017, USA (+1-212-687 2163) (fax 983 0098) (info@rfp.org) (religionsforpeace.org). Formerly World Conference of Religions for Peace. Regional offices in Asia, Europe, Latin America, Africa.

Researchers for Peace (RE AT DA), c/o Scientists for Global Responsibility, Unit 2.8, Halton Mill, Mill Lane, Halton, Lacaster LA2 6ND, Britain (www.researchersforpeace.eu). Network of 700 European scientists and academics.

School Day of Non-Violence and Peace / Día Escolar de la No-Violencia y la Paz [DENIP] (RE), Apdo Postal 77, 11510 Puerto Real, Spain (denip.pax@gmail.com) (denip.webcindario.com). (30 January, anniversary of Mahatma Gandhi's death).

Sea Shepherd (EL RA), PO Box 8628, Alexadria, VA 22306, USA (+1-818-736 8357) (fax -360-370 5651) (info@seashepherd.org) (seashepherd.org). Nature conservation on the high seas. Use direct action to confront those attacking the ecosystem.

Search for Common Ground - Brussels Office (RE CD CR), Rue Belliard 205 - bte 13, 1040 Bruxelles, Belgium (+32-2 736 7262) (fax 2 732 3033) (brussels@sfcg.org) (www.sfcg.org). Conflict transformation projects in 34 countries. Washington DC Office (+1-202-265 4300); West Africa Office, Freetown (+232-22-223479).

Sennacieca Asocio Tutmonda - Worker Esperantists [SAT] (CD PA EL HR), 67 Av Gambetta, 75020 Paris, France (+33-14797 7190) (kontakto@satesperanto.org) (www.satesperanto.org). *Sennaciulo*.

Servas International [SI] (CD PO), c/o Jonny Sågänger, Reimersholmsgatan 47 - plan 2, 11740 Stockholm, Sweden (helpdesk@servas.org) (www.servas.org). World hospitality network for peace and goodwill. Building understanding by facilitating personal contacts between people of different nationalities.

Service Civil International - International Office [SCI] (WC PA TW PO HR), Belgiëlei 37, 2018 Antwerpen, Belgium (+32-3 226 5727) (fax 3 232 0344) (info@sciint.org) (www.sciint.org).

Sikh Human Rights Group (HR CR), 89 South Rd, Southall UB1, Middlesex, Britain (shrg@shrg.net) (shrg.net).

Statewatch (HR CD), 356 Holloway Rd, London N7 6PA, Britain (+44-20-7697 4266) (office@statewatch.org) (www.statewatch.org). Covers Europe. Critical research in fields of state, justice, home affairs, accountability, etc.

Stockholm International Peace Research Institute [SIPRI] (RE), Signalistgatan 9, 16972 Solna, Sweden (+46-8-655 9700) (sipri@sipri.org) (www.sipri.org). *SIPRI Yearbook*.

Third World Network [TWN] (TW), 131 Jalan Macalister, 10400 Penang, Malaysia (+60-4-226 6728) (fax 226 4505) (twn@twnetwork.org) (www.twn.my). *Third World Resurgence*; *Third World Network Features*. Latin America Secretariat: ITEM, Av 18 de Julio 2095/301, Montevideo 11200, Uruguay. Africa Secretariat: 9 Ollenu St, PO Box AN 19452, Accra-North, Ghana (fax +233-21-511188). Also publishes *South-North Development Monitor* (*SUNS*).

Transnational Institute [TNI] (HR ND RE TW EL), PO Box 14656, 1001 LD Amsterdam, Netherlands (+31-20-662 6608) (fax 675 7176) (tni@tni.org) (www.tni.org). *Transnational Institute Series*. Research in support of social movements.

UN Non-Governmental Liaison Service (New York Office) [UN-NGLS] (EL HR PO TW), Room DC1-1106, United Nations, New York, NY 10017, USA (+1-212-963 3125) (fax 963 8712) (info@un-ngls.org) (www.un-ngls.org).

Unfold Zero (ND), c/o Basel Peace Office, University of Basel, Petersgraben 27, 4051 Basel, Switzerland (www.unfoldzero.org). Network for nuclear weapons abolition. Focus on action through UN system. Joint project of various national and international disarmament campaigns.

UNICEF, 3 United Nations Plaza, New York, NY 10017, USA (+1-212-326 7000) (fax 887 7465) (aaltamirano@unicef.org) (www.unicef.org).

United Nations Department for Disarmament Affairs (AT CR ND DA), UN

INTERNATIONAL ORGANISATIONS

Headquarters Bldg (Rm DN25-12), New York, NY 10017, USA (+1-212-963 1570) (fax 963 4066) (www.un.org/disarmament).
United Nations Institute for Disarmament Research [UNIDIR] (RE), Palais des Nations, 1211 Genève 10, Switzerland (+41-22 917 1141) (fax 22 917 0176) (unidir@unog.ch) (www.unidir.org).
Universala Esperanto-Asocio [UEA] (HR CD PO), Nieuwe Binnenweg 176, 3015 BJ Rotterdam, Netherlands (+31-10-436 1044) (fax 436 1751) (uea@co.uea.org) (www.uea.org).
Esperanto; *Kontakto*.
War Resisters' International [WRI] (PA RA HR TR CR), 5 Caledonian Rd, London N1 9DX, Britain (+44-20-7278 4040) (fax 7278 0444) (info@wri-irg.org) (wri-irg.org).
The Broken Rifle; *CO Update*; *War Profiteers News*.
Network of organisations of nonviolent activists, pacifists, conscientious objectors, etc. Also, tel +44-20-3355 2364.
Women Living Under Muslim Laws – International Solidarity Network [WLUML] (HR CD), PO Box 28455, London N19 5JT, Britain (+44-20-7263 0285) (fax 7561 9882) (wluml@wluml.org) (www.wluml.org).
Africa and Middle East office: PO Box 5330, Dakar Fann, Dakar, Senegal (grefels@gmail.com).
Asia office: PO Box 5192, Lahore, Pakistan (sgah@sgah.org.pk).
Includes Violence is Not our Culture campaign (www.violenceisnotourculture.org).
Women's International League for Peace and Freedom [WILPF] (PA HR AT ND), CP 28, 1 rue de Varembé, 1211 Genève 20, Switzerland (+41-22 919 7080) (fax 22 919 7081) (secretariat@wilpf.ch) (www.wilpf.org).
WILPF UN Office: 777 UN Plaza - 6th Floor, New York, NY 10017, USA (+1-212-682 1265) (fax 286 8211).
Projects of UN office include (www.peacewomen.org) and (www.reachingcriticalwill.org).
World Congress of Faiths (RP), 21 Maple St, London W1T 4BE, Britain (+44-1935-864055) (enquiries@worldfaiths.org) (www.worldfaiths.org).
World Federalist Movement - Institute for Global Polivy [WFM-IGP] (WF HR RE TW), 708 3rd Ave - Suite 1715, New York, NY 10017, USA (+1-212-599 1320) (fax 599 1332) (info@wfm-igp.org) (www.wfm-igp.org). Also: Bezuidenhoutseweg 99A, 2594 AC Den Haag, Netherlands (+31-70-363 4484).
World Federation of United Nations Associations / Fédération Mondiale des Associations pour les NU [WFUNA/FMANU] (TW HR), Palais des Nations - Room E4-2A, 1211 Genève 10, Switzerland (+41-22 917 3239) (info@wfuna.org) (www.wfuna.org).
Also: 1 United Nations Plaza - Rm 1177, New York, NY 10017, USA (+1-212-963 5610) (wfunany@wfuna.org).
World Future Council Foundation (WF EL), Dorotheenstr 15, 22301 Hamburg, Germany (+49-40-3070 91420) (fax 3070 91414) (info@worldfuturecouncil.org) (www.worldfuturecouncil.org).
Promotes sustainable future.
Other offices: UN (Geneva) (+41-22 555 0950); UK (+44-20-3356 2771) (info.uk@worldfuturecouncil.org); China (+86-10-6500 8172) (info.china@worldfuturecouncil.org).
World Information Service on Energy [WISE] (EL ND RA), Postbus 59636, 1040 LC Amsterdam, Netherlands (+31-20-612 6368) (info@wiseinternational.org) (www.wiseinternational.org). *WISE/NIRS Nuclear Monitor*. Grassroots-oriented antinuclear information. Works with NIRS in USA.
World Orchestra for Peace [WOP] (CD UN PO), c/o Charles Kaye, 26 Lyndale Ave, London NW2 2QA, Britain (+44-20-7317 8433) (ckconsult19@gmail.com) (www.worldorchestraforpeace.com). Also tel +44-7967-108974. Established 1995. Designated UNESCO Artist for Peace in 2010.
World Peace Council / Consejo Mondial de la Paz [WPC] (ND TW), Othonos St 10, 10557 Athinai, Greece (+30-210 3316 326) (fax 210 3251 576) (wpc@otenet.gr) (www.wpc-in.org).
World Rainforest Movement (EL HR), Avenida General María Paz 1615 - Of 3, 11400 Montevideo, Uruguay (+598-2-605 6943) (fax) (wrm@wrm.org.uy) (wrm.org.uy).
World Service Authority [WSA] (WF HR PA CD), 5 Thomas Circle NW - Suite 300, Washington, DC 20005, USA (+1-202-638 2662) (fax 638 0638) (info@worldservice.org) (www.worldservice.org). *World Citizen News*.
World Student Christian Federation – Inter-Regional Office [WSCF] (TW RP HR), Ecumenical Centre, BP 2251, 1211 Genève 2, Switzerland (+41-22 791 6358) (fax 22 791 6221) (wscf@wscf.ch) (www.wscfglobal.org). *Federation News*; *Student World*.
Youth for Exchange and Understanding [YEU] (CD), Ave du Suffrage Universel 49, 1030 Bruxelles, Belgium (+32-2 649 2048) (fax) (info@yeu-international.org) (www.yeu-international.org). Also Portugal office (+351-289-813074).

NATIONAL ORGANISATIONS

AFGHANISTAN
Co-operation for Peace and Unity [CPAU] (RE HR CR), House 997, Second Street, Kolola Pushta Rd, Kabul (+93-700 278891) (info@cpau.org.af) (www.cpau.org.af). Promoting peace, justice, human rights.
Revolutionary Association of the Women of Afghanistan [RAWA] (HR), see under Pakistan (www.rawa.org).
Women, Peace & Security Research Institute [RIWPS] (RE), Taimani, Street 8 – House 43, Kabul (+93-792 615421) (info@riwps-afghanistan.org) (www.riwps-afghanistan.org).

ALBANIA
Albanian Human Rights Group [AHRG] (HR), St Ibrahim Rugova – 2/39, Green Park, Tiranë (+355-42-225060) (el.ballauri@gmail.com) (www.ahrg-al.org).
Fondacioni Shqiptar Zgjidhja e Konflikteve dhe Pajtimi i Mosmarrëveshjeve [AFCR] (RE CR), Rr "Him Kolli" – Pall PF Trade – Nr 5, Tiranë (+355-4-226 4681) (fax 226 4837) (mediationalb@abcom.al) (www.mediationalb.org). *Pajtimi*.
Komiteti Shqiptar i Helsinkit / Albanian Helsinki Committee (HR), Rr Brigada VIII – Pll Tekno Projekt – Shk 2 – Ap 10, Tiranë (+355-4-223 3671) (fax) (office@ahc.org.al) (www.ahc.org.al).
Women's International League for Peace and Freedom – Albania (WL), Rruga Naim Fresheri – P 84 – Sh2 – Ap31, Tiranë (+355-42-229738) (fax) (tkurtiqi@hotmail.com).

ANDORRA
Partit Verds d'Andorra (EL), Apartat de Correus 2136, Andorra la Vella AD500 (+376-363797) (andorraverds@gmail.com) (www.verds.ad). Green Party.

ANGOLA
Search for Common Ground in Angola (CR CD), 15 rua D2 – Capolo II, Kilamba-Kiaxi, Luanda (angola@sfcg.org) (www.sfcg.org).

ARGENTINA
Fundación Servicio Paz y Justicia [SERPAJ] (FR IB HR), Piedras 730, 1070 Buenos Aires (+54-11-4361 5745) (secinstitucional@serpaj.org.ar) (serpaj.org.ar).
Greenpeace Argentina (GP), Zabala 3873, 1427 Buenos Aires (+54-11-4551 8811) (fax) (activismo@infogreenpeace.org.ar) (www.greenpeace.org/argentina).

For explanation of codes and abbreviations, see introduction

ARMENIA
Civil Society Institute [CSI] (HR), 43 Aygestan 11th St, Yerevan 0025 (+374-10-574317) (csi@csi.am) (www.csi.am).

AUSTRALIA
Act for Peace [AFP] (RP RE TW DA), c/o National Council of Churches in Australia, Locked Bag Q199, Sydney, NSW 1230 (+61-2-8259 0800) (www.actforpeace.org.au).
Alternatives to Violence Project (CR), c/o AVP(NSW), PO Box 161, Lane Cove, NSW 1595 (+61-2-9449 8415) (avpaus@avp.org.au) (www.avp.org.au).
Amnesty International Australia (AI), Locked Bag 23, Broadway, NSW 2007 (+61-2-8396 7600) (fax 9217 7663) (supporter@amnesty.org.au) (www.amnesty.org.au).
Anabaptist Association of Australia and New Zealand (ΠP), PO Box 738, Mona Vale, NSW 1660 (+61-2-8919 0367) (aaanz.info@gmail.com) (www.anabaptist.asn.au).
Anglican Pacifist Fellowship – Australia [APF] (RP), c/o Philip Huggins, 5 Docker St, Richmond, Vic 2121 (phuggins@melbourne.anglican.com.au).
Anti-Nuclear Alliance of Western Australia [ANAWA] (ND EL), 5 King William St, Bayswater, WA 6053 (+61-8-9272 4252) (admin@anawa.org.au) (www.anawa.org.au).
Australia East Timor Friendship Assocaiation – South Australia [AEFTA-SA] (HR), PO Box 240, Goodwood, SA 5034 (+61-8-8344 3511) (www.aetfa.org.au).
Australia West Papua Association (HR), PO Box 105, Bunbury, WA 6231 (ash@freewestpapua.org) (www.freewestpapua.org).
Australian Anti-Bases Campaign Coalition [AABCC] (IB WP AT ND RA), PO Box A899, Sydney South, NSW 1235 (+61-2-9698 5617) (denis@anti-bases.org) (www.anti-bases.org).
Australian Nuclear Free Alliance (EL), c/o Friends of the Earth, PO Box 222, Fitzroy, Vic 3065 (+61-3-9419 8700) (fax 9416 2081) (anfacommittee@gmail.com) (www.anfa.org.au).
Burma Campaign Australia (HR), c/o 4 Goulburn St – Level 1 – Suite 110, Sydney, NSW 2000 (+61-2-9264 7694) (admin@aucampaignforburma.org) (www.aucampaignforburma.org).
Centre for Peace Studies (RE EL SD), University of New England, Armidale, NSW 2351 (+61-2-6773 2442) (fax 6773 3350) (hware@une.edu.au) (www.une.edu.au/study/peace-studies). Organise annual Nonviolence Film Festival.
Christian Peacemaker Teams Australasia [CPTA] (RP RA CR), PO Box 738, Mona

AUSTRALIA

Vale, NSW 1660 (+61-2-9997 4632)
(doug.hynd@netspeed.com.au).
An initiative of various church groups.
**Coalition for Justice & Peace in Palestine
[CJPP]** (HR), PO Box 144, Glebe, NSW
2037 (cjpp@coalitionforpalestine.org)
(www.coalitionforpalestine.org).
Conflict Resolution Network [CRN] (CR UN
RE), PO Box 1016, Chatswood, NSW 2057
(+61-2-9419 8500) (fax 9413 1148)
(crn@crnhq.org) (www.crnhq.org).
**Ecumenical Accompaniment Programme in
Palestine and Israel – Australia** (RP HR),
c/o National Council of Churches in Australia,
Locked Bag Q199, Sydney, NSW 1230
(+61-2-8259 0800) (www.ncca.org.au/eappi).
Footprints for Peace (ND EL), PO Box 632,
Fremantle South, WA 6162
(marcus@footprintsforpeace.org)
(www.footprintsforpeace.net).
Friends of the Earth (FE RA PO), PO Box
222, Fitzroy, Vic 3065 (+61-3-9419 8700)
(fax 9416 2081) (foe@foe.org.au)
(www.foe.org.au).
Greenpeace Australia Pacific (GP), 33
Mountain St, Ultimo, NSW 2007
(+61-2-9281 6100) (fax 9280 0380)
(support.au@greenpeace.org)
(www.greenpeace.org.au).
Greens (WA) (EL HR DA), PO Box 3022, East
Perth, WA 6892 (+61-8-9221 8333)
(fax 9221 8433) (office@wa.greens.org.au)
(www.wa.greens.org.au).
Green Issue.
**Independent and Peaceful Australia
Network [IPAN]** (PA DA), PO Box 573,
Coorparoo, Qld 4151 (+61-431-597256)
(ipan.australia@gmail.com) (ipan.org.au).
Opposes overseas military bases.
International Volunteers for Peace [IVP]
(SC), 499 Elizabeth St, Surry Hills, NSW
2010 (+61-2-9699 1129) (fax 9318 0918)
(admin@ivp.org.au) (www.ivp.org.au).
**Medical Association for Prevention of War
[MAPW]** (IP), PO Box 1379, Carlton, Vic
3053 (+61-3-9023 1958)
(mapw@mapw.org.au) (www.mapw.org.au).
Nonlethal Security for Peace Campaign (DA
RE WF), PO Box 724, Avalon Beach, NSW
2107 (info@tamingwar.com)
(www.nonlethalsecurityforpeace.com).
Pace e Bene Australia [PeBA] (PA RP), 5/63
Roslyn St, Brighton, Vic 3186
(+61-3-9592 5247) (d.hess@ozemail.com.au)
(www.paceebene.org.au). For nonviolence
and cultural transformation.
Pax Christi (PC IB), PO Box 31, Carlton
South, Vic 3053 (+61-3-9893 4946)
(fax 9379 1711) (pax@paxchristi.org.au)
(www.paxchristi.org.au).
Disarming Times.
Also NSW (+61-2-9550 3845).

**People for Nuclear Disarmament – Western
Australia [PND]** (IB ND), 5 King William St,
Bayswater, WA 6053 (+61-8-9272 4252)
(jovall@iinet.net.au).
**People's Charter to Create a Nonviolent
World** (PA TW EL), PO Box 68, Daylesford,
Vic 3460 (flametree@riseup.net)
(thepeoplesnonviolencecharter.wordpress.com).
Quaker Service Australia (SF TW), 119
Devonshire St, Surry Hills, NSW 2010
(+61-2-9698 9103) (fax 9225 9241)
(administration@qsa.org.au)
(www.qsa.org.au).
Religions for Peace Australia (RP), 71
Wellington St, Flemington, Vic 3031
(wcrpaust@iinet.net.au)
(religionsforpeaceaustralia.org.au).
Reprieve Australia (HR), PO Box 4296,
Melbourne, VIC 3001 (+61-3-9670 4108)
(contact@reprieve.org.au)
(www.reprieve.org.au).
Campaigns against death penalty.
SafeGround (DA), PO Box 2143,
Morphettville, SA 5043
(info@safeground.org.au)
(safeground.org.au). Work to reduce impact
of explosive remnants of war.
Schweik Action Wollongong (SD), PO Box
U129, Wollongong, NSW 2500
(+61-2-4228 7860) (fax 4221 5341)
(brian_martin@uow.edu.au)
(www.bmartin.cc/others/SAW.html).
Servas Australia (SE), c/o Pam Webster, 2
Warili Rd, Frenchs Forest, 2076
(+61-2-9451 9669) (secretary@servas.org.au)
(www.servas.org.au).
Society of Friends (SF), PO Box 556,
Kenmore, Qld 4069
(ymsecretary@quakers.org.au)
(www.quakers.org.au).
**Tasmanian Quaker Peace & Justice
Committee [TQPJC]** (SF PA), PO Box 388,
North Hobart, Tas 7002 (+61-400-925385).
**Universal Peace Federation – Australia
[UPF]** (RP), PO Box 642, Burwood, NSW
1805 (oceaniahq@gmail.com) (www.upf.org).
War Resisters' League [WRL] (WR AL HR),
PO Box 451, North Hobart, Tas 7002
(+61-3-6278 2380) (pdpjones@mpx.com.au).
**Women's International League for Peace
and Freedom [WILPF]** (WL ND), PO Box
934, Dickson, ACT 2602
(wilpf.australia@wilpf.org.au) (wilpf.org.au).
Peace & Freedom.
**World Citizens Association (Australia)
[WCAA]** (WF), PO Box 6318, University of
New South Wales, Sydney, NSW 1466
(C.Hamer@unsw.edu.au)
(www.worldcitizens.org.au). *The Bulletin.*

AUSTRIA

Amnesty International Österreich (AI),
Möringgasse 10, 1150 Wien (+43-1-78008)
(fax 780 0844) (office@amnesty.at)
(www.amnesty.at).

Arbeitsgemeinschaft für Wehrdienstverweigerung und Gewaltfreiheit [ARGE WDV] (WR), Schotteng 3A/1/59, 1010 Wien (+43-1-535 9109) (fax 532 7416) (argewdv@verweigert.at) (www.verweigert.at).

Bürgermeister für den Frieden in Deutschland und Österreich (CD ND DA), see under Germany.

Begegnungszentrum für Aktive Gewaltlosigkeit / Centre for Encounter and Active Nonviolence [BFAG] (WR TW EL), Wolfgangerstr 26, 4820 Bad Ischl (+43-6132-24590) (info@begegnungszentrum.at) (www.begegnungszentrum.at). *Rundbrief.*

Die Grünen (EL AL PO), Rooseveltplatz 4-5, 1090 Wien (+43-1-2363 9980) (fax 526 9110) (bundesbuero@gruene.at) (www.gruene.at). Green Party.

Franz Jägerstätter House (PC), St Radegund 31, 5121 Ostermiething (+43-6278-8219) (pfarre.stradegund@dioezese-linz.at).

Internationaler Versöhnungsbund [IVB] (FR), Lederergasse 23/III/27, 1080 Wien (+43-1-408 5332) (fax) (office@versoehnungsbund.at) (www.versoehnungsbund.at).

IPPNW Österreich [OMEGA] (IP), Schulgasse 40/17, 1180 Wien (+43-2988-6236) (office@ippnw.at) (www.ippnw.at).

Konfliktkultur (CR PO), Breitenfeldergasse 2/14, 1080 Wien (+43-699-1944 1313) (office@konfliktkultur.at) (www.konfliktkultur.at).

Österreichische Gesellschaft für Aussenpolitik und die Vereinten Nationen [OEGAVN] (UN), Reitschulgasse 2/2, Hofburg/Stallburg, 1010 Wien (+43-1-535 4627) (office@oegavn.org) (www.una-austria.org).

Österreichisches Netzwerk für Frieden und Gewaltfreiheit (RE), c/o IVB, Lederergasse 23/III/27, 1080 Wien (www.friedensnetzwerk.at).

Österreichisches Studienzentrum für Frieden und Konfliktlösung [ÖSFK/ASPR] (HR PA RE CR), Rochusplatz 1, 7461 Stadtschlaining, Burg (+43-3355-2498) (fax 2662) (aspr@aspr.ac.at) (www.aspr.ac.at). Study Centre for Peace and Conflict Resolution.

Peace Museum Vienna (RE), Blutgasse 3/1, 1010 Wien (office@peacemuseumvienna.com) (www.peacemuseumvienna.com). Includes Windows for Peace project in city streets.

AZERBAIJAN

Azerbaycan Insan Huquqlarini Mudafie Merkezi / Human Rights Centre of Azerbaijan [AIHMM/HRCA] (HR), PO Box 31, Baku 1000 (+994-12-492 1369) (fax) (eldar.hrca@gmail.com) (penitentiary.ucoz.ru). *Human Rights in Azerbaijan.*

BANGLADESH

Bangladesh Interreligious Council for Peace and Justice [BICPAJ] (FR IB PC CR EL), 14/20 Iqbal Rd, Mohammadpur, Dhaka 1207 (+880-2-914 1410) (fax 812 2010) (bicpaj@bijoy.net) (www.bicpaj.org).

Manush Manusher Jonnyo (HR EL CD PO TW), Nahar Peace Garden, 202/1 Tutpara Main Rd, Khulna Metro 9100 (fax +880-41-725071) (manusmanusherjonnyo@gmail.com). *Ideas for a Better Bangladesh.*

Service Civil International [SCI] (SC), 57/15 East Razabazar, Panthapath West, Dhaka 1215 (+880-2-935 3993) (scibangladesh@gmail.com) (scibangladesh.org).

BARBADOS

Barbados Inter-Religious Organisation [BIRO] (RP), c/o Roman Catholic Diocese of Bridgetown, PO Box 1223, Bridgetown (vincentblackett@hotmail.com). Affiliated to Religions for Peace International.

BELARUS

Alternativnaya Grazhdanskaya Sluzhba / Campaign for Alternative Civilian Service in Belarus [AGS] (HR PA), Bakinskaya Str 8-44, 220007 Minsk (+375-25-999 4699) (ags.belarus@gmail.com) (ags.by).

Belarusian Helsinki Committee (HR), Karl Liebknecht St 68 – off 1201, 220036 Minsk (+375-17-222 4800) (fax 222 4801) (office@belhelcom.org) (www.belhelcom.org).

Belrad Institute of Radiation Safety (EL), 2 Marusinsky – pereulok 27, Minsk 220053 (+375-17-289 0383) (fax 289 0384) (belrad@nsys.by) (www.belrad-institute.org).

Green Cross Belarus (EL TW DA CR), Oktiabrsky St 16 – Building 3, 220030 Minsk (+375-17-210 0062) (fax 227 1146) (gcb@greencross.by) (www.greencross.by).

BELGIUM

Abolition 2000 Belgium (ND), c/o Vredesactie, Patriottenstr 27, 2600 Berchem (+32-3-281 6839) (lene@vredesactie.be) (www.abolition2000.be).

ACAT – Belgique Francophone (HR), Quai aux Foins 53, 1000 Bruxelles (+32-2 223 0159) (fax) (a.cat.belgique@gmail.com) (www.acat-belgique-francophone.be). *ACAT-info.*

ACAT België-Vlaanderen (HR), Zevenkerken 4, 8200 Sint-Andries (+32-50 406132) (info@acat-belgie-vlaanderen.org) (www.acat-belgie-vlaanderen.org).

Agir pour la Paix (WR), 35 rue van Elewyck, Ixelles, 1050 Bruxelles (+32-2 648 5220) (info@agirpourlapaix.be) (agirpourlapaix.be).

BELGIUM

Amis de la Terre / Friends of the Earth Belgium (Wallonia and Brussels) [AT] (FE PO), Rue Nanon 98, 5000 Namur (+32-81 390639) (fax 81 390638) (contact@amisdelaterre.be) (www.amisdelaterre.be). *Saluterreliens.*

Amnesty International Belgique Francophone [AIBF] (AI), Rue Berckmans 9, 1060 Bruxelles (+32-2 538 8177) (fax 2 537 3729) (aibf@aibf.be) (www.amnesty.be). *Libertés!.*

Amnesty International Vlaanderen (AI), Kerkstr 156, 2060 Antwerpen (+32-3 271 1616) (fax 3 235 7812) (amnesty@aivl.be) (www.aivl.be).

Artsen Voor Vrede [AVV] (IP), Karel Van de Woesti St 18, 9300 Aalst. *Gezondheidszorg en Vredesvraagstukken.*

Association Médicale pour la Prévention de la Guerre Nucléaire [AMPGN] (IP), 51 Ave Wolvendael, 1180 Bruxelles (de.salle.philippe@skynet.be) (ampgn-belgium.be).

Brigades de Paix Internationales [BPI/PBI] (HR CR CD RE), 23 rue Lt F Wampach, 1200 Bruxelles (+32-473 878136) (info@pbi-belgium.org) (www.pbibelgium.org).

Climaxi – Friends of the Earth (Flanders & Brussels) (FE ND HR), Maria-Hendrikaplein 5, 9000 Gent (+32-9 242 8752) (fax 9 242 8751) (famke@climaxi.be) (www.climaxi.org).

Comité de Surveillance OTAN [CSO] (ND PA RE), rue des Cultivateurs 62, 1040 Bruxelles (+32-2 511 6310) (fax) (info@csotan.org) (www.csotan.org). *Alerte OTAN.* They keep an eye on NATO.

Commission Justice et Paix – Belgique francophone (RP), Rue Maurice Liétart 31/6, 1150 Bruxelles (+32-2 738 0801) (fax 2 738 0800) (info@justicepaix.be) (www.justicepaix.be).

Flemish War and Peace Museum (RE), Ijzertoren, Ijzerdijk 49, 8600 Diksmuide (+32-51 500286) (info@aandeijzer.be) (www.museumaandeijzer.be).

Greenpeace (GP), Haachtsesteenweg 159, 1030 Brussel (+32-2 274 0200) (fax 2 274 0230) (info.be@greenpeace.org) (www.greenpeace.org/belgium).

Groupe Interconfessionnel de la Réconciliation / Kinshasa [GIR] (FR), Route de Longchamp 26, 1348 Louvain-la-Neuve (buangajos@hotmail.com).

I Stop the Arms Trade (AT RA PA), c/o Vredesactie, Patriottenstr 27, 2600 Berchem (+32-3 281 6839) (ikstopwapenhandel@vredesactie.be) (ikstopwapenhandel.eu). Non-violent direct action against EU arms trade.

Intal Globalize Solidarity (WP TW), 53 Chausée de Haecht, 1210 Bruxelles (+32-2 209 2350) (fax 2 209 2351) (info@intal.be) (www.intal.be).

Moeders voor Vrede / Mères pour la Paix / Mothers for Peace, Grote Markt 34, 8900 Ieper (+32-483 599395) (info@mothersforpeace.be) (www.mothersforpeace.be).

Pax Christi Vlaanderen [PCV] (PC RE CD ND CR), Italiëlei 98A, 2000 Antwerpen (+32-3 225 1000) (fax 3 225 0799) (paxchristi@paxchristi.be) (www.paxchristi.be). *Koerier.*

Pax Christi Wallonie-Bruxelles [PCWB] (PC), Rue Maurice Liétart 31/1, 1150 Bruxelles (+32-2 738 0804) (fax 2 738 0800) (info@paxchristiwb.be) (www.paxchristiwb.be). *Signes des Temps.*

Register van Wereldburgers / Registry of World Citizens [RW] (WF PA TW), Vredestr 65, 2540 Hove (+32-3 455 7763) (verstraeten.jean@belgacom.net) (www.recim.org/cdm). *Overleven door Wereldrecht / Survival by World Law.*

Religions for Peace – Belgium (RP), Av de la Reine 7, 1030 Bruxelles (fmdali@wcrp.be)

Say No (PA), A Beernaertstr 28a, 1170 Brussel (+32-497 934716) (info@desertie.be) (www.sayno.be). Anti-militarist choral project.

Servas – Belgium & Luxembourg (SE), c/o Rita Dessauvage, Kloosterweg 30, 1652 Beersel-Alsemberg (belgium@servas.org) (belgium.servas.org).

Sortir de la Violence [SDV] (FR CR RE), Blvd du Souverain 199, 1160 Bruxelles (+32-2 679 0644) (info@sortirdelaviolence.org) (www.sortirdelaviolence.org).

VIA (SC WC), Grote Biëlei 37, 2018 Antwerpen (+32-3 707 1614) (via@viavzw.be) (www.viavzw.be).

Vlaams Vredesinstituut / Flemish Peace Institute (RE), Leuvenseweg 86, 1000 Brussel (+32-2 552 4591) (fax 2 552 4408) (vredesinstituut@vlaamsparlement.be) (www.vlaamsvredesinstituut.eu). Also www.flemishpeaceinstitute.eu.

Vredesactie (WR AT ND), Patriottenstr 27, 2600 Berchem, Antwerpen (+32-3 281 6839) (info@vredesactie.be) (www.vredesactie.be). *Vredesactie.*

Vrouwen in 't Zwart / Femmes en Noir / Women in Black [WiB] (PA DA HR), c/o Ria Convents, Vismarkt 8, 3000 Leuven (+32-16 291314) (marianne.vandegoorberg@telnet.be) (snellings.telenet.be/womeninblackleuven).

BERMUDA

Amnesty International Bermuda (AI), PO Box HM 2136, Hamilton HM JX (+1441-296 3249) (fax) (director@amnestybermuda.org).

BHUTAN
People's Forum for Human Rights (HR), see under Nepal.

BOSNIA-HERZEGOVINA
Centar za ivotnu Sredinu [CZZS] (FE), Miša Stupara 5, 78000 Banja Luka (+387-5143 3140) (fax 5143 3141) (info@czzs.org) (czzs.org).

Centar za Nenasilnu Akciju / Centre for Nonviolent Action [CNA] (CD CR PA RE), Kranjcevicevа 33, 71000 Sarajevo (+387-3326 0876) (fax 3326 0875) (cna.sarajevo@nenasilje.org) (www.nenasilje.org). See also in Serbia.

Nansen Dialogue Centre Sarajevo [NDC Sarajevo] (CR), Hakije Kulenovica 10, 71000 Sarajevo (+387-33-556846) (fax 556845) (ndcsarajevo@nansen-dialogue.net) (www.ndcsarajevo.org).

WhyNjet / Why Not (WR), Demala Bijedica 309, 71000 Sarajevo (+387-33-618461) (info@zastone.ba) (www.zastone.ba). Formerly Kampanja za Prigovor Savjesti u BiH.

BOTSWANA
Society of Friends (Quakers) (SF), c/o Shelagh Willet, Box 20166, Gaborone (+267-394 7147) (willet.shelagh@botsnet.bw).

BRAZIL
ACAT Brasil (HR), Praça Clovis Bevilaqua 351 – sala 701, 01018-001 São Paulo – SP (+55-11-3101 6084) (fax) (acatbrasil.international@gmail.com). Affiliated to FIACAT.

Associação das Nações Unidas – Brasil [ANUBRA] (UN), Av Brigadeiro Faria Lima 1485 – North Tower – 19th Floor, 01452-002 São Paulo – SP (+55-11-3094 7984) (fax) (unab@unab.org.br) (www.unab.org.br).

Centro Brasileiro de Solidariedade aos Povos e Luta pela Paz [CEBRAPAZ] (WP CD SD ND), Rua Marconi 34 – Conj 51, República, 01047-000 São Paulo – SP (+55-11-3223 3469) (cebrapaz@cebrapaz.org.br) (cebrapaz.org.br).

Commissão Pastoral da Terra [CPT] (PC), Edificio Dom Abel – 1º andar, Rua 19 – Nº 35, 74030-090 Centro Goiânia, Goiás (+55-62-4008 6466) (fax 4008 6405) (cpt@cptnacional.org.br) (www.cptnacional.org.br).

Green Cross Brazil (EL TW DA HR), Centro Empresarial Brasilia – SRTVS – Q 701 – Bloco A – Salas 311 e 31, 70340-907 Brasilia (+55-61-3226 4613) (greencrossbrasil.gcb@gmail.com) (gcint.org.br).

Instituto Sou da Paz (CR DA), Rua Luis Murat 260 – VI, Madalena, 05436-050 São Paulo – SP (+55-11-3093 7333) (fax) (atendimento@soudapaz.org) (www.soudapaz.org).

Serviço de Paz [SERPAZ] (RE DA CR), Rua 1º de Março 776 – sala 4 – Centro, 93010-210 São Leopoldo – RS (+55-51-3592 6106) (fax 2111 1411) (serpaz@serpaz.org.br) (www.serpaz.org.br).

Serviço Voluntário Internacional [SVI-Brasil] (SC), Rua Ribeiro Junqueira 161 – Sl 3, Mangabeiras, Belo Horizonte – MG (+55-11-99493 1794) (pedro@svibrasil.org) (www.svibrasil.org).

BRITAIN
38 Degrees (EL HR TW), Room 134, 40 Bowling Green Lane, London EC1 (+44-20-7970 6023) (emailtheteam@38degrees.org.uk) (www.38degrees.org.uk). Organises internet lobbying on progressive issues.

Abolition 2000 UK (ND), 162 Holloway Rd, London N7 (mail@abolition2000uk.org) (www.abolition2000uk.org).

Acronym Institute for Disarmament Diplomacy (RE), Werks Central, 15-17 Middle St, Brighton BN1, Sussex (+44-20-7503 8857) (info@acronym.org.uk) (acronym.org.uk).

Action by Christians Against Torture [ACAT-UK] (HR), c/o 19 The Square, Knowle Park, Bristol BS4 (+44-117-971 0379) (uk.acat@gmail.com) (www.acatuk.org.uk). Newsletter.

Action on Armed Violence (AT DA TW HR), 405 Mile End Rd, Bow, London E3 (info@aoav.org.uk) (aoav.org.uk).

Ahmadiyya Muslim Community (RP HR), c/o Baitul Futuh Mosque, 181 London Rd, Morden, Surrey SM4 (+44-333-240 0490) (enquiries@ahmadiyya.org.uk) (Ahmadiyya.org.uk). Anti-violence and pro freedom of thought group.

Aldermaston Women's Peace Camp(aign) [AWPC] (WR ND RA), c/o 8 Millar House, Merchants Rd, Bristol BS8 4HA (info@aldermaston.net) (www.aldermaston.net). Monthly Aldermaston peace camps; and other actions.

Alternatives to Violence Project – Britain [AVP Britain] (CR PO), 28 Charles Sq, London N1 6HT (+44-20-7324 4755) (info@avpbritain.org.uk) (www.avpbritain.org.uk).

Amnesty International – UK Section [AIUK] (AI), Human Rights Action Centre, 17-25 New Inn Yard, London EC2A 3EA (+44-20-7033 1500) (fax 7033 1503) (info@amnesty.org.uk) (www.amnesty.org.uk).

Anabaptist Network (RP), PO Box 68073, London N22 9HS (admin@anabaptistnetwork.com) (www.anabaptistnetwork.com).

For explanation of codes and abbreviations, see introduction

BRITAIN

Anglican Pacifist Fellowship [APF] (WR IB RP PA), Peace House, 19 Paradise St, Oxford OX1 1LD (enquiries@anglicanpeacemaker.org.uk) (www.anglicanpeacemaker.org.uk). *The Anglican Peacemaker.*

Article 36 (DA), 19 Barnardo Road, Exeter EX2 4ND (info@article36.org) (www.article36.org). Working to change law relating to weapons.

At Ease (HR), Bunhill Fields Meeting House, Quaker Court, Banner St, London EC1Y 8QQ (+44-20-7490 5223) (info@atease.org.uk) (www.atease.org.uk). Advice, counselling for military personnel.

Baby Milk Action (TW PO EL), 4 Brooklands Ave, Cambridge CB2 8BB (+44-1223-464420) (info@babymilkaction.org) (www.babymilkaction.org). *BMA Update.*

Bahá'í Community UK (RP), 27 Rutland Gate, London SW7 1DP (+44-20-7584 2566) (fax 7584 9402) (opa@bahai.org.uk) (www.bahai.org.uk).

Balkans Peace Park Project – UK Committee [B3P] (CD EL), c/o Rylstone Lodge, Rylstone, Skipton BD23 6LH, N Yorks (+44-1756-730231) (j.dyer@leeds.ac.uk) (www.balkanspeacepark.org).

Baptist Peace Fellowship [BPF] (FR), c/o 21 Kingshill, Cirencester GL7 1DE, Gloucestershire (bobgardiner@yahoo.co.uk) (www.baptist-peace.org.uk). *BPF Newsletter.*

Before You Sign Up, 11 Manor Rd, Stratford-upon-Avon, Warwickshire CV37 (info@beforeyousignup.info) (www.beforeyousignup.info). For people thinking of joining the armed forces.

Bertrand Russell Peace Foundation [BRPF] (RE PA ND), Russell House, Bulwell Lane, Nottingham NG6 0BT (+44-115-978 4504) (fax 942 0433) (elfeuro@compuserve.com) (www.russfound.org). *The Spokesman.*

Bloomsbury Ad Hoc Committee [BADHOC] (EL HR PA), c/o 26 Museum Chambers, Little Russell St, London WC1A 9PD (badhoc@activist.com).

Boycott Israel Network [BIN] (HR TW), c/o PSC, Box BM PSA, London WC1N 3XX (info@boycottisraelnetwork.net) (www.boycottisraelnetwork.net). Expansion of the Boycott Israeli Goods Campaign.

Bradford University Department of Peace Studies (RE CR TW), Bradford BD7 1DP, West Yorks (+44-1274-235235) (fax 235240) (www.brad.ac.uk/acad/peace/).

Brighton Peace & Environment Centre [BPEC] (RE EL), 39-41 Surrey St, Brighton BN1, Sussex (+44-1273-766610) (info@bpec.org) (www.bpec.org).

British American Security Information Council [BASIC] (RE AT ND), 3 Whitehall Court, London SW1 (+44-20-7766 3461) (basicuk@basicint.org) (www.basicint.org). *BASIC Reports.*

Building Bridges for Peace (CR), c/o 2 Crossways, Cott Lane, Dartington, Totnes TQ9 6HE, Devon (info@buildingbridgesforpeace.org) (www.buildingbridgesforpeace.org). Conflict transformation through empathy.

Campaign Against Arms Trade [CAAT] (WR AT IB RA), Unit 4, 5-7 Wells Terrace, London N4 3JU (+44-20-7281 0297) (enquiries@caat.org.uk) (www.caat.org.uk). *CAAT News.*

Campaign against Climate Change [CCC] (EL RA), Top Floor, 5 Caledonian Rd, London N1 9DX (+44-20-7833 9311) (info@campaigncc.org) (www.campaigncc.org).

Campaign Against Criminalising Communities [CAMPACC] (HR), c/o 44 Ainger Rd, London NW3 (+44-20-7586 5892) (estella24@tiscali.co.uk) (www.campacc.org.uk).

Campaign for a Nuclear-Free Middle East [CNFME] (ND), Mordechai Vanunu House, 162 Holloway Rd, London N7 8DQ (+44-20-8672 9698) (david.lrcnd@cnduk.org).

Campaign for Earth Federation / World Federalist Party (WF), c/o Ian Hackett, 1 Kenilworth Rd, London W5 5PB (+44-20-8579 7706) (worldfederalistparty@gmail.com) (www.federalunion.org.uk).

Campaign for Homosexual Equality [CHE] (HR), c/o 86 Caledonian Rd, London N1 9DN (+44-7941-914340) (info@c-h-e.org.uk) (www.c-h-e.org.uk).

Campaign for Human Rights in the Philippines [CHRP UK] (HR), c/o Kanlungan Filipino Consortium, Unit 1, Fountayne Business Centre, Broad Lane, London N15 (info@chrp.org.uk) (www.chrp.org.uk).

Campaign for Human Rights in Turkey (HR), c/o Turkish & Kurdish Community Centre, Former Library, Howard Rd, London N16 8PU (+44-20-7275 8440) (fax 7275 7245).

Campaign for Nuclear Disarmament [CND] (IB ND RA RE), 162 Holloway Rd, London N7 8DQ (+44-20-7700 2393) (enquiries@cnduk.org) (www.cnduk.org). *Campaign!.*

Campaign for Nuclear Disarmament Cymru / Yr Ymgyrch dros Ddiarfogi Niwclear [CND Cymru] (ND RA AT DA), c/o 72 Heol Gwyn, Yr Alltwen, Pontardawe SA8 3AN (+44-1792-830330) (heddwch@cndcymru.org) (www.cndcymru.org). *Heddwch.*

Campaign for Press and Broadcasting Freedom [CPBF] (HR), 2nd floor, 23 Orford

Rd, Walthamstow, London E17 9NL (freepress@cpbf.org.uk) (www.cpbf.org.uk). *Free Press.*
Campaign for the Accountability of American Bases [CAAB] (ND PA RA), 59 Swarcliffe Rd, Harrogate HG1, Yorks (+44-1423-884076) (mail@caab.corner.org.uk) (www.caab.org.uk).
Campaign Opposing Police Surveillance [COPS] (HR RA), 5 Caledonian Rd, London N1 9DX (campaignopposingpolicesurveillance.com).
Campaign to Protect Rural England (EL PO), 5-11 Lavington St, London SE1 0NZ (+44-20-7981 2800) (fax 7981 2899) (info@cpre.org.uk) (www.cpre.org.uk). Campaigns include opposing fracking.
Centre for Alternative Technology / Canolfan y Dechnoleg Amgen [CAT] (EL PO AL), Machynlleth, Powys SY20 9AZ (+44-1654-705950) (fax 702782) (info@cat.org.uk) (www.cat.org.uk). *Clean Slate.*
Centre for Global Education York (HR TW), York St John University, Lord Mayor's Walk, York YO31 7EX (+44-1904-876839) (fax 612512) (cge@yorksj.ac.uk) (www.centreforglobaleducation.org).
Centre for International Peacebuilding (CR RE TW EL), The White House, 46 High St, Buntingford, Herts SG9 9AH (+44-1763-272662) (eirwenhartbottle@gmail.com).
Centre for Trust, Peace and Social Relations [CTPSR] (RE), 5 Innovation Village, Coventry University Technology Park, Cheetah Rd, Coventry CV1 2TT (+44-24-7765 1182) (info.ctpsr@coventry.ac.uk) (www.coventry.ac.uk).
Centre of Religion, Reconciliation and Peace (RE RP), University of Winchester, Sparkford Rd, Winchester SO22, Hampshire (+44-1962-841515) (fax 842280) (www.winchester.ac.uk).
Chernobyl Children's Project (UK) (PO EL CD), Kinder House, Fitzalan St, Glossop SK13, Derbyshire (+44-1457-863534) (ccprojectuk@gmail.com) (www.chernobyl-children.org.uk).
Children are Unbeatable! Alliance (HR), 125-127 Westminster Business Square, 1-45 Durham St, London SE11 (+44-20-7713 0569) (info@endcorporalpunishment.org) (www.childrenareunbeatable.org.uk). For abolition of all physical punishment.
Children of Peace (CR HR), 1st Floor, The Roller Mill, Mill Lane, Uckfield TN22 5AA, Sussex (+44-1825-768074) (info@childrenofpeace.org.uk) (www.childrenofpeace.org.uk). Charity working in Israel, Palestine, Jordan.
Christian Aid (TW), 35-41 Lower Marsh, London SE1 (+44-20-7620 4444) (fax 7620 0719) (info@christian-aid.org) (www.christianaid.org.uk).

Christian Campaign for Nuclear Disarmament [CCND] (ND RP), 162 Holloway Rd, London N7 8DQ (+44-20-7700 4200) (fax 7700 2357) (christians@cnduk.org) (www.christiancnd.org.uk). *Ploughshare.*
Christian International Peace Service [CHIPS] (RP CR PO RE), 17 Hopton House, Loughborough Estate, London SW9 7SP (+44-20-7078 7439) (info@chipspeace.org) (www.chipspeace.org).
Church & Peace (RP CR RE), 39 Postwood Green, Hertford Heath SG13 7QJ (+44-1992-416442) (IntlOffice@church-and-peace.org) (www.church-and-peace.org).
City to Sea (EL PO), Unit D, Albion Dockside Studios, Hanovr Place, Bristol BS1 6UT (info@citytosea.org.uk) (www.citytosea.org.uk). Campaign to stop plastic pollution at source.
Climate Outreach (EL), The Old Music Hall, 106-108 Cowley Rd, Oxford OX4 1JE (+44-1865-403334) (info@climateoutreach.org) (climateoutreach.org). Formerly Climate Outreach and Information Network.
Close Capenhurst Campaign (EL), c/o News From Nowhere, 96 Bold St, Liverpool L1 (closecapenhurst@gmail.com) (close-capenhurst.org.uk). Opposes uranium enrichment plant in Cheshire.
Co-operation Ireland (GB) (CD), Windy Ridge, Courtlands Hill, Pangbourne RG8, Berkshire (+44-118-976 7790) (fax) (murphy992@btinternet.com) (www.cooperationireland.org).
Coal Action Network (EL RA), Steade Rd, Sheffield S7 (info@coalaction.org.uk) (www.coalaction.org).
Commonweal Collection (RE AL PA EL), c/o J B Priestley Library, Bradford University, Bradford BD7 1DP, Yorks (+44-1274-233404) (commonweal@riseup.net) (bradford.ac.uk/library/libraries-and-collections/). Peace library.
Community for Reconciliation [CfR] (RP), Barnes Close, Chadwich, Malthouse Lane, Bromsgrove, Worcs B61 0RA (+44-1562-710231) (fax 710278) (cfrenquiry@aol.com) (www.cfrbarnesclose.co.uk). *Newslink.*
Conciliation Resources (CR), 173 Upper St, Islington, London N1 1RG (+44-20-7359 7728) (cr@c-r.org) (www.c-r.org). *Accord.*
Concord Media (PA EL TW), 22 Hines Rd, Ipswich IP3 9BG, Suffolk (+44-1473-726012) (sales@concordmedia.org.uk) (www.concordmedia.org.uk).
Conflict and Environment Observatory [CEOBS] (DA EL RE), Bridge 5 Mill, 22a Beswick St, Ancoats, Manchester M4 (ceobs.org). Previously Toxic Remnants of War Project.
Conflict Research Society [CRS] (RE), c/o Hugh Miall, 45 Ethelbert Rd, Canterbury CT1 3NF, Kent (conflictresearchsociety@kent.ac.uk) (www.conflictresearchsociety.org).

BRITAIN

Conscience – Taxes for Peace not War (TR WR HR), 17 North Square, Hampstead Garden Suburb, London NW11 (+44-20-3515 9132) (campaign@conscienceonline.org.uk) (www.conscienceonline.org.uk). *Conscience Update*.

Conway Hall Ethical Society (HR RE), Conway Hall, Red Lion Sq, London WC1 4RL (+44-20-7405 1818) (admin@conwayhall.org.uk) (www.conwayhall.org.uk). *Ethical Record*. Formerly South Place Ethical Society.

Cord (TW CR), Floor 9, Eaton House, 1 Eaton Rd, Coventry CV1 2FJ (+44-24-7708 7777) (info@cord.org.uk) (www.cord.org.uk). International peacebuilding charity.

Corporate Occupation (HR RA TW), c/o Corporate Watch, 84b Whitechapel High St, London E1 7QX (tom@shoalcollective.org) (www.corporateoccupation.org). Opposes occupation of Palestine.

Corporate Watch (EL RA AL), c/o Freedom Press, Angel Alley, 84b Whitechapel High St, London E1 7QX (+44-20-7426 0005) (contact@corporatewatch.org) (www.corporatewatch.org). *News Update*.

Cuba Solidarity Campaign (TW WC), c/o UNITE, 33-37 Moreland St, London EC1V 8BB (+44-20-7490 5715) (fax 7490 3556) (office@cuba-solidarity.org.uk) (www.cuba-solidarity.org.uk). *Cuba Si*.

Cumbrians Opposed to a Radioactive Environment [CORE] (EL), Dry Hall, Broughton Mills, Broughton-in-Furness, Cumbria LA20 (+44-1229-716523) (fax) (martin@corecumbria.co.uk) (www.corecumbria.co.uk).

Cymdeithas y Cymod / FoR Wales (FR PA CR), c/o 3 Tai Minffordd, Rhostryfan, Caernarfon, Gwynedd LL54 7NF (+44-1286-830913) (cymdeithasycymod@gmail.com) (www.cymdeithasycymod.org.uk).

Cymru dros Heddwch / Wales for Peace (RE DA), c/o Welsh Centre for International Affairs, Temple of Peace, Cathays Park, Cardiff CF10 (+44-29-2082 1051) (walesforpeace@wcia.org.uk) (www.walesforpeace.org). Partnership of 10 organisations.

Cynghrair Wrth-Niwclear Cymru / Welsh Anti-Nuclear Alliance [CWNC/WANA] (EL), PO Box 90, Llandrindod Wells, Powys LD1 9BP (info@wana.wales) (www.wana.wales).

Darvell Bruderhof (RP PA PO), Brightling Rd, Robertsbridge, Sussex TN32 5DR (+44-1580-883330) (darvell@bruderhof.com) (www.bruderhof.com). Anabaptist community.

Defend the Right to Protest [DTRTP] (HR), BM DTRTP, London WC1N 3XX (info@defendtherighttoprotest.org) (www.defendtherighttoprotest.org).

Drone Campaign Network (DA), c/o Peace House, 19 Paradise St, Oxford OX1 (DroneCampaignNetwork@riseup.net) (www.dronecampaignnetwork.org.uk). Network of organisations and academics.

Drone Wars UK (DA HR), c/o FoR, 19 Paradise St, Oxford OX1 (chris@dronewars.net) (www.dronewars.net). Opposes growing British use of armed drones.

East London Against the Arms Fair [ELAAF] (AT), c/o Garden Cafe, 7 Cundy Rd, Custom House, London E16 (elaaf@hotmail.co.uk) (elaaf.org). Opposing regular massive arms fair in Docklands.

Economic Issues Programme of the Society of Friends (SF HR EL), QPSW, Friends House, 175 Euston Rd, London NW1 2BJ (+44-20-7663 1000) (suzannei@quaker.org.uk) (www.quaker.org.uk/economic-jutice). *Earth & Economy* newsletter.

Ecumenical Accompaniment Programme in Palestine and Israel – British and Irish Group [EAPPI] (RP HR SF SD), c/o QPSW, Friends House, 173 Euston Rd, London NW1 2BJ (+44-20-7663 1144) (eappi@quaker.org.uk) (www.quaker.org.uk/eappi).

Edinburgh Peace and Justice Centre (CR ND PA RE HR), 5 Upper Bow, Edinburgh EH1 2JN (+44-131-629 1058) (contact@peaceandjustice.org.uk) (peaceandjustice.org.uk). *Peace and Justice News*. Promotes nonviolence, conflict resolution.

Egypt Solidarity Initiative (HR), c/o MENA Solidarity Network, Unit 193, 15-17 Caledonian Rd, London N1 (campaign@egyptsolidarityinitiative.net) (egyptsolidarityinitiative.org).

Ekklesia (RP RE), 235 Shaftesbury Ave, London WC2 (+44-20-7836 3930) (info@ekklesia.co.uk) (www.ekklesia.co.uk).

End Violence Against Women Coalition (HR), 17-25 New Inn Yard, London EC2 (+44-20-7033 1559) (admin@evaw.org.uk) (www.endviolenceagainstwomen.org.uk).

Environmental Investigation Agency [EIA] (EL), 62/63 Upper St, London N1 (+44-20-7354 7960) (ukinfo@eia-international.org) (www.eia-international.org). Also operates in USA.

Environmental Network for Central America [ENCA] (EL HR), c/o Janet Bye, 5 St Edmund's Place, Ipswich IP1 (+44-20-8769 0492) (enca.info@gmail.com) (www.enca.org.uk). *ENCA*. Works with affected communities.

Equity and Peace (CR), c/o 9 The Arcade, Belsay, Northumberland NE20 (+44-1661-881894) (www.equityandpeace.com).

Esperanto-Asocio de Britio [EAB] (PO HR), Esperanto House, Station Rd, Barlaston, Stoke-on-Trent, Staffs ST12 9DE (+44-1782-372141) (eab@esperanto.org.uk) (www.esperanto.org.uk).
EAB Update; La Brita Esperantisto.

Ethical Consumer Research Association (EL PO AL), Unit 21, 41 Old Birley St, Manchester M15 (+44-161-226 2929) (fax 226 6277) (enquiries@ethicalconsumer.org) (www.ethicalconsumer.org).
Ethical Consumer.

EuroPal Forum (HR), 21 Chalton St, London NW1 1JD (+44-20-3289 6057) (admin@europalforum.org.uk) (europalforum.org.uk).
Mobilises in support of Palestinian rights.

Extinction Rebellion / Rising Up (EL RA PO), The Exchange, Brick Row, Stroud GL5 1DF, Glos (extinctionrebellion@risingup.org.uk) (www.risingup.org.uk).
Actions for climate and economic justice.

Faith & Resistance Network (RP RA), c/o QPSW, Friends House, 175 Euston Rd, London NW1 (faithandresistanceblog.wordpress.com).

Faslane Peace Camp (ND RA AL), Shandon, Helensburgh, Dunbartonshire, G84 8NT (+44-1436-820901) (faslane30@gmail.com) (faslanepeacecamp.wordpress.com).

Fellowship of Reconciliation [FoR] (FR WR), Peace House, 19 Paradise St, Oxford OX1 1LD (+44-1865-250781) (office@for.org.uk) (www.for.org.uk).
Peacelinks; Peace by Peace.
Covers England and Scotland.

Fitnah – Movement for Women's Liberation (HR), BM Box 1919, London WC1N 3XX (fitnah.movement@gmail.com) (www.fitnah.org).
Fitnah. Opposes misogynist cultural and religious customs.

Fly Kites Not Drones (CD HR), c/o VCNV-UK, 31 Carisbrooke Rd, St Leonards-on-Sea TN38, Sussex (kitesnotdrones@gmail.com) (www.flykitesnotdrones.org).
Non-violence project for young people.

ForcesWatch (PA HR RE), 5 Caledonian Rd, London N1 (+44-20-7837 2822) (office@forceswatch.net) (www.forceswatch.net).

Forum for the Future (EL), 9 Imperial Sq, Cheltenham, Glos GL50 1QB (+44-1242-262737) (info@forumforthefuture.org) (www.forumforthefuture.org).
Charity working for sustainability.

Free Tibet Campaign (HR TW EL), 28 Charles Sq, London N1 6HT (+44-20-7324 4605) (fax 7324 4606) (mail@freetibet.org) (www.freetibet.org). *Free Tibet.*

Freedom from Torture (HR), 111 Isledon Rd, London N7 (+44-20-7697 7777) (fax 7697 7799) (www.freedomfromtorture.org).
Survivor. Supports survivors of torture.

Friends of Lebanon [FOL] (CR RE SD), Unit 35, 61 Praed St, London W2 1NS (+44-1923-606385) (mail@friendsoflebanon.org) (www.friendsoflebanon.org).

Friends of the Earth – England, Wales and Northern Ireland [FOE] (FE PO), The Printworks, 1st Floor, 139 Clapham Rd, London SW9 0HP (+44-20-7490 1555) (fax 7490 0881) (info@foe.co.uk) (friendsoftheearth.uk).

Friends of the Earth Cymru / Cyfeillion y Ddaear Cymru (FE), 33 The Balcony, Castle Arcade, Cardiff CF10 1BY (+44-29-2022 9577) (cymru@foe.co.uk) (www.foecymru.co.uk).

Friends of the Earth Scotland (FE), Thorn House, 5 Rose St, Edinburgh EH2 2PR (+44-131-243 2700) (fax 243 2725) (info@foe-scotland.org.uk) (www.foe-scotland.org.uk).

Gandhi Foundation (HR RE PO), Kingsley Hall, Powis Rd, Bromley-by-Bow, London E3 3HJ (contact@gandhifoundation.org) (www.gandhifoundation.org).
The Gandhi Way.

Gender Action for Peace and Security UK [GAPS] (HR RE), c/o Women for Women International UK, 32-36 Loman St, London SE1 0EH (+44-20-7549 0360) (info@gaps-uk.org) (gaps-uk.org).
Network of organisations and individual experts.

GeneWatch UK (EL HR), 60 Lightwood Rd, Buxton, Derbyshire SK17 (+44-1298-24300) (fax) (mail@genewatch.org) (www.genewatch.org).
Monitors genetic engineering.

Global Justice Now (TW), 66 Offley Rd, London SW9 0LS (+44-20-7820 4900) (fax 7820 4949) (offleyroad@globaljustice.org.uk) (www.globaljustice.org).
Ninety Nine. Formerly World Development Movement.

Global Witness (EL HR TW CR), Lloyds Chambers, 1 Portsoken St, London E1 (+44-20-7492 5820) (fax 7492 5821) (mail@globalwitness.org) (www.globalwitness.org). Also in USA.

GM Freeze (EL), c/o 80 Cyprus St, Stretford, Manchester M32 (info@gmfreeze.org) (www.gmfreeze.org). Umbrella body.

GM Watch (EL), c/o 26 Pottergate, Norwich NR2 1DX, Norfolk (+44-1603-624021) (fax 766552) (ngin@gmwatch.org) (www.gmwatch.org).
Analyses and counters GM industry propaganda.

GM-Free Cymru (EL), c/o Dyffryn Dwarch, Abermawr, nr Mathry, Pembrokeshire SA62 (gm@caerhys.co.uk) (www.gmfreecymru.org).

GM-free Scotland (EL), c/o 35 Hamilton Drive, Glasgow G12 (gmfreescotland@yahoo.co.uk) (gmfreescotland.blogspot.com).

BRITAIN

Greater Manchester & District CND [GM&DCND] (ND), Bridge 5 Mill, 22a Beswick St, Ancoats, Manchester M4 7HR (+44-161-273 8283) (fax 273 8293) (gmdcnd@gn.apc.org) (www.gmdcnd.org.uk). *Nuclear Alert.*

Green Christian [GC] (EL PO), 97 Plumpton Ave, Hornchurch RM12 6BB, Essex (info@greenchristian.org.uk) (www.greenchristian.org.uk). *Green Christian.*

Green CND (ND), c/o CND, 162 Holloway Rd, London N7 (+44-20-7700 2393).

Green Party of England and Wales (EL ND HR RA), The Biscuit Factory – A Block (201), 100 Clements Rd, London SE16 4DG (+44-20-3691 9400) (office@greenparty.org.uk) (www.greenparty.org.uk). *Green World.*

Greener UK (EL), c/o Green Alliance, 4th Floor, Victoria Charity Centre, 11 Belgrave Rd, London SW1V 1RB (amount@green-alliance.org.uk) (greeneruk.org). Tracking environmental implications of BREXIT.

GreenNet (TW HR PO), The Green House, 244-254 Cambridge Heath Rd, London E2 9DA (+44-330-335 4011) (info@gn.apc.org) (www.gn.apc.org).

Greenpeace UK (GP), Canonbury Villas, London N1 2PN (+44-20-7865 8100) (fax 7865 8200) (info.uk@greenpeace.org) (www.greenpeace.org.uk). *Connect.*

Gun Control Network (AT RE PO EL), PO Box 11495, London N3 2FE (gcn-uk@btconnect.com) (www.gun-control-network.org).

Housmans Bookshop (WR EL AL HR), 5 Caledonian Rd, Kings Cross, London N1 9DX (+44-20-7837 4473) (fax 7278 0444) (shop@housmans.com) (www.housmans.com). *Peace Diary & World Peace Directory.*
Peace/political books, magazines, cards, etc.

Human Rights Watch – London Office (HR), First Floor, Audrey House, 16-20 Ely Place, London EC1 (+44-20-7618 4700) (londonoutreach@hrw.org) (www.hrw.org/london).

Humanists UK (HR PO), 39 Moreland St, London EC1V 8BB (+44-20-7324 3060) (fax 7324 3061) (info@humanists.uk) (humanism.org.uk).
Formerly British Humanist Association.

Humanity United for Universal Demilitarisation [HUFUD] (PA PO DA), 14a Lakeside Rd, London W14 0DU (info.hufud@gmail.com) (www.hufud.org). For universal abolition of militarism and weapons.

Index on Censorship (HR RA TW), 292 Vauxhall Bridge Rd, London SW1V 1AE (+44-20-7963 7262) (david@indexoncensorship.org) (www.indexoncensorship.org). *Index on Censorship.*

Inter Faith Network for the UK (RP CR CD), 2 Grosvenor Gardens, London SW1W 0DH (+44-20-7730 0410) (fax 7730 0414) (ifnet@interfaith.org.uk) (www.interfaith.org.uk).

International Alert [IA] (RE CR HR CD), 346 Clapham Rd, London SW9 (+44-20-7627 6800) (fax 7627 6900) (general@international-alert.org) (www.international-alert.org).

International Association for Religious Freedom – British Chapter (HR), c/o Pejman Khojasteh, c/o Essex Hall, 1 Essex St, London WC2R 3HY (Pejman_Khojasteh@btinternet.com) (www.iarf.net). *IARF World.*

International Campaign to Abolish Nuclear Weapons – UK [ICAN-UK] (ND), c/o MEDACT, 28 Charles Sq, London N1 6HT (infouk@icanw.org) (www.icanw.org/unitedkingdom).

International Friendship League – UK (CD), PO Box 578, Northampton NN5 4WY (www.ifl.org.uk).

International Service [UNAIS] (TW UN), Second Floor, Rougier House, 5 Rougier St, York YO1 6HZ (+44-1904-647799) (fax 652353) (contact@internationalservice.org.uk) (www.internationalservice.org.uk).

International Voluntary Service [IVS] (SC), Thorn House, 5 Rose St, Edinburgh EH2 2PR (+44-131-243 2745) (fax 243 2747) (info@ivsgb.org) (ivsgb.org). *Interactions.*

Iona Community (FR PA HR), 21 Carlton Court, Glasgow G5 9JP (+44-141-429 7281) (admin@iona.org) (www.iona.org.uk). *The Coracle.* (On Iona: +44-1681-700404).

Israeli Committee Against House Demolitions UK [ICAHD UK] (HR RA), BM ICAHD UK, London WC1N 3XX (+44-20-3740 2208) (info@icahduk.org) (www.icahduk.org). Opposes Israeli occupation of Palestinian land.

JD Bernal Peace Library (RE), c/o Marx Memorial Library, 37a Clerkenwell Green, London EC1R 0DU (+44-20-7253 1485) (archives@mml.xyz) (www.marx-memorial-library.org). *Theory and Struggle.*

Jews for Justice for Palestinians [JfJfP] (HR), 20-22 Wenlock Rd, London N1 7GU (jfjfp@jfjfp.com) (jfjfp.com).

Jubilee Debt Campaign (TW), The Grayston Centre, 28 Charles Sq, London N1 6HT (+44-20-7324 4722) (fax 7324 4723) (info@jubileedebt.org.uk) (jubileedebt.org.uk). *Drop It!.*

Jubilee Scotland (TW), 41 George IV Bridge, Edinburgh EH1 1EL (+44-131-225 4321) (mail@jubileescotland.org.uk) (www.jubileescotland.org.uk). Successor to Jubilee 2000 Scottish Coalition.

Justice & Peace Scotland / Ceartas agus Sith (RP), 65 Bath St, Glasgow G2 2BX (+44-141-333 0238) (fax 331 2409) (office@justiceandpeacescotland.org.uk) (justiceandpeacescotland.org.uk).

Justice, Peace and Integrity of Creation project of the Columban Fathers [JPIC] (RP), St Joseph's, Waford Way, Hendon, London NW4 4TY (+44-20-8202 2555) (fax 8202 5775) (jpicssc@btconnect.com) (www.columbans.co.uk). *Vocation for Justice.*

Khulisa – Breaking the cycle of violence (CD CR PO), Wells House (Unit 7), 5-7 Wells Terrace, London N4 (+44-20-7561 3727) (info@khulisa.co.uk) (www.khulisa.co.uk). Modelled on programmes in South Africa.

Kick Nuclear (EL RA), c/o LRCND, 162 Holloway Rd, London N7 8DQ (+44-20-7607 2302) (kicknuclearlondon@gmail.com) (kicknuclear.com). Opposes UK's addiction to nuclear power.

Labour CND (ND), c/o 480 Lymington Rd, Highcliffe, Christchurch BH23 5HG (+44-1425-279307) (info@labourcnd.org.uk) (www.labourcnd.org.uk).

Land Justice Network (HR EL RA), c/o The Land Magazine, Monkton Wyld Court, Charmouth, Bridport, Dorset DT6 (landjusticeuk@gmail.com) (www.landjustice.uk). Network challenging use and ownership of land.

Liberation (HR TW DA CR), 77 St John St, Clerkenwell, London EC1M 4NN (+44-20-7324 2498) (info@liberationorg.co.uk) (www.liberationorg.co.uk). *Liberation.*

Liberty – The National Council for Civil Liberties (HR), Liberty House, 26-30 Strutton Ground, London SW1P 2HR (+44-20-7403 3888) (fax 7799 5306) (www.liberty-human-rights.org.uk).

Living Streets (EL HR PO), 4th Floor, Universal House, 88-94 Wentworth St, London E1 7SA (+44-20-7377 4900) (info@livingstreets.org.uk) (www.livingstreets.org.uk).

Local Futures / ISEC [ISEC-UK] (EL), PO Box 239, Totnes TQ9 9DP (+44-1392-581175) (info@localfutures.org) (www.localfutures.org).

London Catholic Worker [LCW] (RP RA PA AL), 49 Mattison Rd, London N4 (+44-20-8348 8212) (londoncatholicworker@yahoo.co.uk) (www.londoncatholicworker.org). *London Catholic Worker.*

London Mining Network [LMN] (HR EL), Finfuture, 225-229 Seven Sisters Rd, London N4 (contact@londonminingnetwork.org) (www.londonminingnetwork.org).

London Region CND [LRCND] (ND), Mordechai Vanunu House, 162 Holloway Rd, London N7 8DQ (+44-20-7607 2302) (www.londoncnd.org.uk). *Peaceline.*

Low-Impact Living Initiative [LILI] (PO EL), Redfield Community, Winslow MK18, Bucks (+44-1296-714184) (fax) (lili@lowimpact.org) (www.lowimpact.org).

Low-Level Radiation Campaign [LLRC] (EL), Times Building, South Crescent, Llandrindod Wells, Powys LD1 5DH (+44-1597-824771) (lowradcampaign@gmail.com) (www.llrc.org).

MEDACT (IP IB EL), The Grayston Centre, 28 Charles Sq, London N1 6HT (+44-20-7324 4739) (fax 7324 4734) (office@medact.org) (www.medact.org). *Communique.*

MENA Solidarity Network (HR), Unit 193, 15-17 Caledonian Rd, London N1 (menasolidarity@gmail.com) (www.menasolidaritynetwork.org).

Merseyside CND (ND), 151 Dale St, Liverpool L2 2AH (+44-151-229 5282) (mcnd@care4free.net) (www.mcnd.org.uk).

Methodist Peace Fellowship [MPF] (FR PA), c/o Marie Dove, 17 Fangdale Court, Bridlington, Yorks YO16 (+44-1262-679612) (marie.dove@gmail.com) (mpf.org.uk). *Peace in the 21st Century.*

Milton Keynes Peace & Justice Network (ND HR), 300 Saxon Gate West, Central Milton Keynes, Bucks MK9 2ES (+44-1908-561365) (office@mkpeaceandjustice.org.uk) (www.mkpeaceandjustice.org.uk). *MK Network News.*

Mines Advisory Group [MAG] (DA TW PO), Suite 3A, South Central, 11 Peter St, Manchester M2 5QR (+44-161-236 4311) (fax 236 6244) (info@maginternational.org) (www.maginternational.org).

Mothers Against Murder And Aggression [MAMAA UK], PO Box 778, Borehamwood WD6 9LF, Herts (+44-20-8207 0702) (info@mamaa.org) (www.mamaa.org).

Movement for Compassionate Living [MCL] (PO EL), 105 Cyfyng Rd, Ystalyfera, Swansea SA9 2BT (+44-1639-841223) (mcl.ystalyfera@googlemail.com) (www.MCLveganway.org.uk). *New Leaves.*

Movement for the Abolition of War [MAW] (IB), c/o 11 Venetia Rd, London N1 1EJ (+44-20-3397 3019) (info@abolishwar.org.uk) (www.abolishwar.org.uk). *Abolish War.*

Musicians for Peace and Disarmament [MPD] (IB ND DA), c/o Tony Lamb, 37 Bolton Gdns, Teddington TW11 9AX (info.mpdconcerts@gmail.com) (www.mpdconcerts.org). *Newsletter.*

National Federation of Atheist, Humanist and Secularist Student Societies [AHS] (HR), 39 Moreland St, London EC1 (communications@ahsstudents.org.uk) (ahsstudents.org.uk).

National Justice & Peace Network [NJPN] (RP), 39 Eccleston Sq, London SW1V 1BX (+44-20-7901 4864) (fax 7901 4821) (admin@justice-and-peace.org.uk) (www.justice-and-peace.org.uk). *Justice and Peace.*

BRITAIN

National Secular Society [NSS] (HR), 25 Red Lion Sq, London WC1R 4RL (+44-20-7404 3126) (enquiries@secularism.org.uk) (www.secularism.org.uk).

Navigate: Facilitation for Social Change (RA AL CR EL), Old Music Hall, 106-108 Cowley Rd, Oxford OX4 (+44-1865-403134) (hello@navigate.org.uk) (www.navigate.org.uk).
Formerly part of Seeds for Change network.

Network for Peace [NfP] (DA ND PA), 5 Caledonian Rd, London N1 9DX (mail@networkforpeace.org.uk) (www.networkforpeace.org.uk).

Network of Christian Peace Organisations [NCPO] (RP), c/o FOR, Peace House, 19 Paradise St, Oxford OX1 1LD (+44-1865-250781) (ncpo@for.org.uk) (ncpo.org.uk).

New Economics Foundation [NEF] (EL CD PO), 10 Salamanca Place, London SE1 7HB (+44-20-7820 6300) (info@neweconomics.org) (www.neweconomics.org).

New Economy Organisers Network [NEON] (EL HR PO), 10 Salamanca Place, London SE1 7HB (hello@neweconomyorganisers.org) (neweconomyorganisers.org).
Network of organisers.

New Israel Fund UK (HR), Unit 2, Bedford Mews, London N2 9DF (+44-20-7724 2266) (fax 7724 2299) (info@uknif.org) (uknif.org). Supports progressive civil society in Israel.

Nicaragua Solidarity Campaign [NSC] (HR TW WC), 86 Durham Rd, London N7 7DT (+44-20-7561 4836) (nsc@nicaraguasc.org.uk) (www.nicaraguasc.org.uk). *Nicaragua Now*.

Nipponzan Myohoji (RP), Peace Pagoda, Willen, Milton Keynes MK15 0BA, Bucks (+44-1908-663652) (fax). Also in London: +44-20-7228 9620.

No 2 Nuclear Power (EL), c/o Pete Roche, Friends of the Earth Scotland, Thorn House, 5 Rose Street, Edinburgh EH2 (rochepete8@aol.com) (www.no2nuclearpower.org.uk).
Provides key website and nuclear information.

No Sweat (HR RA TW), 5 Caledonian Rd, London N1 (admin@nosweat.org.uk) (www.nosweat.org.uk). Against sweatshops; for workers' and TU rights.

NO2ID (HR), Box 412, 19-21 Crawford St, London W1H 1PJ (+44-20-7340 6077) (office@no2id.net) (www.no2id.net). *NO2ID Newsletter*.
Opposes ID cards and the database state.

Non-Violent Resistance Network [NVRN] (RA ND PA), c/o David Polden, CND, 162 Holloway Rd, London N7 8DQ (+44-20-7607 2302) (david.lrcnd@cnduk.org). *Newsletter*.

Northern Friends Peace Board [NFPB] (SF), Victoria Hall, Knowsley St, Bolton BL1 2AS (+44-1204-382330) (nfpb@gn.apc.org) (nfpb.org.uk). *The Peace Board*.

Norwich Environment Resource Centre (EL PO), The Greenhouse, 42-46 Bethel St, Norwich NR2 1NR (+44-1603-631007) (www.GreenhouseTrust.co.uk).

Nuclear Awareness Group [NAG] (EL), 16 Back St, Winchester SO23 9SB, Hants (+44-1962-890160) (fax) (nucleareawarenessgroup.org.uk). *Newsletter*.

Nuclear Information Service [NIS] (RE ND), 35-39 London St, Reading RG1 4PS (+44-118-327 4935) (fax) (office@nuclearinfo.org) (nuclearinfo.org).

Nuclear Morality Flowchart Project (ND), c/o Martin Birdseye, 88 Fern Lane, Hounslow TW5 0HJ, Middlesex (+44-20-8571 1691) (info@nuclearmorality.org) (nuclearmorality.com). Helps people to think about ethical accountability.

Nuclear Trains Action Group [NTAG] (ND RA), c/o Mordechai Vanunu House, 162 Holloway Rd, London N7 8DR (+44-20-7607 2302) (david.lrcnd@cnduk.org) (www.nonucleartrains.org.uk). *Newletter*.
Working Group of London Region CND.

Nuclear-Free Local Authorities Secretariat [NFLA] (ND EL), c/o Manchester City Council, Town Hall, Manchester M60 3NY (+44-161-234 3244) (fax 274 7379) (s.morris4@manchester.gov.uk) (www.nuclearpolicy.info).

Nukewatch UK (ND RA), c/o Edinburgh Peace & Justice Centre, 5 Upper Bow, Edinburgh EH1 2JN (+44-345 458 8364) (spotters@nukewatch.org.uk) (www.nukewatch.org.uk).

Oasis of Peace UK (CD CR HR), 192B Station Rd, Edgware HA8 7AR, Middx (+44-20-8952 4717) (office@oasisofpeace.org.uk) (www.oasisofpeaceuk.org).
Formerly British Friends of NSWaS.

One World Week (HR TW EL), 35-39 London St, Reading RG1 4PS, Berks (+44-118-939 4933) (oww@oneworldweek.org) (www.oneworldweek.org).

OneVoice Movement – Europe (CD CR), Unit 4, Benwell Studios, 11-13 Benwell Rd, London N7 7BL (+44-20-8004 6431) (europe@OneVoiceMovement.org.uk) (www.onevoicemovement.org). See also under Israel, Palestine, and USA.

Orthodox Peace Fellowship UK [OPF] (RP), c/o Seraphim Honeywell, "Birchenhoe", Crowfield, nr Brackley NN13 5TW, Northants (oxpeacefp@aol.com) (www.incommunion.org). *In Communion*.

Palestine Solidarity Campaign [PSC] (TW CR), Box BM PSA, London WC1N 3XX (+44-20-7700 6192) (fax 7700 5747) (info@palestinecampaign.org) (www.palestinecampaign.org).

Pax Christi (PC PA RE), Christian Peace Education Centre, St Joseph's, Watford Way, Hendon, London NW4 4TY (+44-20-8203 4884) (fax 8203 5234) (info@paxchristi.org.uk) (www.paxchristi.org.uk). *Justpeace.*

Peace Brigades International – UK Section [PBI UK] (PA RE HR CD), 1b Waterloo Rd, London N19 5NJ (+44-20-7281 5370) (fax) (admin@peacebrigades.org.uk) (peacebrigades.org.uk).

Peace Direct (CR RE), Studio 302, 203-213 Mare St, London E8 (+44-20-3422 5549) (info@peacedirect.org) (www.peacedirect.org).

Peace Education Network (RE), c/o Pax Christi, St Joseph's, Watford Way, London NW4 4TY (+44-20-8203 4884) (education@paxchristi.org.uk) (www.peace-education.org.uk).

Peace Hub – Quaker Peace and Justice Centre, 41 Bull St, Birmingham B4 6AF (+44-121-238 2869) (office@peacehub.org.uk).

Peace in Kurdistan (HR), 44 Ainger Rd, London NW3 3AT (+44-20-7586 5892) (estella24@tiscali.co.uk) (www.peaceinkurdistancampaign.com).

Peace Museum UK (RE PA CR), 10 Piece Hall Yard, off Hustlergate, Bradford BD1 1PJ (+44-1274-780241) (info@peacemuseum.org.uk) (www.peacemuseum.org.uk).

Peace News – for nonviolent revolution **/PN]** (WR HR AL RA ND), 5 Caledonian Rd, London N1 9DY (+44-20-7278 3344) (fax 7278 0444) (editorial@peacenews.info) (www.peacenews.info).

Peace One Day (CR PO RE), St George's House, 15 St George's Rd, Richmond, Surrey TW9 (+44-20-8334 9900) (fax 8948 0545) (info@peaceoneday.org) (www.peaceoneday.org).

Peace Party – Non-violence, Justice, Environment (PA RE EL), c/o John Morris, 39 Sheepfold Rd, Guildford GU2 9TT, Surrey (+44-1483-576400) (info@peaceparty.org.uk) (www.peaceparty.org.uk). *Peace.* Secular pacifist electoral movement.

Peace Pledge Union [PPU] (WR RE), 1 Peace Passage, Brecknock Rd, London N7 0BT (+44-20-7424 9444) (mail@ppu.org.uk) (www.ppu.org.uk). *Peace Matters.*

Peace Tax Seven (TR), c/o Woodlands, Ledge Hill, Market Lavington, Wilts SN10 (info@peacetaxseven.com) (www.peacetaxseven.com).

People & Planet (TW HR EL), The Old Music Hall, 106-108 Cowley Rd, Oxford OX4 1JE (+44-1865-403225) (people@peopleandplanet.org) (peopleandplanet.org). National student network.

People Against Rio Tinto and its Subsidiaries [PARtizans] (HR EL TW), 41A Thornhill Sq, London N1 1BE (+44-20-7700 6189) (fax) (partizans@gn.apc.org) (www.minesandcommunities.org).

Police Spies Out of Lives (HR), c/o 84b Whitechapel High St, London E1 7QX (cotact@policespiesoflives.org.uk) (policespiesoutoflives.org.uk). Supports women abused by undercover police.

Practical Action (PO TW), Schumacher Centre for Technology and Development, Bourton Hall, Bourton-on-Dunsmore, Rugby, Warwickshire CV23 9QZ (+44-1926-634400) (fax 634401) (enquiries@practicalaction.org.uk) (www.practicalaction.org).

Pugwash Conferences on Science and World Affairs (DA EL RE TW CR), Ground Floor Flat, 63A Great Russell St, London WC1B 3BJ (+44-20-7405 6661) (office@britishpugwash.org) (britishpugwash). *Pugwash Newsletter.* Part of international Pugwash network.

Quaker Concern for the Abolition of Torture [Q-CAT] (SF HR), c/o 38 The Mount, Heswall CH60 4RA, Wirral (+44-151-342 4425) (chasraws@onetel.com) (q-cat.org.uk).

Quaker Peace & Social Witness [QPSW] (SF DA PA), Friends House, 175 Euston Rd, London NW1 2BJ (+44-20-7663 1000) (qpsw@quaker.org.uk) (www.quaker.org.uk/qpsw).

Quaker Sustainability and Peace Programme (SF EL RE DA PA), QPSW, Friends House, 175 Euston Rd, London NW1 2BJ (+44-20-7663 1067) (fax 7663 1001) (survival@quaker.org.uk) (www.quaker.org.uk). Previously Peace and Disarmament Programme.

Radical Routes (AL PO), c/o Cornerstone Resource Centre, 16 Sholebroke Ave, Leeds LS7 3HB (+44-1603-776445) (enquiries@radicalroutes.org.uk) (www.radicalroutes.org.uk). Network of radical housing, worker & other co-ops.

Redress (HR), 87 Vauxhall Walk, London SE11 (+44-20-7793 1777) (fax 7793 1719) (info@redress.org) (www.redress.org). Seeks justice for torture survivors.

Religions for Peace [WCRP-UK] (RP RE), c/o 18 Little Acres, Ware SG12 9JW, Hertfordshire (+44-1920-465714) (fax) (secretary@religionsforpeace.org.uk) (www.religionsforpeace.org.uk).

Religious Society of Friends in Britain (Quakers) (SF), Friends House, Euston Rd, London NW1 2BJ (+44-20-7663 1000) (fax 7663 1001) (www.quaker.org.uk). *Quaker News; The Friend; Quaker Voices.*

Remote Control Project (DA RE), c/o Oxford Research Group, Development House, 56-64 Leonard St, London EC2A 4LT (+44-20-7549 0298) (remotecontrolproject.org). Challenges "behind the scenes" warfare.

Reprieve (HR), PO Box 72054, London EC3P 3BZ (+44-20-7553 8140) (info@reprieve.org.uk) (www.reprieve.org.uk).

BRITAIN

Responding to Conflict [RTC] (CR RE), 1046 Bristol Rd, Selly Oak, Birmingham B29 6LJ (+44-121-415 5641) (fax 415 4119) (enquiries@respond.org) (www.respond.org). Training and resources.

Rethinking Security (RE DA EL), c/o Saferworld, The Grayston Centre, 28 Charles Sq, London N1 (celia@rethinkingsecurity.org.uk) (rethinkingsecurity.org.uk). Network of academics, activists, organisations.

Rising Tide UK [RTUK] (EL RA AL), c/o London Action Resource Centre, 62 Fieldgate St, Whitechapel, London E1 1ES (info@risingtide.org.uk) (www.risingtide.org.uk). Direct action for climate justice.

RoadPeace (EL RE HR), Shakespeare Business Centre, 245a Coldharbour Lane, London SW9 8RR (+44-20-7733 1603) (info@roadpeace.org) (roadpeace.org). Supports road traffic victims and families.

Saferworld (RE AT), The Grayston Centre, 28 Charles Sq, London N1 (+44-20-7324 4646) (fax 7324 4647) (general@saferworld.org.uk) (www.saferworld.org.uk). Helping people turn away from armed violence.

Scientists for Global Responsibility [SGR] (RE ND EL AT DA), Unit 2.8, Halton Mill, Mill Lane, Halton, Lancaster LA2 6ND, Lancashire (+44-1524-812073) (info@sgr.org.uk) (www.sgr.org.uk). *SGR Newsletter*.

Scotland's for Peace (ND RE AT), c/o 77 Southpark Ave, Glasgow G12 (+44-141-357 1529) (info@scotland4peace.org) (www.scotland4peace.org). Umbrella body.

Scottish Campaign for Nuclear Disarmament [SCND] (ND), 77 Southpark Ave, Glasgow G12 8LE (+44-141-357 1529) (scnd@banthebomb.org) (www.banthebomb.org). *Nuclear Free Scotland*.

Scottish Friends of Palestine (HR TW), 31 Tinto Rd, Glasgow G43 2AL (+44-141-637 8046) (info@scottish-friends-of-palestine.org) (www.scottishfriendsofpalestine.org).

Scottish Green Party (EL), Bonnington Mill, 72 Newhaven Rd, Edinburgh EH6 5QG (greens.scot).

Scrap Trident Coalition (ND PA RA), c/o Edinburgh Peace and Justice Centre, 5 Upper Bow, Edinburgh EH1 2JN (+44-131-629 1058) (scraptrident@gmail.com) (scraptrident.org). Network in Scotland.

Sea Shepherd UK (EL RA), 27 Old Gloucester St, London WC1N 3AX (+44-300-111 0501) (admin@seashepherduk.org) (www.seashepherduk.org). Conserving nature on the high seas.

Seeds for Change (RA AL), Storey Institute, Meeting House Lane, Lancaster LA1 (+44-1524-509002) (contact@seedsforchange.org.uk) (www.seedsforchange.org.uk). Training for actions, campaigns, setting up co-ops.

Servas Britain (SE), c/o Nash Villa, Nash Lane, Marnhull, Sturminster Newton DT10, Dorset (info@servasbritain.net) (www.servasbritain.net).

Share The World's Resources [STWR] (TW EL), PO Box 52662, London N7 8UX (+44-20-7609 3034) (info@sharing.org) (www.sharing.org). Sustainable economics to end global poverty.

Smash EDO (RA AT), c/o Unemployed Centre, 6 Tilbury Place, Brighton BN2 0GY, Sussex (smashedo@riseup.net) (smashedo.org.uk).

Soil Association (EL PO TW), South Plaza, Marlborough St, Bristol BS1 (+44-117-314 5000) (fax 314 5001) (memb@soilassociation.org) (www.soilassociation.org). Scotland office: +44-131-666 2474.

South Cheshire & North Staffs CND [SCANS CND] (ND), Groundwork Enterprise Centre, Albany Works, Moorland Rd, Burslem, Stoke-on-Trent ST6 1EB, Staffs (+44-1782-829913) (scanscnd@ymail.com) (www.scanscnd.com). *Banner*.

Southdowns Peace Group (DA), c/o Vida, 22 Beaufort Rd, Bedhampton, Havant PO9 3HU (+44-23-9234 6696) (vida.henning@ntlworld.com).

Southern Region CND (ND), 3 Harpsichord Place, Oxford OX4 1BY (+44-1865-248357) (oxfordcnd@phonecoop.coop).

St Ethelburga's Centre for Reconciliation and Peace (CD CR RE RP), 78 Bishopsgate, London EC2N 4AG (+44-20-7496 1610) (fax 7638 1440) (enquiries@stethelburgas.org) (www.stethelburgas.org).

Stop Arming Israel (AT), c/o CAAT, Unit 4, 5-7 Wells Terrace, London N4 3JU (+44-20-7281 0297) (israel@caat.org.uk) (www.stoparmingisrael.org). Joint campaign of peace, solidarity, etc, groups.

Stop Climate Chaos Coalition [SCCS] (EL), 2nd Floor, Thorn House, 5 Rose St, Edinburgh EH2 2PR (+44-131-243 2701) (info@stopclimatechaosscotland.org) (www.stopclimatechaos.org/scotland). Development, environment, etc, groups' coalition.

Stop Hinkley (EL), 8 The Bartons, Yeabridge, South Petherton TA13 5LW, Somerset (+44-1749-860767) (admin@stophinkley.org) (www.stophinkley.org). Against nuclear power in south-west England.

Stop New Nuclear Alliance (EL RA), c/o Kick Nuclear, LRCND, 182 Holloway Rd, London N7 (campaign@stopnewnuclear.org.uk) (stopnewnuclear.org.uk). Alliance of local campaigns opposing new nuclear.

Stop the War Coalition [STWC], 86 Durham Rd, London N7 (+44-20-7561 4830) (office@stopwar.org.uk) (www.stopwar.org.uk).

Student Christian Movement [SCM] (RP), Grays Court, 3 Nursery Rd, Edgbaston, Birmingham B15 3JX (+44-121-426 4918) (scm@movement.org.uk) (www.movement.org.uk).

Surfers Against Sewage [SAS] (EL), Unit 2, Wheal Kitty Workshops, St Agnes TR5 0RD, Cornwall (+44-1872-553001) (fax 552615) (info@sas.org.uk) (www.sas.org.uk). *Pipeline News.*

Syria Peace & Justice Group (CR CD AT DA), c/o LARC, 62 Fieldgate St, London E1 (syriapeaceandjustice@gmail.com) (syriapeaceandjustice.wordpress.com). Anti-militarist human rights campaign.

Syrian Human Rights Committee [SHRC] (HR), PO Box 123, Edgware HA8 0XF, Middlesex (fax +44-870-1377678) (walid@shrc.org) (www.shrc.org). Syrian human rights group in exile.

Tapol (HR AT TW RE), Durham Resource Centre, 86 Durham Rd, London N7 (+44-20-7561 7485) (info@tapol.org) (www.tapol.org).

The Brotherhood Church (WR AL EL), Stapleton, nr Pontefract, Yorkshire WF8 3DF (+44-1977-620381).

The Climate Coalition (EL), c/o Oxfam, 3rd Floor North, Victoria Charity Centre, 11 Belgrave Rd, London SW1 (+44-20-7802 9989) (admin@theclimatecoalition.org) (www.theclimatecoalition.org).

The Corner House (HR TW EL), Station Rd, Sturminster Newton, Dorset DT10 1BB (+44-1258-473795) (fax) (enquiries@thecornerhouse.org.uk) (www.thecornerhouse.org.uk). *Briefing Papers.*

The Forgiveness Project (CR PO), 42a Buckingham Palace Rd, London SW1 (+44-20-7821 0035) (info@theforgivenessproject.com) (www.theforgivenessproject.com).

"The Right to Refuse to Kill" Group [RRK] (PA HR), c/o PPU, 1 Peace Passage, London N7 0BT (+44-20-7237 3731) (edna.mathieson1@btinternet.com) (www.rrk.freeuk.com).

Tibet Foundation (HR), Room 304, 5 Westminster Bridge Rd, London SE1 (+44-20-7930 6001) (info@tibet-foundation.org) (www.tibet-foundation.org).

Tibet Society (HR TW CR), 2 Baltic Place, London N1 5AQ (+44-20-7923 0021) (info@tibetsociety.com) (www.tibetsociety.com). Campaigns for Tibetan self-determination.

Tolerance International – UK (CR HR RE), Scandinavian House, 2-6 Cannon St, London EC4 (+44-20-7097 5167) (fax) (tolernace@toleranceinternational.org.uk) (www.toleranceinternational.org.uk).

Tools for Self Reliance (TW PO WC), Ringwood Rd, Netley Marsh, Southampton SO40 7GY (+44-23-8086 9697) (fax 8086 8544) (info@tfsr.org) (www.tfsr.org). *Forging Links.*

Tourism Concern (TW HR EL), The Lansdowne Building, 2 Lansdowne Rd, Croydon CR9 (+44-20-8263 6007) (fax 8263 6001) (info@tourismconcern.org.uk) (www.tourismconcern.org.uk).

Town and Country Planning Association [TCPA] (EL), 17 Carlton House Terr, London SW1Y 5AS (+44-20-7930 8903) (fax 7930 3280) (tcpa@tcpa.org.uk) (www.tcpa.org.uk). *Town & Country Planning.*

Trade Justice Movement (TW HR EL), c/o Fairtrade Foundation, 3rd Floor, Ibex House, 42-47 Minories, London EC3N 1DY (+44-20-7440 8560) (mail@tjm.org.uk) (www.tjm.org.uk).

Trident Ploughshares (WR ND RA), c/o Edinburgh Peace & Justice Centre, 5 Upper Bow, Edinburgh EH1 2JN (+44-345 458 8361) (tp2000@gn.apc.org) (tridentploughshares.org).

Turning the Tide (SF PO RA), Friends House, Euston Rd, London NW1 2BJ (+44-20-7663 1064) (fax 7663 1049) (stevew@quaker.org) (www.turning-the-tide.org). *Making Waves.* Offers workshops, nonviolence training, etc.

Tyne & Wear CND (ND), 1 Rectory Ave, Gosforth, Newcastle-upon-Tyne NE3 1XS (+44-191-285 1290) (rhpg@btinternet.com).

UK Committee for UNICEF [UNICEF UK] (TW HR), UNICEF House, 30a Great Sutton St, London EC1 (+44-20-7490 2388) (fax 7250 1733) (www.unicef.org.uk).

UNA Exchange (UN WC PO), Temple of Peace, Cathays Park, Cardiff CF10 3AP (+44-29-2022 3088) (fax 2022 2540) (info@unaexchange.org) (www.unaexchange.org). *Opinions.*

UNA-UK Members for Civil Society Link with UN General Assembly [UNGA-Link UK] (UN), 11 Wilberforce House, 119 Worple Rd, London SW20 8ET (+44-20-8944 0574) (fax) (info@ungalink.org.uk) (www.ungalink.org.uk).

Unitarian and Free Christian Peace Fellowship [UPF] (RP), c/o Sue Woolley, 5 Martins Rd, Piddinton, Northampton NN7 2DN (+44-1455-636602) (www.unitariansocieties.org.uk/peace).

United Nations Association – UK [UNA-UK] (UN HR RE TW), 3 Whitehall Court, London SW1A 2EL (+44-20-7766 3454) (fax 7000 1381) (info@una.org.uk) (www.una.org.uk). *UNA-UK.*

United Reformed Church Peace Fellowship [URCPF] (RP), c/o Church and Society, United Reformed Church, 86 Tavistock Pl, London WC1H 9RT (+44-20-7916 8632) (fax 7916 2021) (church.society@urc.org.uk) (www.urc.org.uk/mission/peace-fellowship.html).

BRITAIN

Uniting for Peace [UfP] (DA ND CD AT RE), 14 Cavell St, London E1 2HP (+44-20-7791 1717) (info@unitingforpeace.com) (unitingforpeace.com). *Uniting for Peace.* Also in Edinburgh (+44-131-446 9545).

Vegan Society (EL TW PO HR), Donald Watson House, 21 Hylton St, Hockley, Birmingham B18 6HJ (+44-121-523 1730) (info@vegansociety.com) (www.vegansociety.com). *The Vegan.*

Vegetarian Society of the UK (EL TW PO), Parkdale, Dunham Rd, Altrincham, Cheshire (+44-161-925 2000) (fax 926 9182) (info@vegsoc.org) (www.vegsoc.org). *The Vegetarian.*

Veggies (PO EL), c/o Sumac Centre, 245 Gladstone St, Nottingham NG7 (+44-115-960 8254) (info@veggies.org.uk) (www.veggies.org.uk).

Veterans for Peace UK [VFP UK] (PA RA RE), 12 Dixon Rd, London SE25 6TZ (coord@vfpuk.org) (veteransforpeace.org.uk).

Voices for Creative Non-Violence UK [VCNV-UK] (PA CR), 31 Carisbrooke Rd, St Leonards-on-Sea TN38 0JN, Sussex (vcnvuk@gmail.com) (www.vcnv.org.uk).

Voluntary Service Overseas [VSO] (TW), 100 London Rd, Kingston-upon-Thames KT2, Surrey (+44-20-8780 7500) (enquiry@vsoint.org) (www.vsointernational.org).

Volunteer Action for Peace [VAP UK] (WC HR EL), 16 Overhill Rd, East Dulwich, London SE22 0PH (action@vap.org.uk) (www.vap.org.uk). Within UK, tel 0844-209 0927.

Volunteering Matters (PO CD), The Levy Centre, 18-24 Lower Clapton Rd, London E5 (+44-20-3780 5870) (information@volunteeringmatters.org.uk) (volunteeringmatters.org.uk). Formerly Community Service Volunteers.

War Child (RE PA PO), Studio 320, Highgate Studios, 53-79 Highgate Rd, London NW5 1TL (+44-20-7112 2555) (info@warchild.org.uk) (www.warchild.org.uk). Aid organisation for children in war zones.

War On Want [WOW] (TW), 44-48 Shepherdess Walk, London N1 7JP (+44-20-7324 5040) (fax 7324 5041) (support@waronwant.org) (www.waronwant.org).

Week of Prayer for World Peace (RP), c/o 126 Manor Green Rd, Epsom KT19 8LN, Surrey (+44-1628-530309) (j.jackson215@btinternet.com) (www.weekofprayerforworldpeace.com).

West Midlands CND [WMCND] (ND), 54 Allison St, Digbeth, Birmingham B5 5TH (+44-121-643 4617) (wmcndall@gmail.com) (www.wmcnd.org.uk).

West Midlands Quaker Peace Education Project [WMQPEP] (SF RE CR), 41 Bull St, Birmingham B4 6AF (+44-121-236 4796) (office@peacemakers.org.uk) (www.peacemakers.org.uk).

Western Sahara Campaign UK (HR TW), Manora, Cwmystwyth, Aberystwyth SY23 4AF (+44-1974-282575) (coordinator@wsahara.org.uk) (www.wsahara.org.uk).

White Ribbon Campaign (PO), White Ribbon House, 1 New Rd, Mytholmroyd, Hebden Bridge HX7 5DZ (+44-1422-886545) (info@whiteribboncampaign.co.uk) (www.whiteribboncampaign.co.uk).

WMD Awareness Programme (RE DA), c/o Pugwash Office, Bell Push 13, 63A Great Russell St, London WC1B 3BJ (+44-20-7405 6661) (office@wmdawareness.org.uk) (www.wmdawareness.org.uk).

Women in Black, c/o 24 Colvestone Cres, London E8 (wibinfo@gn.apc.org) (www.womeninblack.org).

Women's International League for Peace and Freedom [UK WILPF] (WL), 52-54 Featherstone St, London EC1Y 8RT (+44-20-7250 1968) (ukwilpf.peace@gmail.com) (www.wilpf.org.uk). Also Scottish office (scottishwilpf@yahoo.co.uk).

Woodcraft Folk (PA EL PO RE TW), Units 9/10, 83 Crampton St, London SE17 (+44-20-7703 4173) (fax 7358 6370) (info@woodcraft.org.uk) (www.woodcraft.org.uk). *The Courier.* Co-operative children's and youth organisation.

Working Group on Conscientious Objection in the UK (HR), c/o ForcesWatch, 5 Caledonian Rd, London N1 (office@forceswatch.net). Network of pacifist and human rights groups.

World Future Council – UK Office (WF EL DA ND), 4th Floor, Rex House, 4-12 Regent St, London SW1Y 4PE (info.uk@worldfuturecouncil.org) (www.worldfuturecouncil.org). Promotes sustainable future.

World Harmony Orchestra (CD PO), 12d Princess Crescent, London N4 2HJ (www.worldharmonyorchestra.com). Raises funds for humanitarian cuases.

World Peace Campaign, Hill House, Cookley, Kidderminster DY10 3UW, Worcs (+44-1562-851101) (fax 851824) (office@worldpeacecampaign.co.uk) (www.worldpeacecampaign.co.uk).

World Peace Prayer Society [WPPS] (RP PO EL RE), Allanton Sanctuary, Auldgirth, Dumfries DG2 0RY (+44-1387-740642) (allanton@worldpeace-uk.org) (www.worldpeace-uk.org). Promote the message "May peace prevail on earth".

Yorkshire CND (ND), The Deaf Centre, 25 Hallfield Rd, Bradford BD1 3RP, W Yorks (+44-1274-730795)

(info@yorkshirecnd.org.uk) (www.yorkshirecnd.org.uk). *Action for Peace.*
Youth and Student CND [YSCND] (ND RA), 162 Holloway Rd, London N7 8DQ (+44-20-7700 2393) (yscnd@riseup.net) (www.yscnd.org).

BURMA
Peace Way Foundation (HR), see under Thailand.

BURUNDI
Shalom – Educating for Peace (RE), Bujumbura (for postal address see Rwanda office) (hareprime@yahoo.fr).

CAMBODIA
Centre for Peace and Conflict Studies (RE), PO Box 93066, Siem Reap City (info@centrepeace.asia) (www.centrepeaceconflictstudies.org).

CANADA
Action by Christians Against Torture / Action des Chrétiens pour l'Abolition de la torture [ACAT-Canada] (HR), 2715 chemin de la Côte-Ste-Catherine, Montréal, QC, H3T 1B6 (+1-514-890 6169) (fax 890 6484) (info@acatcanada.org) (www.acatcanada.org).
Amnesty International Canadian Section – English Speaking (AI), 312 Laurier Ave E, Ottawa, ON, K1N 1H9 (+1-613-744 7667) (fax 746 2411) (members@amnesty.ca) (www.amnesty.ca). *The Activist.*
Amnistie Internationale – Section Canadienne Francophone (AI), 50 rue Ste-Catherine Ouest – bureau 500, Montréal, QC, H2X 3V4 (+1-514-766 9766) (fax 766 2088) (www.amnistie.qc.ca).
Antennes de Paix – Montréal (PC), 2450 chemin de la Cote Sainte-Catherine – bureau 310, Montréal, Québec H3T 1B1 (+1-514-271 9198) (antennesdepaix@gmail.com) (antennesdepaixmontreal.blogspot.com).
Artistes pour la Paix (PA ND AT), CP 867 – Succursale C, Montréal, QC, H2L 4L6 (artistespourlapaix.org).
Baptist Peace Fellowship of North America – Bautistas por la Paz (RP), see under USA.
Canadian Coalition for Nuclear Responsibility / Regroupement pour la Surveillance du Nucléaire [CCNR] (ND EL CD), 53 Dufferin Rd, Hampstead, QC, H3X 2X8 (+1-514-489 5118) (ccnr@web.ca) (www.ccnr.org).
Canadian Peace Congress (WP), 125 Brandon Ave, Toronto, ON, M6H 2E2 (info@CanadianPeaceCongress.ca) (www.canadianpeacecongress.ca).
Canadian Secular Alliance [CSA] (HR), 802 – 195 St Patrick St, Toronto, ON, M5T 2Y8 (+1-416-402 8856) (info@secularalliance.ca) (secularalliance.ca).

Centre de Ressources sur la Non-violence [CRNV] (WR EL), 75 Rue du Square Sir George étienne Carter, Montréal, QC, H4C 3A1 (+1-514-504 5012) (crnv@nonviolence.ca) (nonviolence.ca).
Christian Peacemaker Teams [CPT Canada] (RP PA RA), 140 Westmounth Rd N, Waterloo, ON, N2L 3G6 (+1-647-339 0991) (canada@cpt.org) (www.cpt.org).
Civilian Peace Service Canada (CD PO), 2106-1025 Richmond Rd, Ottawa, ON, K2B 8G8 (+1-613-721 9829) (gbreedyk@civilianpeaceservice.org) (civilianpeaceservice.ca).
Coalition for Gun Control, PO Box 90062, 1488 Queen St West, Toronto, ON, M6K 3K3 (+1-416-604 0209) (coalitionforguncontrol@gmail.com) (guncontrol.ca). Also in Montreal (+1-514-528 2360).
Coalition to Oppose the Arms Trade [COAT] (AT), 191 James St, Ottawa, ON, K1R 5M6 (+1-613-231 3076) (overcoat@rogers.com) (coat.ncf.ca).
Collectif échec à la Guerre (PA RE DA), 5055A rue Rivard, Montréal, QC, H2J 2N9 (+1-514-919 7249) (info@echecalaguerre.org) (echecalaguerre.org).
Edmonton Peace Council (WP), 392 Meadowview Drive, Fort Saskatchewan, Alberta T8L 0N9 (+1-587-873 9739) (canadianpeace@gmail.com). *Alberta Peace News.*
Friends of the Earth / Les Ami(e)s de la Terre [FoE] (FE), 260 St Patrick St – Suite 300, Ottawa, ON, K1N 5K5 (+1-613-241 0085) (fax 241 7998) (foe@intranet.ca) (www.foecanada.org).
Greenpeace Canada (GP), 33 Cecil St, Toronto, ON, M5T 1N1 (+1-416-597 8408) (fax 597 8422) (supporter.ca@greenpeace.org) (www.greenpeace.ca).
Mines Action Canada / Action Mines Canada (AT HR DA), 86A Renfrew Ave, Ottawa, ON, K1S 1Z8 (+1-613-241 3777) (fax 244 3410) (info@minesactioncanada.org) (www.minesactioncanada.org).
Pace e Bene Canada (PA RP), 4058 Rivard, Montreal, Quebec, H2L 4H9 (veronow@sympatico.ca).
Peace Brigades International – Canada [PBI-Canada] (CR RE SD), 211 Bronson Ave – Suite 220, Ottawa, ON, K1R 6H5 (+1-613-237 6968) (info@pbicanada.org) (www.pbicanada.org).
Peace Magazine (PA AT CR), Box 248, Toronto P, Toronto, ON, M5S 2S7 (+1-416-789 2294) (office@peacemagazine.org) (www.peacemagazine.org). 4 yrly, Can$20 (Can$24 US, Can$35 elsewhere).

For explanation of codes and abbreviations, see introduction

CANADA

PeaceWorks, c/o MSCU Centre for Peace Advancement, CGUC, University of Waterloo, 140 Westmount Road North, Waterloo, ON, N2L 3G6 (+1-519-591 1365) (mail@peaceworks.tv) (peaceworks.tv). Youth movement.

Physicians for Global Survival (Canada) / Médecins pour la Survie Mondiale (Canada) [PGS] (IP IB), 30 Cleary Ave, Ottawa, ON, K2A 4A1 (+1-613-233 1982) (pgsadmin@web.ca) (pgs.ca).

Project Ploughshares (RE AT ND RP DA), 140 Westmount Road North, Waterloo, ON, N2L 3G6 (+1-519-888 6541) (fax 888 0018) (plough@ploughshares.ca) (www.ploughshares.ca).

Religions for Peace – Canada / Religions pour la Paix – Canada (RP RE PA), 3333 Queen Mary Rd 490-1, Montréal, QC, H3Z 1A2 (pascale.fremond@videotron.ca).

Toronto Action for Social Change / Homes not Bombs [TASC] (RA AL), PO Box 2090, 57 Foster St, Perth, ON, K7H 1R0 (+1-613-267 3998) (tasc@web.ca) (www.homesnotbombs.blogspot.ca). *Resources for Radicals.*

Trudeau Centre for Peace, Conflict and Justice (RE), Monk School of Global Affairs, University of Toronto, 1 Devonshire Place, Toronto, ON, M5S 3K7 (+1-416-946 0326) (pcj.programme@utoronto.ca) (www.munkschool.utoronto.ca/trudeaucentre).

United Nations Association in Canada / Association canadienne pour les Nations-Unies [UNAC/ACNU] (UN EL RE HR CD), 309 Cooper St – Suit 300, Ottawa, ON, K2P 0G5 (+1-613-232 5751) (fax 563 2455) (info@unac.org) (unac.org).

USCC Doukhobors (RP CD PA), Box 760, Grand Forks, BC, V0H 1H0 (+1-250-442 8252) (fax 442 3433) (info@usccdoukhobors.org) (www.usccdoukhobors.org). *Iskra.* Union of Spiritual Communities of Christ.

Women's International League for Peace and Freedom [WILPF] (WL), PO Box 365, 916 West Broadway, Vancouver, BC, V5Z 1K7 (+1-604-224 1517) (judydavis@telus.net).

World Federalist Movement – Canada / Mouvement Fédéraliste Mondial (Canada) (WF), Suite 207, 110 – 323 Chapel St, Ottawa, ON, K1N 7Z2 (+1-613-232 0647) (wfcnat@web.ca) (www.worldfederalistscanada.org). *Mondial.*

CHAD

Tchad Non-Violence [TNV] (WR FR), BP 1266, N'Djamena (astnv@yahoo.fr).

CHILE

Comité Nacional pro Defensa de la Flora y Fauna [CODEFF] (FE), Ernesto Reyes 035, Providencia, Santiago (+56-2-777 2534) (administra@codeff.cl) (www.codeff.cl).

Grupo de Objeción de Conciencia "Ni Casco Ni Uniforme" (WR), Bremen 585, Nuñoa, Santiago (+56-2-556 6066) (objetores@yahoo.com) (nicasconiuniforme.wordpress.com).

Grupo de Objeción de Conciencia – Rompiendo Filas (WR), Prat 289 – Oficina 2-A, Temuco (rompiendofilas@entodaspartes.org).

Servicio Paz y Justicia – Chile [SERPAJ] (FR), Orella Nº 1015, Valparaíso (+56-32-215 8239) (serpaj@serpajchile.cl) (serpajchile.cl).

CHINA

China Committee on Religion and Peace [CCRP] (RP), 23 Taipingqiao St, Xichen District, Beijing 100811 (+86-10-6619 1655) (fax 6619 1645) (ccrp1994@hotmail.com) (www.cppcc.gov.cn/ccrp).

Friends of Nature [FON] (EL), Rm 406, Building C, Huazhan Guoji Gongyu, 12 Yumin Road, Chaoyang District, Beijing 100029 (+86-10-6523 2040) (office@fonchina.org) (www.fon.org.cn).

Greenpeace China (GP), 3/F – Julong Office Building – Block 7, Julong Gardens, 68 Xinzhong St, Dongcheng District, Beijing 100027 (+86-10-6554 6931) (fax 6554 6932) (greenpeace.cn@greenpeace.org) (www.greenpeace.org/china). See also under Hong Kong for head office.

COLOMBIA

Acción Colectiva de Objetores y Objetoras de Conciencia [ACOOC] (WR), Cr 19 – No 33A – 26/1, Bogotá (+57-1-560 5058) (objecion@objetoresbogota.org) (objetoresbogota.org).

Liga Internacional de Mujeres pro Paz y Libertad [LIMPAL] (WL), Calle 44 – No 19-28 – Of 201, Bogotá (+57-1-285 0062) (limpal@limpalcolombia.org) (limpalcolombia.org).

CONGO, DEMOCRATIC REPUBLIC OF

Cercle des Jeunes Leaders pour la Paix / Circle of Young Leaders for Peace (RP), Av Kwango – No 7, Kintambo Magasin, Ngaliema, Dist Lukunga, Kinshasa (+243-81-514 0938) (jcsaki2000@yahoo.fr).

Groupe Interconfessionnel de la Réconciliation / Kinshasa [GIR] (FR), see under Belgium.

Life & Peace Institute (CR RP), Bukavu (for postal address see under Rwanda (pieter.vanholder@life-peace.org).

Peace & Conflict Resolution Project (CR), for postal address see under Rwanda (+243-993-463279) (peacecrp@yahoo.com) (www.peaceconflictresolutionproject.webs.com). Based in Bukavu.

COSTA RICA
Centro de Estudios Para la Paz [CEPPA] (RE), Apdo 8-4820, 1000 San José (+506-2234 0524) (fax) (info@ceppacr.org) (www.ceppacr.org).
Monteverde Friends Meeting (SF), Monteverde 5655, Puntarenas (+506-2645 5530) (fax 2645 5302) (MonteverdeQuakers@gmail.com) (MonteverdeQuakers.org).
Religions for Peace – Costa Rica (RP), Apdo Postal 7288, 1000 San Jose (eduardoenrique_69@msn.com).

CROATIA
Centar za ene rtve Rata / Centre for Women War Victims – ROSA [C R] (CR HR), Kralja DHslava 2, 10000 Zagreb (+385-1-455 1142) (fax 455 1128) (cenzena@zamir.net) (www.czzzr.hr). Feminist, anti-militarist.
Centar Za Mir, Nenasilje i Ljudska Prava – Osijek / Centre for Peace, Nonviolence and Human Rights (CR HR PC RE), Trg Augusta Šenoe 1, 31000 Osijek (+385-31-206886) (fax 206889) (centar-za-mir@centar-za-mir.hr) (www.centar-za-mir.hr).
Centar za Mirovne Studije / Centre for Peace Studies [CMS] (WR CR RE HR), Selska cesta 112a, 10000 Zagreb (+385-1-482 0094) (fax) (cms@cms.hr) (www.cms.hr).
Dalmatinski Komitet za Ljudska Prava [DK] (HR), Trumbucac 19, 21000 Split (+385-21-482805) (dkomit@cryptolab.net) (dalmatinskikomitet.com). Dalmatian Committee for Human Rights.

CUBA
Moviemiento Cubano por la Paz y la Soberanía de los Pueblos (WP), Calle C No 670, e/ 27 y 29, Vedado, Habana (+53-7-831 9429) (secretariat@movpaz.cu) (www.movpaz.cu).

CYPRUS
Conciliation – Peace Economics Network (CR), PO Box 20209, Nicosia 1665 (costas@highwaycommunications.com).
Hands Across the Divide – Women Building Bridges in Cyprus (HR CD CR DA), Ellispontos 10, Dasoupolis 2015, Nicosia (handsacrossthedivide@gmail.com) (www.handsacrossthedivide.org). Supports feminist values and demilitaristion.
Oikiologiki Kinisi Kyprou / Ecological Movement of Cyprus (EL), TK 28948, Nicosia 2084 (+357-2251 8787) (fax 2251 2710) (ecological_movement@cytanet.com.cy) (www.ecologicalmovement.org.cy). *Ecologiki Enimerosi.*
Philoi tis Gis (Kypros) / Friends of the Earth (Cyprus) [FOE] (FE), PO Box 53411, 361B St Andrews St, Lemesos 3035 (+357-2534 7042) (fax 2534 7043) (contact@foecyprus.org) (www.foecyprus.org).

CYPRUS (NORTHERN)
Hands Across the Divide – Women Building Bridges in Cyprus (HR CD CR DA), see under Cyprus (www.handsacrossthedivide.org). Supports feminist values and demilitaristion.

CZECH REPUBLIC
České Mírové Hnutí / Czech Peace Movement (WP), Josefa Houdka 123, 15531 Praha (mirovehnuti@email.cz) (www.mirovehnuti.cz).
Hnutí DUHA (FE RA), údolní 33, 60200 Brno (+420-5 4521 4431) (fax 5 4521 4429) (info@hnutiduha.cz) (hnutiduha.cz). *Evergreen.*
Lékaři za Bezpečný ivot na Zemi / Physicians for Global Security (IP), c/o Vaclav Stukavec, Jlhí 222, 46801 Jablonec nad Nisou 8 (+420-603 364224) (stukav@volny.cz).
Nezávislé Sociálně Ekologické Hnutí / Independent Socio-Ecological Movement [NESEHNUTÍ] (WR EL HR AT), třída Kpt Jaroše 18, 60200 Brno (+420-5 4324 5342) (brno@nesehnuti.cz) (nesehnuti.cz). Social Ecological Movement.
Památník Mohyla Míru / Cairn of Peace Memorial (RE), K Mohyle Míru 200, 66458 Peace (+420-54 424 4724) (www.muzeumbrnenska.cz).

DENMARK
Aldrig Mere Krig [AMK] (WR AT IB), Nørremarksvej 4, 6880 Tarm (+45-9737 3163) (info@aldridmerekrig.dk) (aldridmerekrig.dk). *Ikkevold.*
Amnesty International (AI), Gammeltorv 8 – 5 sal, 1457 København K (+45-3345 6565) (amnesty@amnesty.dk) (www.amnesty.dk).
Center for Konfliktløsning / Danish Centre for Conflict Resolution (CR RE), Dronning Olgas Vej 30, 2000 Frederiksberg (+45-3520 0550) (center@konfliktloesning.dk) (www.konfliktloesning.dk).
Danske Laeger Mod Kernevåben [DLMK] (IP), Langdalsvej 40, 8220 Brabrand, Aarhus (+45-8626 4717) (povl.revsbech@gmail.com) (www.dlmk.dk). *Danske Laeger Mod Kernevåben.*
FN-Forbundet (UN WF), Tordenskjoldsgade 25 st th, 1055 København K (+45-3346 4690) (fax 3646 4649) (fnforbundet@fnforbundet.dk) (www.fnforbundet.dk).
Green Cross Denmark (EL TW DA HR), Abel Cathrines Gade 3 – 1 sal, 1654 København V (+45-2639 1555) (kbi@greencross.dk) (greencross.dk).

DENMARK

Klimabevaegelsen i Danmark / Climate Movement Denmark (EL), c/o Thomas Meinart Larsen, JC Christensens Gade 2A – 3TV, 2300 København S (sek@klimabevaegelsen.dk) (www.klimabevaegeksen.dk).

Kvaekercentret (SF), Drejervej 15 – 4, 2400 København NV.

Kvindernes Internationale Liga for Fred og Frihed [KILFF] (WL RE), Vesterbrogade 10 – 2, 1620 København V (+45-3323 1097) (wilpfdk@gmail.com) (kvindefredsliga.dk).

NOAH / Friends of the Earth Denmark (FE), Nørrebrogade 39 – 1, 2200 København N (+45-3536 1212) (fax 3536 1217) (noah@noah.dk) (www.noah.dk).

Plums Fond for Fred, Økologi og Baeredygtighed / Plums Foundation for Peace, Ecology and Sustainability (DA HR EL), Dronningensgade 14, 1420 København K (+45-3295 4417) (plumsfond@plumsfond.dk) Previously Danish Peace Foundation / Fredsfonden.

Servas Danmark (SE), c/o Jan Degrauwe, Højbakkevej 32, 9440 Aabybro (+45-2048 5087) (info@servas.dk) (www.servas.dk).

EAST TIMOR

Haburas Foundation / Friends of the Earth Timor Leste (FE), PO Box 390, Dili (+670-331 0103) (haburaslorosae@yahoo.com) (www.haburasfoundation.org).

ECUADOR

Servicio Paz y Justicia del Ecuador [SERPAJ] (WR RP), Casilla 17-03-1567, Quito (+593-22-257 1521) (fax) (serpaj@ecuanex.org.ec) (www.serpaj.org.ec).

EGYPT

Arab Organisation for Human Rights [AOHR] (HR), 91 Merghani St, Heliopolis, Cairo 11341 (+20-2-2418 1396) (fax 2418 5346) (alaa.shalaby@aohr.net) (www.aohr.net).

No to Compulsory Military Service Movement (WR), [post should be sent via the WRI office in London] (+49-1763-141 5934) (NoMilService@gmail.com) (www.nomilservice.com).

EL SALVADOR

Centro Salvadoreño de Tecnologia Apropiada [CESTA] (FE), Apdo 3065, San Salvador (+503-2213 1400) (fax 2220 6479) (cesta@cesta-foe.org.sv) (www.cesta-foe.org.sv).

ESTONIA

Eestimaa Rohelised / Estonian Green Party (EL), Postkast 4740, 13503 Tallinn (+372-502 6816) (info@erakond.ee) (www.erakond.ee).

United Nations Association of Estonia (UN), Veski 42, 50409 Tartu (+372-527 1051) (una.estonia@gmail.com) (www.una.ee).

FIJI

Greenpeace Pacific – Fiji Office (GP), 1st Floor, Old Town Hall, Victoria Parade, Suva (+679-331 2861) (fax 331 2784) (support.au@greenpeace.org).

FINLAND

Ålands Fredsinstitut / Åland Islands Peace Institute (RE HR CR), PB 85, 22101 Mariehamn, Åland (+358-18-15570) (peace@peace.ax) (www.peace.ax).

Committee of 100 / Sadankomitea (WR IB ND AT RE), Rauhanasema, Veturitori, 00520 Helsinki (sadankomitea@sadankomitea.fi) (www.sadankomitea.fi).

Greenpeace Finland (GP), Iso Roobertinkatu 20-22 A (5 frs), 00120 Helsinki (+358-9-6229 2200) (fax 6229 2222) (info.finland@greenpeace.org) (www.greenpeace.fi).

Laajan Turvallisuuden Verkosto / Wider Security Network [WISE] (CR DA), Siltasaarenkatu 4 – 7th floor, 00530 Helsinki (+358-9-260 0131) (info@widersecurity.fi). Formerly Civil Society Conflict Prevention Network.

Maan Ystävät / Friends of the Earth (FE), Mechelininkatu 36 B 1, 00260 Helsinki (+358-45-886 3958) (fax -2-237 1670) (toimisto@maanystavat.fi) (www.maanystavat.fi).

Peace Union of Finland / Suomen Rauhanliitto / Finlands Fredsförbundet (IB FR ND AT RE), Peace Station, Veturitori, 00520 Helsinki (+358-9-7568 2828) (fax 147297) (rauhanliitto@rauhanliitto.fi).

Physicians for Social Responsibility / Lääkärin Sosiaalinen Vastuu / Läkarens Sociala Ansvar [PSR/LSV] (IP EL), Caloniusenkatu 9 D 64, 00100 Helsinki (+358-45-350 8516) (lsv@lsv.fi) (lsv.fi).

Sitoutumaton Vasemmisto / Independent Left (WR EL HR), Mannerheimintie 5B 7krs, 00100 Helsinki (sitvas-hallitus@helsinki.fi) (sitvasfi.wordpress.com).

Suomen Luonnonsuojeluliitto / Finnish Association for Nature Conservation [FANC] (EL), Itälahdenkatu 22-b A, 00210 Helsinki (+358-9-2280 8224) (toimisto@sll.fi) (www.sll.fi).

Union of Conscientious Objectors / Aseistakieltäytyjäliitto [AKL] (WR), Rauhanasema, Veturitori 3, 00520 Helsinki (+358-9-7568 2444) (fax 147297) (toimisto@akl-web.fi) (www.akl-web.fi).

Women's International League for Peace and Freedom – Finnish Section [WILPF] (WL), PL 1174, 00101 Helsinki (wilpf@wilpf.fi) (wilpf.fi).

For explanation of codes and abbreviations, see introduction

FRANCE

Action des Chrétiens pour l'Abolition de la Torture [ACAT] (HR), 7 rue Georges Lardennois, 75019 Paris (+33-14040 4243) (fax 14040 4244) (acat@acatfrance.fr) (www.acatfrance.fr).

Action des Citoyens pour le Désarmement Nucléaire [ACDN] (ND), 31 Rue du Cormier, 17100 Saintes (+33-673 507661) (contact@acdn.net) (www.acdn.net). Opposes both military and civilian nukes.

Alternatives Non-Violentes [ANV] (PA RE CR), Centre 308, 82 rue Jeanne d'Arc, 76000 Rouen (+33-235 752344) (contact@alternatives-non-violentes.org) (alternatives-non-violentes.org).

Amis de la Terre – France (FE), Mundo M, 47 ave Pasteur, 93100 Montreuil (+33-14851 3222) (fax 14851 9512) (france@amisdelaterre.org) (www.amisdelaterre.org).

Association des Médecins Français pour la Prévention de la Guerre Nucléaire [AMF-PGN] (IP), 5 Rue Las Cases, 75007 Paris (+33-14336 7781) (revue@amfpgn.org) (amfpgn.org). *Médecine et Guerre Nucléaire*.

Association française pour les Nations Unies (UN), 26 Av Charles Floquet, 75007 Paris (+33-17716 2454) (contact@afnu.fr) (afnu.fr).

Brigades de Paix Internationales [PBI-France] (HR PO RE CD), 21ter, rue Voltaire, 75011 Paris (+33-14373 4960) (pbi.france@free.fr) (www.pbi-france.org).

Centre Français d'Enregistrement des Citoyens du Monde (WF), 15 rue Victor Duruy, 75015 Paris (+33-14531 2999) (contact@citoyensdumonde.net) (www.citoyensdumonde.net). *Citoyens du Monde*.

Centre mondial de la Paix, des Libertés et des Droits de l'Homme (RE), Place Monseigneur, BP 10183, 55100 Verdun (+33-329 865500) (fax 329 861514) (contact@cmpaix.eu) (www.centremondialdelapaix.eu).

Cesser d'Alimenter la Guerre / Stop Fuelling War [SFW] (AT RA), c/o Centre Quaker de Paris, 114 rue de Vaugirard, 75006 Paris (stopfuellingwar@gmail.com) (stopfuellingwar.org). Countering the normalisation of the trade in arms.

Coordination pour l'éducation à la Non-violence et la Paix (RE), 148 rue du Faubourg Saint-Denis, 75010 Paris (+33-14633 4156) (education-nvp.org).

Greenpeace (GP), 13 rue d'Enghien, 75010 Paris (+33-18096 9696) (fax) (contact.fr@greenpeace.org) (www.greenpeace.org/france).

Groupement pour les Droits des Minorités [GDM] (HR), 212 rue St-Martin, 75003 Paris (+33-14575 0137) (fax 14579 8046) (yplasseraud@wanadoo.fr). *La Lettre du GDM*.

Institut de Recherche sur la Résolution Non-violente des Conflits [IRNC] (RE SD CR PA), 14 rue des Meuniers, 93100 Montreuil-sous-Bois (+33-14287 9469) (fax) (irnc@irnc.org) (www.irnc.org). *Alternatives Non-violentes*.

Ligue d'Amitié Internationale (CD), Les Champs Fleuris – Nº 4, 14 rue Maurice Boyau, 91220 Bretigny-sur-Orge (+33-160 853407) (www.ifl-france.org). Affiliate of the International Friendship League.

Ligue Internationale des Femmes pour la Paix et la Liberté – Section française [LIFPL/WILPF] (WL ND RE), 114 rue de Vaugirard, 75006 Paris (+33-14844 6711) (wilpf-france.net).

Mémorial de Caen Museum – Cité de l'Histoire pour la Paix / Centre for History and Peace (PO RE), Esplanade Eisenhower, BP 55026, 14050 Caen Cedex 4 (+33-231 060644) (fax 231 060670) (contact@memorial-caen.fr) (www.memorial-caen.fr).

Mouvement de la Paix (IB WP ND PA AT), 9 Rue Dulcie September, 93400 Saint-Ouen (+33-14012 0912) (national@mvtpaix.org) (www.mvtpaix.org). *Planète Paix*; *La Paix en Mouvement*.

Mouvement International de la Réconciliation (FR WR), 68 rue de Babylone, 75007 Paris (+33-14753 8405) (mirfr@club-internet.fr) (www.mirfrance.org). *Cahiers de la Réconciliation*.

Mouvement pour une Alternative Non-violente [MAN] (WR SD CR AT RA), 47 ave Pasteur, 93100 Montreuil (+33-14544 4825) (man@nonviolence.fr) (www.nonviolence.fr).

Non-Violence Actualité [NVA] (CR HR RE), Centre de Ressources sur la Gestion non-violente des Relations et des Conflits, BP 241, 45202 Montargis cedex (+33-238 936722) (fax 975 385985) (Nonviolence.Actualite@wanadoo.fr) (www.nonviolence-actualite.org). 6 yrly, €43 pa.

Non-Violence XXI (PA RE), 47 Ave Pasteur, 93100 Montreuil (+33-14548 3762) (fax 14544 4825) (coordination@nonviolence21.org) (www.nonviolence21.com).

Pax Christi France (PC), 5 rue Morère, 75014 Paris (+33-14449 0636) (accueil@paxchristi.cef.fr) (www.paxchristi.cef.fr). *Journal de la Paix*.

Peace Lines / Messageries de la Paix (CR RE), 51310 Esternay (+33-326 819115) (peacelines@gmail.com) (www.peacelines.org). *The Messengers' Mail / Le Courrier des Messageries*.

Réseau "Sortir du Nucléaire" / Network for a Nuclear Phase-Out (EL RA PO), 9 rue Dumenge, 69317 Lyon cedex 04 (+33-47828 2922) (fax 47207 7004) (contact@sortirdunucleaire.org) (www.sortirdunucleaire.org). Network of groups in France against nuclear energy.

FRANCE

Religions pour la Paix (RP), 8 bis Rue Jean Bart, 75006 Paris (Religionspourlapaix@yahoo.fr) (religionspourlapaix.org).
Service Civil International [SCI-F] (SC), 75 rue du Chevalier Français, 59800 Lille (+33-320 552258) (sci@sci-france.org) (www.sci-france.org).
Silence (EL AL PA PO), 9 Rue Dumenge, 69317 Lyon cedex 04 (+33-478 395533) (www.revuesilence.net). Mthly, Eu55 pa.
Société Religieuse des Amis (SF), Centre Quaker International, 114 Rue de Vaugirard, 75006 Paris (+33-14548 7423) (assembleedefrance@gmail.com) (www.QuakersEnFrance.org). *Lettre des Amis.*
Solidarités Jeunesses (WC CD), 10 Rue du 8 Mai 1945, 75010 Paris (+33-15526 8877) (fax 15326 0326) (secretariat@solidaritesjeunesses.org) (www.solidaritesjeunesses.org).
Sortir de la Violence – France (RP), 11 rue de la Chaise, 75007 Paris (sdv-France@sortirdelaviolence.org) (www.sortirdelaviolence.org).
Union Pacifiste de France [UPF] (WR AT), BP 40196, 75624 Paris cédex 13 (+33-14586 0875) (union.pacifiste@orange.fr) (www.unionpacifiste.org). *Union Pacifiste.*

FRENCH POLYNESIA

Ligue Internationale des Femmes pour la Paix et la Liberté – Section Polynésienne [LIFPL] (WL), Faaone pk 49.2, Côté Montagne, 98713 Faaone, Tahiti (+689-264729) (wilpf.polynesie@gmail.com).

GEORGIA

Sakhartvelos Mtsvaneta Modzraoba / Green Movement of Georgia (FE), 55 Kandelaki St, 0160 Tbilisi (+995-32-386978) (info@greens.ge) (www.greens.ge).
War Resisters' International – Georgian Section (WR), 45 Kavtaradze St – Apt 45, Tbilisi 0186 (+995-577-117878) (uchananua@yahoo.com).

GERMANY

Aktion Sühnezeichen Friedensdienste [ASF] (WC RP HR CD), Auguststr 80, 10117 Berlin-Mitte (+49-30-2839 5184) (fax 2839 5135) (asf@asf-ev.de) (www.asf-ev.de). *Zeichen.*
Aktion Völkerrecht / International Law Campaign (WF ND CD), c/o Peter Kolbe, Werderstr 36, 69120 Heidelberg (buero@a-vr.org) (www.aktion-voelkerrecht.de).
Aktionsgemeinschaft Dienst für den Frieden [AGDF] (WC PA RP), Endenicher Str 41, 53115 Bonn (+49-228-249990) (fax 249 9920) (agdf@friedensdienst.de) (www.friedensdienst.de). Voluntary service co-ordination agency.
Amnesty International (AI), Zinnowitzer Str, 10115 Berlin (+49-30-420 2480) (fax 4202 48488) (info@amnesty.de) (www.amnesty.de). *ai-Journal.*
Anti-Kriegs-Museum / Anti-War Museum (WR), Brüsseler Str 21, 13353 Berlin (+49-30-4549 0110) (Anti-Kriegs-Museum@gmx.de) (www.anti-kriegs-museum.de).
Arbeitsgemeinschaft für Friedens- und Konfliktforschung / German Association for Peace and Conflict Studies [AFK] (RE), c/o Fakultät Gesellschaft und Ökonomie, Hochschule Rhein-Waal, 47533 Kleve (+49-2821-806739793) (fax 8067 3162) (afk-gf@afk-web.de) (afk-web.de).
Archiv Aktiv für gewaltfreie Bewegungen (WR RE EL), Normannenweg 17-21, 20537 Hamburg (+49-40-430 2046) (email@archiv-aktiv.de) (www.archiv-aktiv.de).
ausgestrahlt (EL RA ND), Grosse Bergstr 189, 22767 Hamburg (+49-40-2531 3913) (fax 2531 8944) (info@ausgestrahlt.de) (www.ausgestrahlt.de). *.ausgestrahlt-magazin.* Anti-nuclear direct action network.
Bürgermeister für den Frieden in Deutschland und Österreich (CD ND DA), c/o Landeshauptstadt Hannover, Büro Oberbürgermeister, Trammplatz 2, 30159 Hannover (+49-511-1684 1446) (fax 1684 4025) (mayorsforpeace@hannover-stadt.de) (www.mayorsforpeace.de).
Berghof Foundation (CR RE), Altensteinstr 48a, 14195 Berlin (+49-30-844 1540) (fax 8441 5499) (info@berghof-conflictresearch.org) (www.berghof-conflictresearch.org). Works to prevent political and social violence.
Bund für Soziale Verteidigung [BSV] (WR SD CR), Schwarzer Weg 8, 32423 Minden (+49-571-29456) (fax 23019) (office@soziale-verteidigung.de) (www.soziale-verteidigung.de). *Soziale Verteidigung.*
Bund für Umwelt und Naturschutz Deutschland [BUND] (FE), Am Köllnischen Park 1, 10179 Berlin (+49-30-275 8640) (fax 2758 6440) (info@bund.net) (www.bund.net).
Connection eV (PA HR), Von-Behring-Str 110, 63075 Offenbach (+49-69-8237 5534) (fax 8237 5535) (office@Connection-eV.org) (www.Connection-eV.org). *KDV im Krieg.* International work for COs and deserters.
Deutsch-Russischer Austausch / Nyemyetsko-Russkiy Obmyen [DRA] (CD), Badstr 44, 13357 Berlin (+49-30-446 6800) (fax 4466 8010) (info@austausch.org) (www.austausch.org). German-Russian Exchange.
Deutsche Friedens-Bücherei (RE PA EL), Postfach 101361, 66013 Saarbrücken (+33-387 950018).

Deutsche Friedensgesellschaft – Internationale der Kriegsdienstgegner [DFG-IdK] (WR DA), Jungfrauenthal 37, 20149 Hamburg (+49-40-453433) (fax 4440 5270) (mail@dfg-idk.de) (www.dfg-idk.de). *Rundbrief.*

Deutsche Friedensgesellschaft – Vereinigte Kriegsdienstgegner [DFG-VK] (WR IB RE), Werastr 10, 70182 Stuttgart (+49-711-5189 2626) (fax 2486 9622) (office@dfg-vk.de) (www.dfg-vk.de).

Deutsche Gesellschaft für die Vereinten Nationen [DGVN] (UN), Zimmerstr 26/27, 10969 Berlin (+49-30-259 3750) (fax 2593 7529) (info@dgvn.de) (www.dgvn.de). *Vereinte Nationen.*

Deutsche Sektion der IPPNW / Ärzte in sozialer Verantwortung (IPPNW Germany) (IP AT DA), Körtestr 10, 10967 Berlin (+49-30-698 0740) (fax 693 8166) (kontakt@ippnw.de) (www.ippnw.de). *Forum.*

Deutscher Friedensrat / German Peace Council (WP), Platz der Vereinten Nationen 7, 10249 Berlin (+49-30-426 5290) (fax 4201 7338) (saefkow-berlin@t-online.de) (www.deutscher-friedensrat.de).

Deutsches Bündnis Kindersoldaten (HR PA), c/o Kindernothilfe, Düsseldorfer Landstr 180, 47249 Duisburg (+49-203-778 9111) (fax 778 9118) (info@kindernothilfe.de) (www.kindernothilfe.de). Campaigns against use of child soldiers.

Forum Ziviler Friedensdienst / Civil Peace Service Forum [forumZFD] (SF CR RE), Am Kölner Brett 8, 50825 Köln (+49-221-912 7320) (fax 9127 3299) (kontakt@forumZFD.de) (www.forumZFD.de). Offers conflict transformation training & courses.

Frauennetzwerk für Frieden (IB), Kaiserstr 201, 53113 Bonn (+49-228-626730) (fax 626780) (fn.frieden@t-online.de) (www.frauennetzwerk-fuer-frieden.de).

Friedensausschuss der Religiösen Gesellschaft der Freunde (Quäker) (SF PA CR DA), Föhrenstieg 8, 22926 Ahrensburg (+49-4102-53337) (helga.tempel@gmx.de). *Quäker.*

Gandhi Information Centre (PA RE), Postfach 210109, 10501 Berlin (mkgandhi@snafu.de) (www.nonviolent-resistance.info). Previously Gandhi-Informations-Zentrum.

GandhiServe Foundation (RE HR), Rathausstr 51a, 12105 Berlin (+49-30-705 4054) (fax 3212-100 3676) (mail@gandhimail.org) (www.gandhiserve.com).

Gewaltfreie Aktion Atomwaffen Abschaffen / Nonviolent Action to Abolish Nuclear Weapons [GAAA] (ND RA), c/o Marion Küpker, Beckstr 14, 20357 Hamburg (+49-40-430 7332) (marion.kuepker@gaaa.org) (www.gaaa.org).

Graswurzelrevolution (WR AL RA), Breul 43, 48143 Münster (+49-251-482 9057) (fax 482 9032) (redaktion@graswurzel.net) (www.graswurzel.net).

Greenpeace (GP), Hongkongstr 10, 20457 Hamburg (+49-40-306180) (fax 3061 8100) (mail@greenpeace.de) (www.greenpeace.de). Berlin: +49-30-308 8990.

Hessische Stiftung Friedens- und Konfliktforschung / Peace Research Institute Frankfurt [HSFK/PRIF] (RE), Baseler Str 27-31, 60329 Frankfurt (+49-69-959 1040) (fax 558481) (info@hsfk.de) (www.hsfk.de). *HSFK-Standpunkt.*

Humanistische Union [HU] (HR), Haus der Demokratie und Menschenrechte, Greifswalder Str 4, 10405 Berlin (+49-30-2045 0256) (fax 2045 0257) (info@humanistische-union.de) (www.humanistische-union.de). *Vorgänge.*

Initiative Musiker/innen gegen Auftritte der Bundeswehrmusikkorps (PA), c/o Dietmar Parchow, Austr 77, 72669 Unterensingen (musikergegenmilitaermusik@idk-berlin.de) (musiker-gegen-militaermusik.jimdo.com). Against public and church use of military bands.

Institut für Friedensarbeit und Gewaltfreie Konfliktaustragung [IFGK] (WR RE CR), Hauptstr 35, 55491 Wahlenau/Hunsrück (+49-6543-980096) (fax 500636) (BMuellerIFGK@t-online.de) (www.ifgk.de). *IFGK Working Papers.*

Institut für Friedenspädagogik Tübingen/ Institute for Peace Education Tübingen (RE CR), Corrensstr 12, 72076 Tübingen (+49-7071-920510) (fax 920 5111) (info-tuebingen@berghof-foundation.org) (www.friedenspaedagogik.de). A branch of the Berghof Foundation.

Institute for International Assistance and Solidarity [IFIAS] (IB CD HR ND), Postfach 170420, 53027 Bonn (+49-228-721 6864) (fax 721 6866) (drake@ifias.eu) (www.ifias.eu). Also in Belgium.

Internationale der Kriegsdienstgegner/innen [IDK] (WR AL), Postfach 280312, 13443 Berlin (info@idk-berlin.de) (www.idk-info.net).

Internationale Frauenliga für Frieden und Freiheit [IFFF] (WL), Haus der Demokratie und Menschenrechte, Greifswalder Str 4, 10405 Berlin (info@wilpf.de) (wilpf.de).

Internationale Jugendgemeinschaftsdienste [IJGD] (WC EL CD), Kasernenstr 48, 53111 Bonn (+49-228-228 0014) (fax 228 0010) (workcamps@ijgd.de) (www.ijgd.de). Workcamps and volunteering in Germany and abroad.

Juristen und Juristinnen gegen Atomare, Biologische und Chemische Waffen – IALANA Deutschland (ND), Marienstr 19-20, 10117 Berlin (+49-30-2065 4857) (fax 2065 4858) (info@ialana.de) (www.ialana.de).

GERMANY

Kampagne gegen Wehrpflicht, Zwangsdienste und Militär (PA RA SD), Kopenhagener Str 71, 10437 Berlin (+49-30-4401 3025) (fax 4401 3029) (info@kampagne.de) (www.kampagne.de).

Komitee für Grundrechte und Demokratie (HR CD RA PA), Aquinostr 7-11 (HH), 50670 Köln (+49-221-972 6920) (fax 972 6931) (info@grundrechtekomitee.de) (www.grundrechtekomitee.de).

Kooperation für den Frieden (DA ND RE), Römerstr 88, 53111 Bonn (+49-228-692905) (fax 692906) (info@koop-frieden.de) (www.koop-frieden.de). Networking organisation in German peace movement.

KURVE Wustrow – Bildungs- und Begegnungsstätte für gewaltfreie Aktion (FR PA CR HR RE), Kirchstr 14, 29462 Wustrow (+49-5843-98710) (fax 987111) (info@kurvewustrow.de) (www.kurvewustrow.org).

Netzwerk Friedenskooperative (ND PA AT), Römerstr 88, 53111 Bonn (+49-228-692904) (fax 692906) (friekoop@friedenskooperative.de) (www.friedenskooperative.de). *Friedensforum*.

Netzwerk Friedenssteuer [NWFS] (TR), Krennerweg 12, 81479 München (+49-8062-725 2395) (fax 725 2396) (info@netzwerk-friedenssteuer.de) (www.netzwerk-friedenssteuer.de). *Friedenssteuer-Nachrichten*.

Ohne Rüstung Leben (AT CR PA ND DA), Arndtstr 31, 70197 Stuttgart (+49-711-608396) (fax 608357) (orl@gaia.de) (www.ohne-ruestung-leben.de). *Ohne Rüstung Leben-Informationen*.

Pax Christi Deutsche Sektion (PC), Hedwigskirchgasse 3, 10117 Berlin (+49-30-2007 6780) (fax 2007 67819) (sekretariat@paxchristi.de) (www.paxchristi.de).

Peace Brigades International Deutscher Zweig [PBI] (CR HR PA), Bahrenfelder Str 101 A, 22765 Hamburg (+49-40-3890 4370) (fax 3890 43729) (info@pbi-deutschland.de) (www.pbideutschland.de).

Pestizid Aktions-Netzwerk [PAN Germany] (EL), Nernstweg 32, 22765 Hamburg (+49-40-3991 9100) (fax 3991 91030) (info@pan-germany.de) (www.pan-germany.org).

RüstungsInformationsBüro [RIB-Büro] (AT PA RE), Stühlinger Str 7, 79016 Freiburg (+49-761-767 8088) (fax 767 8089) (rib-info@rib-ev.de) (www.rib-ev.de). Campaign against small arms.

RfP Deutschland / Religions for Peace (RP), c/o Franz Brendle, Im Schellenkönig 61, 70184 Stuttgart (+49-711-539 0209) (fax 505 8648) (rfp@r-f-p.de) (www.religionsforpeace.de). *Informationen*.

Servas Germany (SE), O'Swaldstr 32, 22111 Hamburg (mail@servas.de) (www.servas.de).

Stiftung die schwelle / Schwelle Foundation – Beiträge zum Frieden (CR TW RE HR), Wachmannstr 79, 28209 Bremen (+49-421-303 2575) (fax 303 2464) (stiftung@dieschwelle.de) (www.dieschwelle.de).

Terre des Femmes – Menschenrechte für die Frau eV (HR), Brunnenstr 128, 13355 Berlin (+49-30-4050 46990) (fax 4050 469999) (info@frauenrechte.de) (www.frauenrechte.de).

Versöhnungsbund [VB] (FR IB PA), Schwarzer Weg 8, 32423 Minden (+49-571-850875) (fax 829 2387) (vb@versoehnungsbund.de) (www.versoehnungsbund.de).

Working Group on Conscientious Objection in War (WR), c/o Franz Nadler, Riethgasse 4, 63075 Offenbach (+49-69-815128) (fax) (office@connection-eV.org) (www.connection-eV.de). *KDV im Krieg*.

GHANA

United Nations Association of Ghana (UN), Private Mail Bag, Ministries Post Office, Accra (+233-30-376 8858) (office@unaghana.org) (www.unaghana.org).

GREECE

Diethnis Amnistia / Amnesty International (AI), 30 Sina Street, 10672 Athinai (+30-210 3600 628) (fax 210 3638 016) (athens@amnesty.org.gr) (www.amnesty.org.gr). *Martyries*.

Elliniki Epitropi gia ti Thiethni Yphesi kai Eirene / Greek Committee for International Detente and Peace [EEDYE] (WP), Themistokleous 48, 10681 Athinai (+30-210 3844 853) (fax 210 3844 879) (eedye@otenet.gr) (eedye.gr).

Enomenes Koinonies ton Valkanion / United Societies of the Balkans [USB] (CD CR HR PO), Adamanas 9, Agios Paulos, 55438 Thessaloniki (+30-231 0215 629) (fax) (info@usbngo.gr) (www.usbngo.gr).

Greenpeace Greece (GP), Kolonou 78, 10437 Athinai (+30-210 3840 774) (fax 210 3804 008) (gpgreece@greenpeace.org) (www.greenpeace.org/greece).

Kinisi Ethelonton / Volunteer Movement [SCI-Hellas] (SC), Pythagora 12, Neos Kosmos, 11743 Athinai (+30-215 5406 504) (info@sci.gr) (www.sci.gr).

Oikologoi Prasinoi / Ecologist Greens (EL), Plateia Eleftherias 14, 10553 Athinai (+30-210 3306 301) (fax 210 3241 825) (ecogreen@otenet.gr) (www.ecogreens.gr). Green Party.

Syndhesmos Antirrision Syneidhisis / Association of Greek Conscientious Objectors [SAS] (WR), Tsamadou 13A, 10683 Athinai (+30-694 4542 228) (fax 210 4622 753) (greekCO@hotmail.com) (www.antirrisies.gr).

HONG KONG

Alternatives to Violence Project – AVP Hong Kong (CR PO), 12a Shun Ho Tower, 24-30 Ice House St, Central (avphongkong@gmail.com) (www.avphongkong.org).

Amnesty International Hong Kong (AI), Unit 3D, Best-O-Best Commercial Centre, 32-36 Ferry St, Kowloon (+852-2300 1250) (fax 2782 0583) (admin-hk@amnesty.org.hk) (www.amnesty.org.hk).

Association for the Advancement of Feminism [AAF] (HR), Flats 119-120, Lai Yeung House, Lei Cheng Uk Estate, Kowloon (+852-2720 0891) (fax 2720 0205) (hkaaf38@gmail.com) (www.aaf.org.hk). *Nuliu*.

Greenpeace China (GP), 8/F Pacific Plaza, 410-418 Des Voeux Rd West (+852-2854 8300) (fax 2745 2426) (enquiry.hk@greenpeace.org) (www.greenpeace.org/china). Also Beijing office: see under China.

Human Rights in China – Hong Kong Office [HRIC] (HR), GPO, PO Box 1778 (+852-2701 8021) (hrichk@hrichina.org) (www.hrichina.org). Main office in New York (+1-212-239 4495).

HUNGARY

ACAT-Hungary (HR), c/o Csaba Kabódi, Eötvös University, Egyetem Tér 1-3, 1364 Budapest (+36-1-252 5961) (fax) (kabodi@ajk.elte.hu).

Bocs Foundation (FR EL TW), Pf 7, 8003 Székesfehérvár (m@bocs.hu) (www.bocs.hu). *Bocsmagazin*.

Magyar Orvosmozgalom a Nukleáris Háború Megelőzéséért (IP), c/o Zita Makoi, Hegedus Gy u 48, 1133 Budapest (zita.makoi@gmail.com).

Magyar Természetvédők Szövetsége [MTVSZ] (FE), Ulloi U 91B – III/21, 1091 Budapest (info@mtvsz.hu) (www.mtvsz.hu).

ICELAND

Amnesty International (AI), Thingholtsstraeti 27, 101 Reykjavík (+354-511 7900) (fax 511 7901) (amnesty@amnesty.is) (www.amnesty.is).

Peace 2000 Institute (CR RE), Vogasel 1, 109 Reykjavík (+354-557 1000) (fax 496 2005) (info@peace2000.org) (peace2000.org). Offices also in Britain, USA.

Samtök Hernadarandstaedinga / Campaign Against Militarism (WR), Njalsgata 87, 101 Reykjavík (+354-554 0900) (sha@fridur.is) (fridur.is).

INDIA

All India Peace and Solidarity Organisation [AIPSO] (WP), c/o AIPSO West Bengal, 5 Sarat Ghosh St (behind Entally Market), Kolkota 700014 (info) (bengalaipso@gmail.com) (www.aipsowb.org).

Anglican Pacifist Fellowship [APF] (RP), c/o John Nagella, Opp SBI Colony, AT Agraharam, Guntur 552004, Andhra Pradesh.

Anuvrat Global Organisation [ANUVIBHA] (IB EL ND PO CR), B01-02, Anuvibha Jaipur Kendra, opp Gaurav Tower, Malviya Nagar 302017, Rajasthan (+91-141-404 9714) (slgandhi@hotmail.com) (www.anuvibha.in).

Atheist Centre (HR RA), Benz Circle, Patamata, Vijayawada 520010, AP (+91-866-247 2330) (fax 248 4850) (atheistcentre@yahoo.com) (www.atheistcentre.in). *Atheist*.

Bombay Sarvodaya Friendship Centre (FR WC SF), 701 Sainath Estate, Opp Lokmanya Vidyalaya, Nilam Nagar-II, Mulund East, Mumbai 400081 (+91-22-2563 1022) (danielm@mtnl.net.in).

Centre for Peace and Development (AT ND RE TW EL), 12/1 BT Rd "A" Cross, Chamarajapet, Bangalore 560018 (+91-80-4153 8790).

Coalition for Nuclear Disarmament and Peace [CNDP] (ND), A-124/6 – First Floor, Katwaria Sarai, New Delhi 110016 (+91-11-6566 3958) (fax 2651 7814) (cndpindia@gmail.com) (www.cndpindia.com). Network of 200 organisations.

Ekta Parishad (HR PO TW), 2/3A – Second Floor – Jungpura-A, New Delhi 10014 (+91-11-2437 3998) (ektaparishad@gmail.com) (www.ektaparishad.com). Federation of thousands of community organisations.

Friends of the Gandhi Museum (RE EL PO), B-4 Puru Society, Airport Rd, Lohegaon, Pune 411032 (+91-937 120 1138) (satyagrahi2000@gmail.com).

Gandhi Book Centre / Mumbai Sarvodaya Mandal (PO), 299 Tardeo Rd, Nana Chowk, Mumbai 400007 (+91-22-2387 2061) (info@mkgandhi.org) (www.mkgandhi.org).

Gandhi Research Foundation (RE), Gandhi Teerth, Jain Hills PO Box 118, Jalgaon 425001, Maharashtra (+91-257-226 0011) (fax 226 1133) (gandhiexam@gandhifoundation.net) (www.gandhifoundation.net).

Gandhian Society Villages Association (WR), Amaravathy Pudur PO, Pasumpon District, Tamil Nadu 623301 (+91-8645-83234).

Greenpeace India (GP), 60 Wellington Rd, Richmond Town, Bangalore 560025, Karnataka (+91-80-2213 1899) (fax 4115 4862) (supporter.services.in@greenpeace.org) (www.greenpeace.org/india). Regional Office in Delhi (+91-11-6666 5000).

Gujarat Vidyapeeth (RE), Ashram Rd (near Income tax), Ahmedabad 380014 (+91-79-2754 0746) (fax 2754 2547) (registrar@gujaratvidyapith.org) (www.gujaratvidyapith.org). Gandhian study centre.

INDIA

Indian Doctors for Peace and Development [IDPD] (IP), 139-E Kitchlu Nagar, Ludhiana 141001, Punjab (+91-161-230 0252) (fax 230 4360) (idpd2001@yahoo.com) (www.idpd.org).

Nagaland Peace Centre (PA CR), D Block, Kohima Town, PO Kohima 797001, Nagaland (+91-370-229 1400).

National Gandhi Museum and Library (RE), Rajghat, New Delhi 110002 (+91-11-2331 1793) (fax 2332 8310) (gandhimuseumdelhi@gmail.com) (www.gandhimuseum.org). Has collection of original relics, books, etc.

Organisation for Nuclear Disarmament, World Peace and Environment [ONDAW-PE] (ND EL), 11 Gautam Palli, Lucknow 226001, UP (+91-522-223 5659) (ammarrizvi505@yahoo.com).

Swadhina / Independence (WR), 34/C Bondel Rd, Ballygunge, Kolkata 700019 (+91-33-3245 1730) (mainoffice.swadhina@gmail.com) (www.swadhina.org.in).

Tibetan Centre for Human Rights and Democracy (FR HR), Narthang Building – Top Floor, Gangchen Kyishong, Dharamsala, HP 176215 (+91-1892-223363) (fax 225874) (office@tchrd.org) (www.tchrd.org). Works for human rights of Tibetans in Tibet.

War Resisters of India/West (WR), c/o Swati & Michael, Juna Mozda, Dediapada, Dt Narmada, Gujarat 393040 (+91-2649-290249) (mozdam@gmail.com).

Women's International League for Peace and Freedom – India [WILPF] (WL), c/o Peace Research Centre, Gujatat Vidyapith, Ahmedabad 380014.

IRAN

Iranian Physicians for Social Responsibility [PSR-Iran] (IP), PO Box 11155-18747, Tehran Peace Museum, Parke shahr, Tehran (+98-21-6675 6945) (fax 6693 9992) (info@irpsr.org).

Islamic Human Rights Commission [IHRC] (HR), PO Box 13165-137, Tehran (+98-21-8852 9742) (fax 8876 8807) (ihrc@ihrc.ir) (www.ihrc.ir).

IRELAND, NORTHERN

NOTE: Organisations working on an all-Ireland basis (ie covering both the Republic of Ireland and Northern Ireland), with their office address in the Irish Republic, will be found listed there. Similarly, groups operating on a United Kingdom-wide basis (ie covering both Britain and Northern Ireland), with a British-based office, will be found listed under Britain.

Amnesty International – NI Region [AI-NI] (AI), 397 Ormeau Rd, Belfast BT7 (+44-28-9064 3000) (fax 9069 0989) (nireland@amnesty.org.uk) (www.amnesty.org.uk).

Bahá'í Council for Northern Ireland (RP), Apt 4, 2 Lower Windsor Ave, Belfast BT9 (+44-28-9016 0457) (bcni@bahai.org.uk) (www.bahaicouncil-ni.org.uk).

Centre for Democracy and Peacebuilding (HR CR), 55 Knock Rd, Belfast BT5 (info@democracyandpeace.org) (democracyandpeace.org). Sharing peacebuilding expertise internationally.

Children are Unbeatable! Alliance (HR), Unit 9, 40 Montgomery Rd, Belfast BT6 (+44-28-9040 1290) (carolconlin@btinternet.com) (www.childrenareunbeatable.org.uk). For abolition of all physical punishment.

Christian Aid Ireland (TW), Linden House, Beechill Business Park, 96 Beechill Rd, Belfast BT8 7QN (+44-28-9064 8133) (belfast@christian-aid.org) (www.christianaid.ie).

Co-operation Ireland (CD), 5 Weavers Court Business Park, Linfield Rd, Belfast BT12 (+44-28-9032 1462) (info@cooperationireland.org) (www.cooperationireland.org). Works for tolerance and acceptance of differences.

Committee on the Administration of Justice [CAJ] (HR), Community House, Citylink Business Park, 6A Albert St, Belfast BT12 (+44-28-9031 6000) (fax 9031 4583) (info@caj.org.uk) (www.caj.org.uk). *Just News.*

Conflict Resolution and Reconciliation Studies Programme (RE CR RP), Irish School of Ecumenics (of Trinity College Dublin), 683 Antrim Rd, Belfast BT15 (+44-28-9077 5010) (fax 9037 3986) (reconsec@tcd.ie) (www.tcd.ie/ise). Research, teaching and outreach.

Corrymeela Community (RP), 83 University St, Belfast BT7 1HP (+44-28-9050 8080) (fax 9050 8070) (belfast@corrymeela.org) (www.corrymeela.org). *Corrymeela.*

Friends of the Earth – NI (FE), 7 Donegall Street Place, Belfast BT1 2FN (+44-28-9023 3488) (fax 9024 7556) (foe-ni@foe.co.uk) (www.foe.co.uk/ni).

Global Peacebuilders (CR), c/o Springboard Opportunities, 2nd Floor, 7 North St, Belfast BT1 1NH (+44-28-9031 5111) (fax 9031 3171) (james@springboard-opps.org) (www.globalpeacebuilders.org).

Green Party in Northern Ireland (EL), 1st Floor, 76 Abbey St, Bangor BT20 4JB (+44-28-9145 9110) (info@greenpartyni.org) (www.greenpartyni.org).

Healing Through Remembering [HTR] (RE), Alexander House, 17a Ormeau Ave, Belfast BT2 8HD (+44-28-9023 8844)

(fax 9023 9944)
(info@healingthroughremembering.org)
(www.healingthroughremembering.org).
Institute for Conflict Research [ICR] (RE), North City Business Centre, 2 Duncairn Gdns, Belfast BT15 (+44-28-9074 2682) (fax 9035 6654) (info@conflictresearch.org.uk) (www.conflictresearch.org.uk).
Institute for the Study of Conflict Transformation and Social Justice [ISCT-SJ] (RE CR), Queen's University Belfast, 19 University Sq, Belfast BT7 (+44-28-9097 3609) (ctsj@qub.ac.uk).
Irish Network for Nonviolent Action Training and Education [INNATE] (WR RA FR), c/o 16 Ravensdene Park, Belfast BT6 0DA (+44-28-9064 7106) (fax) (innate@ntlworld.com) (www.innatenonviolence.org). *Nonviolent News*.
Northern Ireland Community Relations Council [CRC] (CR PO RE), 2nd Floor, Equality House, 7-9 Shaftesbury Sq, Belfast BT2 7DP (+44-28-9022 7500) (info@nicrc.org.uk) (www.community-relations.org.uk).
Northern Ireland Council for Integrated Education [NICIE] (PO HR CD RE), 25 College Gdns, Belfast BT9 (+44-28-9097 2910) (fax 9097 2919) (info@nicie.org.uk) (www.nicie.org.uk).
Oxfam Ireland (TW), 115 North St, Belfast (+44-28-9023 0220) (fax 9023 7771) (info@oxfamireland.org) (www.oxfamireland.org).
Peace People (FR CD HR), 224 Lisburn Rd, Belfast BT9 6GE (+44-28-9066 3465) (info@peacepeople.com) (www.peacepeople.com).
Quaker Service (SF), 541 Lisburn Rd, Belfast BT7 7GQ (+44-28-9020 1444) (fax 9020 1881) (info@quakerservice.com) (www.quakerservice.com).
The Junction (CR PO RE), 8-14 Bishop St, Derry/Londonderry BT48 6PW (+44-28-7136 1942) (info@thejunction-ni.org) (thejunction-ni.org). Community relations, civic empowerment.
TIDES Training (CR), 174 Trust, Duncairn Complex, Duncairn Ave, Belfast BT14 6BP (+44-28-9075 1686) (info@tidestraining.org) (www.tidestraining.org).
Tools for Solidarity – Ireland (TW PO), 55A Sunnyside St, Belfast BT7 (+44-28-9543 5972) (fax) (tools.belfast@myphone.coop) (www.toolsforsolidarity.com). *Solidarity*.
Transitional Justice Institute [TJI] (RE), Ulster University – Jordanstown Campus, Shore Rd, Newtownabbey BT37 (+44-28-9036 6202) (fax 9036 8962) (transitionaljustice@ulster.ac.uk) (www.transitionaljustice.ulster.ac.uk). Also Magee Campus, Londonderry.

IRELAND, REPUBLIC OF

Amnesty International Ireland (AI), Sean MacBride House, 48 Fleet St, Dublin 2 (+353-1-863 8300) (fax 671 9338) (info@amnesty.ie) (www.amnesty.ie). *Amnesty Ireland*.
Chernobyl Children International (PO EL HR), 1A The Stables, Alfred St, Cork City (+353-21-455 8774) (fax 450 5564) (info@chernobyl-ireland.com) (www.chernobyl-international.com).
Co-operation Ireland [CI] (CD), Port Centre, Alexandra Rd, Dublin 1 (+353-1-819 7692) (fax 894 4962) (info@cooperationireland.org) (www.cooperationireland.org). Works for tolerance and acceptance of differences.
Comhlámh – Development Workers and Volunteers in Global Solidarity (TW HR), 12 Parliament St, Dublin 2 (+353-1-478 3490) (info@comhlamh.org) (www.comhlamh.org). Action and education for global justice.
Dublin Quaker Peace Committee (SF), c/o Quaker House, Stocking Lane, Rathfarnham, Dublin 16 (info@dublinquakerpeace.org) (www.dublinquakerpeace.org).
Educate Together (HR RE PO CR), 11-12 Hogan Place, Dublin 2 (+353-1-429 2500) (fax 429 2502) (info@educatetogether.ie) (www.educatetogether.ie).
Friends of the Earth (FE), 9 Upper Mount St, Dublin 2 (+353-1-639 4652) (info@foe.ie) (www.foe.ie).
Friends of the Irish Environment (EL), Kilcatherine, Eyeries, Co Cork (+353-27-74771) (admin@friendsoftheirishenvironment.org) (www.friendsoftheirishenvironment.org).
Irish Anti-War Movement, PO Box 9260, Dublin 1 (+353-1-872 7912) (info@irishantiwar.org) (www.irishantiwar.org).
Irish Campaign for Nuclear Disarmament / Feachtas um Dhí-armáil Eithneach [ICND] (IB ND), PO Box 6327, Dublin 6 (irishcnd@gmail.com) (www.irishcnd.org). *Peacework*.
Irish Centre for Human Rights (HR), National University of Ireland, University Rd, Galway (+353-91-493948) (fax 494575) (humanrights@nuigalway.ie) (www.nuigalway.ie/human_rights).
Irish United Nations Association [IUNA] (UN), 14 Lower Pembroke St, Dublin 2 (+353-1-661 6920) (irelandun@gmail.com).
Pax Christi Ireland (PC HR AT), 52 Lower Rathmines Rd, Dublin 6 (+353-1-496 5293) (www.paxchristi.ie).
Peace and Neutrality Alliance / Comhaontas na Síochána is Neodrachta [PANA] (ND CD), 17 Castle St, Dalkey, Co Dublin (+353-1-235 1512) (info@pana.ie) (www.pana.ie).

IRELAND, Republic

Peace Brigades International – Ireland [PBI] (HR), 12 Parliament St, Temple Bar, Dublin 2 (pbiireland@peacebrigades.org) (www.pbi-ireland.org).

Programme for International Peace Studies (RE), Irish School of Ecumenics – Loyola Institute Building, TCD – Main Campus, Dublin 2 (+353-1-896 4770) (fax 672 5024) (peacesec@tcd.ie) (www.tcd.ie/ise). *Unity.*

Servas (SE), c/o Donal Coleman, 53 Glengara Park, Glenageary, Co Dublin A96 TOF6 (+353-87-915 9635) (ireland@servas.org) (www.servas.org).

ShannonWatch (DA HR), PO Box 476, Limerick DSU, Dock Rd, Limerick (+353-87-822 5087) (shannonwatch@gmail.com) (www.shannonwatch.org).
Monitors foreign military use of Shannon Airport.

Vegetarian Society of Ireland [VSI] (EL PO), c/o Dublin Food Coop, 12 Newmarket, Dublin 8 (info@vegetarian.ie) (www.vegetarian.ie). *The Irish Vegetarian.*

Voluntary Service International [VSI] (SC), 30 Mountjoy Sq, Dublin 1 (+353-1-855 1011) (fax 855 1012) (info@vsi.ie) (www.vsi.ie). *VSI News.*

ISLE OF MAN

Shee Nish! / Peace Now! (AT PA DA), c/o Stuart Hartill, 1 The Sycamores, Walpole Rd, Ramsey IM8 1LU (+44-1624-814496) (stuarth@manx.net).
Widely-based coalition of peace campaigners.

ISRAEL (see also Palestine)

NOTE: Territories allocated to Israel in the United Nations partition of Palestine in 1947, together with further areas annexed by Israel prior to 1967, are included here. Other parts of Palestine occupied by Israel in 1967 or later are listed under Palestine.

Al-Beit – Association for the Defence of Human Rights in Israel (HR CD TW), PO Box 650, Arara 30026 (+972-6-635 4370) (fax 635 4367) (uridavis@actcom.co.il).
Concentrates on right of residence and housing.

Alternative Information Centre [AIC] (HR RE TW AL AT), POB 31417, West Jerusalem 91313 (+972-2-624 1159) (fax 3-762 4664) (connie.hackbarth@alternativenews.org) (www.alternativenews.org). *Economy of the Occupation.* See also Palestine.

Amnesty International Israel (AI), PO Box 5239, Tel-Aviv 66550 (+972-3-525 0005) (fax 525 0001) (info@amnesty.org.il) (amnesty.org.il).

B'Tselem – Israeli Information Centre for Human Rights in the Occupied Territories (HR), PO Box 53132, West Jerusalem 9153002 (+972-2-673 5599) (fax 674 9111) (mail@btselem.org) (www.btselem.org).

Bimkom – Planners for Planning Rights (HR), 13 Ebenezra St – PO Box 7154, West Jerusalem 9107101 (+972-2-566 9655) (fax 566 0551) (bimkom@bimkom.org) (www.bimkom.org).

Coalition of Women for Peace [CWP] (HR CD), POB 29214, Tel Aviv – Jaffa 61292 (+972-3-528 1005) (fax) (cwp@coalitionofwomen.org) (www.coalitionofwomen.org).

Combatants for Peace (CD), PO Box 3049, Beit Yehushua 40591 (office@cfpeace.org) (www.cfpeace.org).
Israeli and Palestinian ex-fighters for peace.

Defence for Children International – Israel [DCI-Israel] (HR), PO Box 2533, West Jerusalem 91024 (+972-2-563 3003) (fax 563 1241) (dci@dci-il.org).

Geneva Initiative (CD CR), c/o HL Education for Peace, 33 Jabotinsky Rd, Ramat-Gan 525108 (+972-3-693 8780) (fax 691 1306) (www.geneva-accord.org). See also Palestine.

Givat Haviva Jewish-Arab Centre for Peace [JACP] (CR HR RE), MP Menashe 37850 (+972-4-630 9289) (fax 630 9305) (givathaviva@givathaviva.org.il) (www.givathaviva.org.il).

Greenpeace Mediterranean – Israel (GP HR), PO Box 20079, Tel Aviv 61200 (+972-3-561 4014) (fax 561 0415) (gpmedisr@greenpeace.org) (www.greenpeace.org/israel).

Gush Shalom / Peace Bloc (CD CR HR RE RA), PO Box 3322, Tel-Aviv 61033 (+972-3-522 1732) (fax 527 1108) (info@gush-shalom.org) (www.gush-shalom.org).

Hamerkaz Hamishpati L'zkhuyot Hami-ut Ha'aravi Beyisrael / Legal Centre for Arab Minority Rights in Israel [Adalah] (HR), 94 Yaffa St, PO Box 8921, Haifa 31090 (+972-4-950 1610) (fax 950 3140) (adalah@adalah.org) (www.adalah.org).
Works for equal rights for Arab citizens in Israel.

Hand in Hand – Centre for Jewish-Arab Education in Israel (PO CD RE), PO Box 10339, Jerusalem 91102 (+972-2-673 5356) (info@handinhand.org.il) (www.handinhandk12.org).
Supports integrated, bilingual education.

Israel-Palestine Creative Regional Initiatives [IPCRI] (RE CR EL CD), see under Palestine (+972-52-238 1715) (www.ipcri.org).

Israeli Committee for a Middle East Free from Atomic, Biological and Chemical Weapons (ND HR), PO Box 16202, Tel Aviv 61161 (+972-3-522 2869) (fax) (spiro@bezeqint.net).

Mossawa Center – Advocacy Center for Arab Citizens in Israel (HR), 5 Saint Lucas St, PO Box 4471, Haifa 31043 (+972-4-855 5901) (fax 855 2772) (programs.mossawa@gmail.com) (www.mossawa.org).

New Profile – Movement for the Demilitarisation of Israeli Society (WR), c/o Sergeiy Sandler, POB 48005, Tel Aviv 61480 (+972-3-696 1137) (newprofile@speedy.co.il) (www.newprofile.org). Feminist movement of women and men.

Ometz Le'sarev / Courage to Refuse, PO Box 16238, Tel Aviv (+972-3-523 3103) (info@seruv.org.il) (www.seruv.org.il). (Zionists) refusing deployment in the Territories.

OneVoice Movement – Israel [OVI] (CD CR), PO Box 29695, Tel Aviv 66881 (+972-3-516 8005) (info@OneVoice.org.il) (www.onevoicemovement.org). See also Palestine.

Palestinian-Israeli Peace NGO Forum (Israeli Office) (CD), c/o The Peres Center for Peace, 132 Kedem St, Jaffa 68066 (+972-3-568 0646) (fax 562 7265) (info@peres-center.org) (www.peacengo.org). See also under Palestine.

Parents' Circle – Families' Forum: Bereaved Israeli and Palestinian Families Supporting Peace and Tolerance (CD CR), 1 Hayasmin St, Ramat-Efal 52960 (+972-3-535 5089) (fax 635 8367) (contact@theparentscircle.org) (www.theparentscircle.com). See also under Palestine.

Public Committee Against Torture in Israel [PCATI] (HR), POB 4634, West Jerusalem 91046 (+972-2-642 9825) (fax 643 2847) (pcati@stoptorture.org.il) (www.stoptorture.org.il).

Rabbis for Human Rights [RHR] (HR), 9 HaRechavim St, West Jerusalem 9346209 (+972-2-648 2757) (fax 678 3611) (info@rhr.israel.net) (www.rhr.israel.net).

Sadaka-Reut – Arab-Jewish Partnership (CR RE HR CD), 35 Shivtey Israel St, PO Box 8523, Jaffa – Tel-Aviv 61084 (+972-3-518 2336) (fax) (info@reutsadaka.org) (www.reutsadaka.org).

Shalom Achshav / Peace Now, PO Box 22651, Tel Aviv 62032 (+972-3-602 3300) (fax 602 3301) (info@peacenow.org.il) (www.peacenow.org.il).

Shatil (CD HR), PO Box 53395, West Jerusalem 91533 (+972-2-672 3597) (fax 673 5149) (shatil@shatil.nif.org.il) (www.shatil.org.il). Also 4 other regional offices.

Shovrim Shtika / Breaking the Silence (HR), PO Box 51027, 6713206 Tel Aviv (info@breakingthesilence.org) (www.shovrimshtika.org). Also www.breakingthesilence.org.il.

Wahat al-Salam – Neve Shalom [WAS-NS] (HR RE CR PO CD), Doar Na / Mobile Post, Shimshon 9976100 (+972-2-999 6305) (fax 991 1072) (info@wasns.info) (wasns.org). "Oasis of Peace".

Windows – Israeli-Palestinian Friendship Centre (CD), PO Box 5195, Tel Aviv – Jaffa (+972-3-620 8324) (fax 629 2570) (office@win-peace.org) (www.win-peace.org). *Windows.* Chlenov 41. See also in Palestine.

ITALY

Amnesty International – Sezione Italiana (AI), Via Magenta 5, 00185 Roma (+39-06 4490210) (fax 06 449 0222) (infoamnesty@amnesty.it) (www.amnesty.it).

Archivio Disarmo [IRIAD] (IB RE AT), Via Paolo Mercuri 8, 00193 Roma (+39-06 3600 0343) (fax 06 3600 0345) (archiviodisarmo@pec.it) (www.archiviodisarmo.it).

Associazione Italiana Medicina per la Prevenzione della Guerra Nucleare [AIMPGN] (IP), Via Bari 4, 64029 Silvi Marina (TE) (+39-085 935 1350) (fax 085 935 3333) (mdipaolantonio55@gmail.com) (www.ippnw-italy.org).

Associazione Memoria Condivisa (CR), Viale 1º Maggio 32, 71100 Foggia (+39-0881 637775) (fax) (info@memoriacondivisa.it) (www.memoriacondivisa.it). Supports non-violence as a response to terrorism.

Associazione Museo Italiano per la Pace / Association of Italian Museums for Peace (RE), Via Ezio Andolfato 1, 20126 Milano (museoitalianoperlapace@gmail.com). Promotes culture of peace in schools.

Azione dei Cristiani per l'Abolizione della Tortura [ACAT] (HR), c/o Rinascita Cristiana, Via della Traspontina 15, 00193 Roma (+39-06 686 5358) (posta@acatitalia.it) (www.acatitalia.it).

Centro Studi Sereno Regis – Italian Peace Research Institute / Rete CCP [IPRI] (RE CR EL), Via Garibaldi 13, 10122 Torino (+39-011 532824) (fax 011 515 8000) (www.serenoregis.it). *IPRI Newsletter.*

Eirene Centro studi per la pace (RE SD), Via Enrico Scuri 1, 24128 Bergamo (+39-035 260073) (fax 035 432 9224) (info@eirene.it) (www.eirene.it).

Gesellschaft für Bedrohte Völker / Associazione per i Popoli Minacciati / Lia por i Popui Manacês (HR), CP 233, 39100 Bozen/Bolzano, Südtirol (+39-0471 972240) (fax) (gfbv.bz@ines.org) (www.gfbv.it). Part of international GFBV network.

Green Cross Italy (EL TW DA HR), Via dei Gracchi 187, 00192 Roma (+39-06 3600 4300) (fax 06 3600 4364) (info@greencross.it) (www.greencrossitalia.org).

Greenpeace (GP), Via Della Cordonata 7, 00187 Roma (+39-06 6813 6061) (fax 06 4543 9793) (info.it@greenpeace.org) (www.greenpeace.org/italy). *GP News.*

ITALY

International School on Disarmament and Research on Conflicts [ISODARCO] (RE CR DA), c/o Prof Carlo Schaerf, via della Rotonda 4, 00186 Roma (+39-06 689 2340) (isodarco@gmail.com) (www.isodarco.it).
Lega degli Obiettori di Coscienza [LOC] (WR), Via Mario Pichi 1, 20143 Milano (+39-02 837 8817) (fax 02 5810 1220) (locosm@tin.it) (ospiti.peacelink.it/loc/).
Movimento Internazionale della Riconciliazione [MIR] (FR), via Garibaldi 13, 10122 Torino (+39-011 532824) (fax 011 515 8000) (segretaria@miritalia.org) (www.miritalia.org).
Movimento Nonviolento [MN] (WR TR EL), Via Spagna 8, 37123 Verona (+39-045 800 9803) (fax) (azionenonviolenta@sis.it) (www.nonviolenti.org). *Azione Nonviolenta.*
Operazione Colomba / Operation Dove (RP CD CR), Via Mameli 5, 47921 Rimini (+39-0541 29005) (fax) (info@operazionecolomba@it) (www.operationdove.org). A project of Associazione Papa Giovanni XXIII.
Pax Christi Italia (PC), via Quintole per le Rose 131, 50029 Tavarnuzze, Firenze (+39-055 202 0375) (fax) (info@paxchristi.it) (www.paxchristi.it). *Mosaico di Pace.*
PBI Italia (PA RA HR), Via Asiago 5/a, 35010 Cadoneghe (PD) (+39-345 269 0132) (info@pbi-italy.org) (www.pbi-italy.org).
Religioni per la Pace Italia (RP), Via Pio VIII 38-D-2, 00185 Roma (+39-333 273 1245) (info@religioniperlapaceitalia.org) (www.religioniperlapaceitalia.org).
Servas Italia (SE), c/o Centro Studi Sereno Regis, Via Garibaldi 13, 10122 Torino (segretario@servas.it) (www.servas.it).
Società Italiana per l'Organizzazione Internazionale [SIOI] (UN), Piazza di San Marco 51, 00186 Roma (+39-06 692 0781) (fax 06 678 9102) (sioi@sioi.org) (www.sioi.org). *La Comunità Internazionale.*

JAPAN

Chikyu no Tomo / Friends of the Earth (FE), 1-21-9 Komone, Itabashi-ku, Tokyo 173-0037 (+81-3-6909 5983) (fax 6909 5986) (info@foejapan.org) (www.foejapan.org).
Goi Peace Foundation / World Peace Prayer Society Japan Office (CD PO), Heiwa-Daiichi Bldg, 1-4-5 Hirakawa-Cho, Chiyoda-ku, Tokyo 102-0093 (+81-3-3265 2071) (fax 3239 0919) (info@goipeace.or.jp) (www.goipeace.or.jp).
Green Action (EL), Suite 103, 22-75 Tanaka Sekiden-cho, Sakyo-ku, Kyoto 606-8203 (+81-75-701 7223) (fax 702 1952) (info@greenaction-japan.org) (www.greenaction-japan.org). Campaigns especially against nuclear fuel cycle.
Greenpeace Japan (GP), N F Bldg 2F 8-13-11, Nishi-Shinjuku, Shinjuku, Tokyo 160-0023 (+81-3-5338 9800) (fax 5338 9817) (www.greenpeace.or.jp).
Himeyuri Peace Museum (RE), 671-1 Ihara, Itoman-shi, Okinawa 901-0344 (+81-98-997 2100) (fax 997 2102) (himeyuri1@himeyuri.or.jp) (www.himeyuri.or.jp).
Hiroshima Peace Culture Foundation [HPCF] (PA ND RE), 1-2 Nakajima-cho, Naka-ku, Hiroshima 730-0811 (+81-82-241 5246) (fax 542 7941) (p-soumu@pcf.city.hiroshima.jp) (www.pcf.city.hiroshima.jp/hpcf). *Peace Culture.*
Hiroshima Peace Memorial Museum (RE), 1-2 Nakajima-cho, Naka-ku, Hiroshima 730-0811 (+81-82-241 4004) (fax 542 7941) (hpcf@pcf.city.hiroshima.jp) (www.pcf.city.hiroshima.jp).
Japan Council Against A & H Bombs – Gensuikyo (IB ND PA), 2-4-4 Yushima, Bunkyo-ku, Tokyo 113-8464 (+81-3-5842 6034) (fax 5842 6033) (antiatom@topaz.plala.or.jp) (www.antiatom.org). *No More Hiroshimas; Gensuikyo Tsushin.* National federation.
Japanese Physicians for the Prevention of Nuclear War [JPPNW] (IP), c/o Hiroshima Prefectural Medical Association, 3-2-3 Futabanosato, Higashi-ku, Hiroshima 732-0057 (+81-82-568 1511) (fax 568 2112) (ippnw-japan@hiroshima.med.or.jp) (www.hiroshima.med.or.jp).
Kyoto Museum for World Peace (RE), Ritsumeikan University, 56-1 Kitamachi, Toji-in, Kyoto 603-8577 (+81-75-465 8151) (fax 465 7899) (peacelib@st.ritsumei.ac.jp) (www.ritsumei.ac.jp/mng/er/wp-museum).
Nihon Hidankyo / Japan Confederation of A- and H-Bomb Sufferers' Organisations (ND CR HR), Gable Bldg 902, 1-3-5 Shiba Daimon, Minato-ku, Tokyo 105-0012 (+81-3-3438 1897) (fax 3431 2113) (kj3t-tnk@asahi-net.or.jp) (www.ne.jp/asahi/hidankyo/nihon). *Hidankyo.*
Nipponzan Myohoji (WR), 7-8 Shinsen-Cho, Shibuya-ku, Tokyo 150-0045 (+81-3-3461 9363) (fax 3461 9367) (info@nipponzanmyohoji.org) (nipponzanmyohoji.org).
Organising Committee – World Conference Against A and H bombs (ND), 2-4-4 Yushima, Bunkyo-ku, Tokyo 113-8464 (+81-3-5842 6034) (fax 5842 6033) (intl@antiatom.org).
Peace Depot – Peace Resources Cooperative (ND PA RE), Hiyoshi Gruene 1st Floor, 1-30-27-4 Hiyoshi Hon-cho, Kohoku-ku, Yokohama 223-0062 (+81-45-563 5101) (fax 563 9907) (office@peacedepot.org) (www.peacedepot.org). *Nuclear Weapon & Nuclear Test Monitor.*

Toda Peace Institute (RE CR PA WF ND), Samon Eleven Bldg – 5th floor, 3-1 Samoncho, Shinjuku-ku, Tokyo 160-0017 (contact@toda.org) (www.toda.org).
United Nations Association (UN), Nippon Building – Rm 427, 2-6-2 Ohtemachi, Chiyoda-ku, Tokyo 100-8699 (+81-3-3270 4731) (info@unaj.or.jp) (www.unaj.or.jp).
WRI Japan (WR HR AL), 666 Ukai-cho, Inuyama-shi, Aichi-ken 468-0085 (+81-568-615850).

KAZAKHSTAN

Servas Kazakhstan (SE), Garibaldi Str 52, Karaganda City (+7-3212-439316) (fax 412021) (kazakhstan@servas.org) (www.servas-kazakhstan.narod.ru).

KENYA

Centre for Research and Dialogue – Somalia [CRD] (CR RE), PO Box 28832, Nairobi (www.crdsomalia.org). Based in Mogadishu, Somalia.
International Friendship League – Kenya [IFL] (CD), PO Box 9929, 00200 Nairobi. Part of international network of groups.
Life & Peace Institute – Somalia and Kenya Programme (RP CR), AACC Commercial Building – 5th floor, off Waiyaki Way, Nairobi (+254-20-444 0431) (fax 444 0433) (michele.cesari@life-peace.org) (www.life-peace.org).
Sudanese Women's Voice for Peace, PO Box 21123, Nairobi.

KOREA, REPUBLIC OF

Greenpeace East Asia – Seoul Office (GP), 2/F – 358-121 Seogyo-dong, Mapo-gu, Seoul (+82-2-3144 1994) (fax 6455 1995) (greenpeace.kr@greenpeace.org) (www.greenpeace.org/eastasia).
International Peace Youth Group [IPYG] (RP), 46 Cheongpa-ro 71-gil, Yongsan-gu, Seoul 04304 (+82-2-514 1963) (info@ipyg.org) (ipyg.org).
Korea Federation for Environmental Movement [KFEM] (FE), 251 Nooha-dong, Jongno-gu, Seoul 110-806 (+82-2-735 7000) (fax 730 1240) (ma@kfem.or.kr) (www.kfem.or.kr). Anti-nuclear movement.
Pyeonghwa wa Tongil Yoneun Saramdeul / Solidarity for Peace and Re-Unification of Korea [SPARK] (PC), 3-47 Beonji 2 Cheung, Chungjeongno 3 ga, Sodaemun-gu, Seoul 120-837 (+82-2-711 7292) (fax 712 8445) (spark946@hanmail.net) (www.peaceone.org). *Pyeonghwamuri.*
World Without War (WR), 422-9 Mangwondong, Mapo-gu, Seoul 121-230 (+82-2-6401 0514) (fax) (peace@withoutwar.org) (www.withoutwar.org).

LATVIA

Latvijas Zemes Draugi (FE), Lapu iela 17, Zemgales Priekšpilseta, Riga 1002 (+371-6722 5112) (zemesdraugi@zemesdraugi.lv) (www.zemesdraugi.lv).

LEBANON

Greenpeace Mediterranean (GP), PO Box 13-6590, Beirut (+961-1-361255) (fax 36 1254) (supporters@greenpeace.org.lb) (www.greenpeace.org/lebanon). See also Israel, Turkey.

LITHUANIA

United Nations Association (UN HR), Lithuanian Culture Research Institute, Saltoniskiu St 58, 08015 Vilnius (+370-5-275 1898) (jurate128@yahoo.de).

LUXEMBOURG

Action des Chrétiens pour l'Abolition de la Torture [ACAT] (HR), 5 Av Marie-Thérèse, 2132 Luxembourg (+352-4474 3558) (fax 4474 3559) (contact@acat.lu) (www.acat.lu).
Association Luxembourgeoise pour les Nations Unies [ALNU] (UN), 3 Rte d'Arlon, 8009 Strassen (+352-461468) (fax 461469) (alnu@pt.lu) (www.alnu.lu).
Greenpeace Luxembourg (GP), BP 229, 4003 Esch/Alzette (+352-546 2521) (fax 545405) (membres.lu@greenpea.org) (www.greenpeace.org/luxembourg).
Iwerliewen fir Bedreete Volleker (HR), BP 98, 6905 Niederanven (+352-2625 8687) (info@iwerliewen.org) (iwerliewen.org).
Mouvement écologique (FE), 6 Rue Vauban, 2663 Luxembourg (+352-439 0301) (fax 4390 3043) (meco@oeko.lu) (www.meco.lu).
Servas (SE), see under Belgium.

MACEDONIA

Dvizenje na ekologistijte na Makedonija / Ecologists' Movement of Macedonia [DEM] (FE), Ul Vasil Gjorgov 39 – 6, 1000 Skopje (+389-2-220518) (fax) (dem@dem.org.mk) (www.dem.org.mk).
Mirovna Aktsiya / Aksioni Paqësor / Peace Action (WR), Joseski Ice, Ul Andon Slabejko Br 138, 75000 Prilep (+389-48-22616) (office@mirovnaakcija.org) (www.mirovnaakcija).
Nansen Dialogue Centre Skopje [NDC Skopje] (CR CD), Str Bahar Mois No 4, 1000 Skopje (+389-2-320 9905) (fax 320 9906) (ndcskopje@nansen-dialogue.net) (ndc.net.mk).
United Nations Association of Macedonia (UN), St Zorz Bize 9-b, 1000 Skopje (+389-2-244 3751) (fpesevi@mt.net.mk) (www.sunamk.org).

MALAWI

Citizens for Justice – Friends of the Earth Malawi (FE), Post Dot Net, Box X100, Crossroads, Lilongwe (+265-176 1887) (fax 176 1886) (info@cfjmalawi.org) (cfjmalawi.org).

MALAWI

International Friendship League – Malawi [IFL] (CD), PO Box 812, Mzuzu (menardkamabga@yahoo.com).

MALAYSIA

Sahabat Alam Malaysia / Friends of the Earth Malaysia [SAM] (FE), 258 Jalan Air Itam, George Town, 10460 Penang (+60-4-228 6930) (fax 228 6932) (sam_inquiry@yahoo.com) (www.foe-malaysia.org).

MALI

Amnesty International Mali [AI Mali] (AI), BP E 3885 ML, Bamako.

MALTA

John XXIII Peace Laboratory [Peacelab] (IB RP RE), Triq Hal-Far, Zurrieq ZRQ 2609 (+356-2168 9504) (fax 2164 1591) (info@peacelab.org) (www.peacelab.org). *It-Tieqa.*

Moviment ghall-Ambjent / Friends of the Earth Malta (FE), PO Box 1013, South Street, Valletta VLT 1000 (+356-7996 1460) (info@foemalta.org) (www.foemalta.org).

MAURITIUS

Lalit (SF WL PA), 153 Main Rd, Grand River North West, Port-Louis (+230-208 2132) (lalitmail@intnet.mu) (www.lalitmauritius.org). Anti-militarist party and campaign.

MEXICO

Médicos Mexicanos para la Prevención de la Guerra Nuclear (IP), Antiguo Claustro – Hospital Juarez – PA, Plaza San Pablo, 06090 Mexico – DF (fromow@servidor.unam.mx).

MOLDOVA

Asociatia de Voluntariat International [AVI] (SC), 129 – 3A Vasile Alecsandri Str, 2012 Chisinau (+373-2-292 7724) (fax 293 0415) (avi@avimd.org) (www.avimd.org).

MONACO

Organisation pour la Paix par le Sport – Peace and Sport (CD), Immeuble les Mandariniers, 42ter Blvd du Jardin Exotique, 98000 (+377-9797 7800) (fax 9797 1891) (contact@peace-sport.org) (www.peace-sport.org).

MONGOLIA

Oyu Tolgoi Watch (EL HR), POB 636, Ulaanbaatar 46A (+976-9918 5828) (otwatch@gmail.com). Opposing devastation by Rio Tinto mining project.

MONTENEGRO

Nansen Dialogue Centre Montenegro (CR CD), Cetinsjki put bb 16/2, 81000 Podgorica (+382-20-290094) (fax) (ndcmontenegro@nansen-dialogue.net) (nansen-dialogue.net/ndcmontenegro).

NAMIBIA

Alternatives to Violence Project [AVP Namibia] (CR), PO Box 50617, Bachbrecht, Windhoek (+264-61-371554) (fax 371555) (vicky@peace.org.na).

Earthlife Namibia [ELA] (EL), PO Box 24892, Windhoek (+264-61-227913) (fax 305213) (earthl@iway.na).

NEPAL

Human Rights and Peace Foundation [HURPEF] (HR), GPO 8975, Epc 5397, Kathmandu (+977-1-438 5231) (hurpef@hons.com.np) (www.hurpef.org.np).

Human Rights Without Frontiers – Nepal (WR HR), PO.Box 10660, Maitidevi-33, Kathmandu (+977-1-444 2367) (fax 443 5331) (hrwfnepal@mail.com.np) (www.hrwfnepal.net.np). *Human Rights Monitor.*

National Land Rights Forum (WR HR), Bhumi-Ghar, Tokha-10, Dhapasi Kathmandu (+977-1-691 4586) (fax 435 7033) (land@nlrfnepal.org) (www.nlrfnepal.org).

Nepal Physicians for Social Responsibility (IP), PO Box 19624, Bagbazar, Kathmandu (psrn@healthnet.org.np).

People's Forum for Human Rights – Bhutan (HR), Anarmani 4, Birtamod, Jhapa (+977-23-540824) (rizal_pfhrb@ntc.net.np).

WILPF (WL), PO Box 13613, Chabahill 7, Mirmire Tole, Kathmandu (+977-11-448 6280) (wilpfnepalsectiom@gmail.com).

NETHERLANDS

Anti-Militaristies Onderzoekskollectief – VD AMOK (WR RE AT ND), Lauwerecht 55, 3515 GN Utrecht (+31-30-890 1341) (info@vdamok.nl) (www.vdamok.nl).

Campagne tegen Wapenhandel (AT), Anna Spenglerstr 71, 1054 NH Amsterdam (+31-20-616 4684) (fax) (info@stopwapenhandel.org) (www.stopwapenhandel.org). Campaign against arms trade.

Centre for International Conflict Analysis and Management [CICAM] (RE), Postbus 9108, 6500 HK Nijmegen (+31-24-361 5687) (cicam@fm.ru.nl) (www.ru.nl/cicam).

Christian Peacemaker Teams – Nederland [CPT-NL] (RP RA PA), c/o Irene van Setten, Bredasingel 70, 6843 RE Arnhem (+31-26-848 1706) (info@cpt-nl.org) (www.cpt-nl.org).

Greenpeace Nederland (GP), NDSM-Plein 32, 1033 WB Amsterdam (+31-20-626 1877) (fax 622 1272) (info@greenpeace.nl) (www.greenpeace.nl).

GroenFront! (EL RA), Postbus 85069, 3508 AB Utrecht (info@groenfront.nl) (www.groenfront.nl). *Frontnieuws.* Earth First!-style group.

Kerk en Vrede (FR PA RE), Joseph Haydnlaan 2a, 3533 AE Utrecht (+31-30-231 6666) (secretariaat@kerkenvrede.nl) (kerkenvrede.nl).

Museum voor Vrede en Geweldloosheid [MVG] (RE PA), Ezelsveldlaan 212, 2611 DK Delft (+31-15-785 0137) (info@vredesmuseum.nl) (www.vredesmuseum.nl). *De Vredesboot.*

Musicians without Borders (RP), Kloveniersburgwal 87, 1011 KA Amsterdam (+31-20-330 5012) (info@musicianswithoutborders.org) (www.musicianswithoutborders.org).

Nederlands Expertisecentrum Alternatieven voor Gewald / Netherlands Expertise Centre Alternatives to Violence [NEAG] (CR), Vossiusstr 20, 1071 AD Amsterdam (+31-20-670 5295) (info@neag.nl) (www.neag.nl). Affiliated to Nonviolent Peaceforce.

Nederlandse Vereniging voor Medische Polemologie [NVMP] (IP), PO Box 199, 4190 CD Geldermalsen (+31-6-4200 9559) (office@nvmp.org) (nvmp.org).

Pax (PC AT RE CD), Sint Jacobsstr 12, 3511 BS Utrecht (+31-30-233 3346) (info@paxforpeace.nl) (www.paxvoorvrede.nl). Also Paxforpeace.nl.

Peace Brigades Nederland [PBI] (RA PO CR RE), de Kargadoor, Oudegracht 36, 3511 AP Utrecht (+31-6-1649 8221) (info@peacebrigades.nl) (www.peacebrigades.nl).

Ploughshares Support Group / Amsterdamse Catholic Worker (PA AT RP HR), Postbus 12622, 1100 AP Amsterdam (+31-20-699 8996) (noelhuis@antenna.nl) (noelhuis.nl). *Nieuwsbrief Jeannette Noelhuis.*

Religieus Genootschap der Vrienden – Quakers Nederland (SF), Postbus 2167, 7420 AD Deventer (+31-570-655229) (secretariaat@dequakers.nl) (www.quakers.nu). *De Vriendenkring.*

Stichting Voor Aktieve Geweldloosheid [SVAG] (SD PO RE), Postbus 288, 5280 AG Boxtel (info@geweldloosactief.nl) (www.geweldlozekracht.nl). *Geweldloze Kracht.*

Stichting Vredesburo Eindhoven (PA RE), Grote Berg 41, 5611 KH Eindhoven (+31-40-244 4707) (fax) (info@vredesburo.nl) (www.vredesburo.nl). *Vredesburo Nieuwsbrief.*

Upact (PO RE), Postbus 19, 3500 AA Utrecht (+31-30-223 8724) (info@upact.nl) (www.upact.nl). *Upact Nieuws.*

Vereniging Milieudefensie (FE), Postbus 19199, 1000 GD Amsterdam (+31-20-550 7300) (fax 550 7310) (service@milieudefensie.nl) (www.milieudefensie.nl). *Down to Earth.*

Vredesbeweging Pais (WR EL), Ezelsveldlaan 212, 2611 DK Delft (+31-15-785 0137) (info@vredesbeweging.nl) (www.vredesbeweging.nl). *vredesmagazine.*

Vrijwillige Internationale Aktie [VIA] (SC), M v B Bastiaansestr 56, 1054 SP Amsterdam (info@stichtingvia.nl) (www.stichtingvia.nl).

Vrouwen en Duurzame Vrede (CR ND SD), Haaksbergerstr 317, 7545 GJ Enschede (+31-53-434 0559) (info@vrouwenenduurzamevrede.nl) (www.vrouwenenduurzamevrede.nl).

Women's International League for Peace and Freedom – Netherlands [WILPF-IVVV] (WL), Laan van Nieuw Oost Indië 252, 2593 CD Den Haag (+31-345-615105) (info@wilpf.nl) (www.wilpf.nl).

NEW ZEALAND / AOTEAROA

Abolition 2000 Aotearoa New Zealand [A2000 ANZ] (ND), c/o Pax Christi, PO Box 68419, Newton, Aukland 1145 (+64-9-377 5541) (abolition2000@ymail.com) (www.a2000.org.nz).

Amnesty International (AI), PO Box 5300, Wellesley St, Aukland 1141 (+64-9-303 4520) (fax 303 4528) (info@amnesty.org.nz) (www.amnesty.org.nz).

Anabaptist Association of Australia and New Zealand (RP), see under Australia (anabaptist.asn.au).

Anglican Pacifist Fellowship [APF] (RP AT TR), c/o Indrea Alexander, 9 Holmes St, Waimate 7924 (apfnzsecretary@gmail.com) (converge.org.nz/pma/apf). *The Anglican Pacifist of Aotearoa New Zealand.*

Anti-Bases Campaign [ABC] (PA RE), Box 2258, Christchurch 8140 (abc@chch.planet.org.nz) (www.converge.org.nz/abc). 2 yrly.

Campaign Against Foreign Control of Aotearoa [CAFCA] (PA RE), PO Box 2258, Christchurch 8140 (cafca@chch.planet.org.nz) (www.cafca.org.nz). *Foreign Control Watchdog.*

Disarmament and Security Centre [DSC] (IB WL RE ND CR), PO Box 8390, Christchurch 8440 (+64-3-348 1353) (fax) (kate@chch.planet.org.nz) (www.disarmsecure.org).

Engineers for Social Responsibility [ESR] (EL ND AT), PO Box 6208, Wellesley Street, Auckland 1141 (www.esr.org.nz).

Green Party of Aotearoa/NZ (EL), PO Box 11652, Wellington 6142 (+64-4-801 5102) (fax 801 5104) (greenparty@greens.org.nz) (www.greens.org.nz). *Te Awa.*

Greenpeace New Zealand (GP), 11 Akiraho St, Mount Eden, Auckland (+64-9-630 6317) (fax 630 7121) (info@greenpeace.org.nz) (www.greenpeace.org/new-zealand).

NEW ZEALAND

New Zealand Burma Support Group (HR EL), 14 Waitati Pl, Mt Albert, Auckland (+64-9-828 4855) (nzburma@xtra.co.nz) *Newsletter.*

Pax Christi Aotearoa/NZ (PC), PO Box 68419, Newton, Aukland (paxnz@xtra.co.nz) (nzpaxchristi.wordpress.com).

Peace Action Wellington (DA AT RA), PO Box 9263, Wellington (peacewellington@riseup.net) (peacewellington.org).
Work includes direct action against arms fairs.

Peace Council of Aotearoa/New Zealand [PCANZ] (WP), 13 Bell St, Otaki 5512 (+64-6-364 8940) (fax) (bt.richards@xtra.co.nz).

Peace Foundation (CR RE), PO Box 8055, Symonds Street, Auckland 1150 (+64-9-373 2379) (fax 379 2668) (peace@peacefoundation.org.nz) (kiaora.peace.net.nz).

Peace Movement Aotearoa [PMA] (AT HR PA RE), PO Box 9314, Wellington 6141 (+64-4-382 8129) (fax 382 8173) (pma@xtra.co.nz) (www.converge.org.nz/pma).
National networking body.

Quaker Peace and Service Aotearoa/New Zealand [QPSANZ] (SF), Quaker Meeting House, 72 Cresswell Ave, Christchurch 8061 (+64-3-980 4884) (www.quaker.org.nz/groups/qpsanz).

Stop the Arms Trade NZ (AT DA), PO Box 9843, Wellington (stop-the-arms-trade@riseup.net) (www.stopthearmstrade.nz).
Actions against weapons expos.

Women's International League for Peace and Freedom [WILPF] (WL), PO Box 2054, Wellington (wilpfaotearoa@gmail.com) (www.wilpf.org.nz).

NICARAGUA

Centro de Prevención de la Violencia [CEPREV] (HR PO DA), Villa Fontana – casa 23, Club Terraza 1/2 c al lago, Managua (fax +505-2278 1637) (www.ceprev.org).
Promotes a culture of peace.

NIGERIA

Alternatives to Violence Project [AVP Nigeria] (WR), 5 Ogunlesi St, off Bode Thomas Rd, Onipanu, Lagos (+234-1-497 1359) (avp@linkserve.com.ng).

Anglican Pacifist Fellowship – Nigeria [APF] (RP), c/o Peter U James, Akwa Ibom Peace Group, PO Box 269, Abak, Akwa Ibom State.

United Nations Association (UN), PO Box 54423, Falomo, Ikoyi, Lagos (+234-1-269 3112) (fax).

NORWAY

Amnesty International (AI), PO Box 702, Sentrum, 0106 Oslo (+47-2240 2200) (fax 2240 2250) (info@amnesty.no) (www.amnesty.no).

Folkereisning Mot Krig [FMK] (WR AT), PO Box 2779, Solli, 0204 Oslo (+47-2246 4670) (fax) (fmk@ikkevold.no) (www.ikkevold.no). *Ikkevold.*

Fred og Forsoning – IFOR Norge (FR), Fredshuset, Møllergata 12, 0179 Oslo (contact@ifor.no) (www.ifor.no).

Informasjonsarbeidere for Fred [IF] (IB AT ND DA), c/o Heffermehl, Stensgaten 24B, 0358 Oslo (+47-9174 4783) (fredpax@online.no) (peaceispossible.info).

Internasjonal Dugnad [ID] (SC), Nordahl Brunsgt 22, 0165 Oslo (+47-2211 3123) (info@internasjonaldugnad.no) (www.internasjonaldugnad.org). *Dugnad Nytt.*

Narviksenteret – Nordnorsk Fredssenter (IB), Postboks 700, 8509 Narvik (+47-9154 7078) (fax 7694 4560) (fred.no).

Nei til Atomvåpen / No to Nuclear Weapons (ND), Postboks 8838, Youngstorget, 0028 Oslo (post@neitilatomvapen.org) (www.neitilatomvapen.no).

Nobels Fredssenter / Nobel Peace Centre (RE), PO Box 1894 Vika, 0124 Oslo (+47-4830 1000) (fax 9142 9238) (post@nobelpeacecenter.org) (www.nobelpeacecenter.org).

Norges Fredslag (DA AT ND RE), Grensen 9B, Postboks 8922, Youngstorget, 0028 Oslo (www.fredslaget.no). Norwegian Peace Association.

Norges Fredsråd / Norwegian Peace Council (IB), Postboks 8940 Youngstorget, 0028 Oslo (+47-9527 4822) (fax 2286 8401) (post@norgesfredsrad.no) (norgesfredsrad.no).

Norwegian Nobel Institute / Det Norske Nobelinstitutt (RE DA CR), Henrik Ibsens gate 51, 0255 Oslo (+47-2212 9300) (fax 9476 1117) (postmaster@nobel.no) (nobelpeaceprize.org).

WILPF Norge – Internasjonal Kvinneliga for Fred og Frihet [IKFF] (WL), Storgata 11, 0155 Oslo (+47-9308 9644) (ikff@ikff.no) (www.ikff.no). *Fred og Frihet.*

PAKISTAN

Human Rights Commission of Pakistan [HRCP] (HR), Aiwan-i-Jamhoor, 107 Tipu Block, New Garden Town, Lahore 54600 (+92-42-3586 4994) (fax 3588 3582) (hrcp@hrcp-web.org) (hrcp-web.org).

Revolutionary Association of the Women of Afghanistan [RAWA] (HR), PO Box 374, Quetta (+92-300-554 1258) (rawa@rawa.org) (www.rawa.org).

Servas Pakistan [SE-PK] (SE), c/o Muhammad Naseem, GPO Box 516, Lahore 54000 (+92-321-444 4516) (fax 42-3532 2223) (servaspakistan@yahoo.com)

(pages.intnet.mu/servas/Pakistan). *Servas Pakistan Newsletter.*
Women's Internationl League for Peace and Freedom (WL), Sharah-e-Kashmir, Gulab Nagar, nr Darbar Saeen Mircho, Sector H-13, Islamabad (+92-51-250 6521) (mossarat_coco@yahoo.com).

PALESTINE (see also Israel)

NOTE: Because all of Palestine is under Israeli control (including areas not under day-to-day occupation), it is advisable to add 'via Israel' to addresses here (as well as 'Palestine').

Al-Watan Centre (CR HR RE), PO Box 158, Hebron, West Bank (+970-2-222 3777) (fax 222 0907) (info@alwatan.org) (www.alwatan.org). Supports popular resistance and nonviolence.

Alternative Information Centre [AIC] (HR RE TW AL AT), Building 111, Main Street, Beit Sahour, West Bank (+972-2-277 5444) (fax 277 5445) (www.alternativenews.org). See also Israel.

Arab Educational Institute – Open Windows [AEI] (RE PC), Paul VI Street, Bethlehem, West Bank (+970-2-274 4030) (fax 277 7554) (info@aeicenter.org) (www.aeicenter.org).

Centre for Conflict Resolution and Reconciliation [CCRR] (FR PC CR CD), PO Box 861, Bethlehem, West Bank (+970-2-276 7745) (fax 274 5475) (ccrr@ccrr-pal.org) (www.ccrr-pal.org). *Tree of Hope.*

Christian Peacemaker Teams [CPT] (RP), c/o Redeemer Church, PO Box 14076, Muristan Rd, Jerusalem 91140 (+972-2-222 8485) (cptheb@cpt.org) (www.cpt.org).

Combatants for Peace (CD), Ramallah (for postal address, see under Israel) (office@cfpeace.org) (www.cfpeace.org). Palestinian and Israeli ex-fighters for peace.

Ecumenical Accompaniment Programme in Palestine and Israel – Jerusalem Office [EAPPI] (RP HR CD CR), PO Box 741, East Jerusalem 91000 (+972-2-628 9402) (communications@eappi.org) (eappi.org).

Geneva Initiative (CD CR), c/o Palestinian Peace Coalition, PO Box 4252, Ramallah (+972-2-297 2535) (fax 297 2538) (www.geneva-accord.org). See also Israel.

Good Shepherd Collective (HR RA CR), Um al-Khair, Hebron Governate, West Bank (info@goodshepherdcollective.org) (goodshepherdcollective.org). Collective resisting military occupation.

International Peace and Co-operation Centre [IPCC] (TW CR), PO Box 24162, Jerusalem 91240 (+972-2-581 1992) (fax 540 0522) (info@ipcc-jerusalem.org) (home.ipcc-jerusalem.org).

Israel-Palestine Creative Regional Initiatives [IPCRI] (RE CR EL CD), PO Box 9321, Jerusalem 91092 (+970-59-856 7287) (ipcri@ipcri.org) (www.ipcri.org). Office is in Ammunition Hill, East Jerusalem.

Middle East Non-Violence and Democracy – FOR Palestine [MEND] (FR HR CR), PO Box 66558, Beit Hanina, East Jerusalem (+970-2-656 7310) (fax 656 7311) (lucynusseibeh@gmail.com) (www.mendonline.org).

Movement Against Israeli Apartheid in Palestine [MAIAP] (HR), see under Israel.

OneVoice Movement – Palestine (CD CR), PO Box 2401, Ramallah, West Bank (+970-2-295 2076) (info@OneVoice.ps) (www.onevoicemovement.org). See also Israel.

Palestinian BDS National Committee (HR RA), c/o PACBI, PO Box 1701, Ramallah, West Bank (pacbi@bdsmovement.net) (bdsmovement.net/bnc).

Palestinian Centre for Human Rights [PCHR] (HR), PO Box 1328, Gaza City, Gaza Strip (+970-8-282 4776) (fax) (pchr@pchrgaza.org) (www.pchrgaza.org).

Palestinian Human Rights Monitoring Group [PHRMG] (HR), PO Box 19918, East Jerusalem 91198 (+970-2-583 8189) (fax 583 7197) (admin@phrmg.org) (www.phrmg.org). Office: Ahmad Jaber House, Beit Hanina.

Palestinian Physicians for the Prevention of Nuclear War [PPPNW] (IP), PO Box 51681, East Jerusalem (azizlabadi@yahoo.com).

Palestinian-Israeli Peace NGO Forum (Palestinian Office) (CD), c/o Panorama, Al Ahliya St, Ramallah 2045 (+972-2-295 9618) (fax 298 1824) (panorama@panoramacenter.org) (www.peacengo.org). See also Israel.

Parents' Circle – Families' Forum: Bereaved Palestinian and Israeli Families Supporting Peace and Tolerance (CD CR), 13 Jamal Abed Al-Nasser St, Al-Ram, East Jerusalem (+972-2-234 4554) (fax 234 4553) (alquds@theparentscircle.org) (www.theparentscircle.com). See also under Israel.

Wi'am – Palestinian Conflict Resolution Centre (FR CR), PO Box 1039, Bethlehem, West Bank (+970-2-277 7333) (fax) (hope@alaslah.org) (www.alaslah.org).

Windows – Israeli-Palestinian Friendship Centre (CD), PO Box 352, Ramallah (office@win-peace.org) (www.win-peace.org). See also in Israel.

PARAGUAY

Amnistía Internacional Paraguay (AI), Dr Hassler 5229 – e/ Cruz del Defensor y Cruz del Chaco, Bsrrio Villa Mora, Asunción (+595-21-604822) (fax 663272) (ai-info@py.amnesty.org) (www.amnesty.org).

Movimiento Objeción de Conciencia – Paraguay [MOC-PY] (WR), Calle Iture Nº 1324 – entre Primera e Secunda Proyectada, Asunción (+598-981-415586) (moc_py@yahoo.com) (moc_py.org).

PARAGUAY

SERPAJ-Paraguay (HR PA), Calle Teniente Prieto 354 – entre Dr Facundo Insfran y Tte Rodi, Asunción (+595-21-481333) (serpajpy@serpajpy.org.py) (www.serpajpy.org.py).

PHILIPPINES

Aksyon para sa Kapayapaan at Katarungan (Action for Peace and Justice)– Center for Active Non-Violence [AKKAPKA-CANV] (FR TW HR EL), Rm 222, Administration Bldg, Pius XII Catholic Centre, 1175 UN Avenue, Paco, 1007 Manila (+63-2-526 0103) (fax 400 0823) (akkapka.canv84@gmail.com).

Task Force Detainees of the Philippines [TFDP] (HR), 45 Saint Mary St, Cubao, 1109 Quezon City (+63-2-437 8054) (fax 911 3643) (main.tfdp.net).

POLAND

Lekarze Przeciw Wojnie Nuklearnej – Sekcja Polska IPPNW (IP), Ul Mokotowska 3 – lok 6, 02640 Warszawa (+48-22-845 5784) (b.wasilewski@ips.pl).

Servas Polska (SE), c/o Joanna Mozga, Ul Kasprzaka 24A m 39, 01211 Warszawa (joanna@servas.pl) (servas.pl).

PORTUGAL

Amnistia Internacional Portugal (AI), Av Infante Santo 42 – 2º, 1350-179 Lisboa (+351-21 386 1652) (fax 21 386 1782) (aiportugal@amnistia-internacional.pt) (www.amnistia-internacional.pt).

Associação das Nações Unidas Portugal (UN), Rua do Almada 679 – 1º – S 103, 4050-039 Porto (+351-22 200 7767) (fax 22 200 7868) (anuportugal@gmail.com) (www.anup.pt).

Associação Livre dos Objectores e Objectoras de Consciência [ALOOC] (WR AL), Rua D Aleixo Corte-Real 394 – 3º D, 1800-166 Lisboa (alooc.portugal@gmail.com).

Conselho Português para a Paz e Cooperação [CPPC] (WP ND DA), Rua Rodrigo da Fonseca 56-2º, 1250-193 Lisboa (+351-21 386 3375) (fax 21 386 3221) (conselhopaz@cppc.pt) (www.cppc.pt).
Portuguese Council for Peace and Co-operation.

Observatório Género e Violência Armada / Observatory on Gender and Armed Violence [OGIVA] (DA HR), Centro Estudos Sociais, Colégio de S Jerónimo, Apartado 3087, 3000-995 Coimbra (+351-239 855593) (fax 239 855589) (ogiva@ces.uc.pt) (www.ces.uc.pt/ogiva).

PUERTO RICO

Pax Christi Puerto Rico (PC), c/o Randolph Rivera Cuevas, HC 3 Box 9695, Gurabo 00778 (+1787-761 1355) (fax) (clidin@bppr.com).

RUSSIA

Bellona Russia – St Petersburg (EL), Suvorovskiy Pr 59, 191015 Sankt-Peterburg (+7-812-275 7761) (fax 719 8843) (mail@bellona.ru) (www.bellona.ru). *Environment and Rights.*
Environmental Rights Centre. Main office in Norway.

Dom Druzeiy v Moskvye / Friends' House Moscow (SF), Sukharevskaya M – pl 6 – str 1, 127051 Moskva (+7-903-664 1075) (dd.moskva@gmail.com) (friendshousemoscow.org).

Dom Mira i Nyenasiliya / House of Peace and Nonviolence (PC), a/ya 33, 191002 Sankt-Peterburg (+7-951-644 8052) (peacehouse.spb@gmail.com) (www.peacehouse.ru).

Federatsiya Mira i Soglasiya / International Federation for Peace and Conciliation [IFPC] (WP), 36 Prospekt Mira, 129090 Moskva (+7-495-680 3576) (fax 688 9587) (vik@ifpc.ru) (www.ifpc.ru). *Mir i Soglasie.*

Fond Zashchitiy Glanosti / Glasnost Defence Foundation (HR), 4 Zubovsky Bulevard – Of 438, 119992 Moskva (+7-495-637 4947) (fax 637 4420) (simonov@gdf.ru) (www.gdf.ru).

Greenpeace Russia (GP), Lyeningradskii prospect – d 26 – k 1, 125040 Moskva (+7-495-988 7460) (fax) (info@greenpeace.ru) (www.greenpeace.org/russia).

Interchurch Partnership – Peace Resarch Centre (PC RE), PO Box 31, 191002 Sankt-Peterburg (+7-812-764 0423) (fax 764 6695) (mshishova@yahoo.com).

Memorial (HR CD), Malyi Karetnyi pereulok 12, 127051 Moskva (+7-495-650 7883) (fax 609 0694) (info@memo.ru) (www.memo.ru).

Nyemyetsko-Russkiy Obmyen / Deutscher-Russischer Austausch [NRO] (CD), Ligovski Pr 87 – Ofis 300, 191040 Sankt-Peterburg (+7-812-718 3793) (fax 718 3791) (nro@obmen.org) (www.obmen.org).
German-Russian Exchange.

Soldatskiye Matyeri Sankt-Peterburg / Soldiers' Mothers of St Petersburg (HR PA PC), Ul Razyezzhaya 9, 191002 Sankt-Peterburg (+7-812-712 4199) (fax 712 5058) (soldiersmothers@yandex.ru) (www.soldiersmothers.ru).

Tsenter po Isledovaniyu Problem Mira / Centre for Peace Research (RE), Russian Academy of Sciences, Profsoyuznaya Str 23, 117859 Moskva. *Ways to Security.*

Tsentr Mezhnatsionalnovo Sotrudnichestva / Centre for Interethnic Co-operation (CR CD), a/ya 8, 127055 Moskva (+7-499-972 6807) (center@interethnic.org) (www.interethnic.org).

RWANDA
Life & Peace Institute – DR Congo (RE RP), PO Box 64, Cyangugu (+243-81-249 4489) (pieter.vanholder@life-peace.org) (www.life-peace.org).

Peace & Conflict Resolution Project (of Bukavu, DR Congo) [PCR] (CR), PO Box 37, Cyangugu (+243-993-463279) (peacecrp@yahoo.com) (www.peaceconflictresolutionproject.webs.com). Operates in Bukavu, eastern Congo.

SERBIA
Beogradski Forum za Svet Ravnopravhih / Belgrade Forum for a World of Equals [Beoforum] (WP), Sremska Broj 6 – IV sprat, 11000 Beograd (+381-11-328 3778) (beoforum@gmail.com) (www.beoforum.rs).

Centar za Nenasilnu Akciju – Beograd / Centre for Nonviolent Action – Belgrade [CNA] (CR PA RE CD), Čika Ljubina 6, 11000 Beograd (+381-11-263 7603) (fax) (cna.beograd@nenasilje.org) (www.nenasilje.org). See also in Bosnia-Herzegovina.

Centre for Applied NonViolent Action and Strategies [CANVAS], Gandijeva 76a, 11070 Novi Beograd (+381-11-222 8331) (fax 222 8336) (office@canvasopedia.org) (www.canvasopedia.org).

ene U Crnom Protiv Rata / Women in Black Against War (WR), Jug Bogdanova 18/V, 11000 Beograd (+381-11-262 3225) (zeneucrnombeograd@gmail.com) (www.zeneucrnom.org).

SINGAPORE
Inter-Religious Organisation – Singapore (RP), Palmer House, 70 Palmer Rd – 05-01/02, Singapore 079427 (+65-6221 9858) (fax 6221 9212) (irosingapore@gmail.com) (iro.sg). Affiliate of Religions for Peace International.

United Nations Association of Singapore [UNAS] (UN), PO Box 351, Tanglin Post Office, Singapore 912412 (+65-6792 0026) (sctham@unas.org.sg) (www.unas.org.sg). *World Forum*.

SLOVAKIA
Pax Christi Bratislava-Pezinok (PC), Kpt Jaroša 15, 90201 Pezinok (+421-33-640 1284) (fax) (molnars@nextra.sk).

Priatelia Zeme Slovensko / Friends of the Earth Slovakia (FE), Komenského 21, 97401 Banská Bystrica (+421-48-412 3859) (fax) (foe@priateliazeme.sk) (www.priateliazeme.sk).

SOMALIA
Centre for Research and Dialogue [CRD] (CR RE), for postal address see under Kenya (+252-1-658666) (fax 5-932355) (crd@crdsomalia.org) (www.crdsomalia.org). Street address: K4 Airport Rd, Mogadishu.

Life & Peace Institute – Somalia and Kenya Programme (RP CR), see under Kenya (michele.cesari@life-peace.org).

SOUTH AFRICA
Action Support Centre [ASC] (CR), Postnet Suite No 145, Private Bag X9, Melville 2109 (+27-11 482 7442) (fax 11 482 2484) (info@asc.org.za) (www.asc.org.za).

African Centre for the Constructive Resolution of Disputes [ACCORD] (RE CD CR), 2 Golf Course Drive, Mount Edgecombe, Durban 4320, Kwazulu-Natal (+27-31 502 3908) (fax 31 502 4160) (info@accord.org.za) (www.accord.org.za). *Conflict Trends*.

Anglican Pacifist Fellowship [APF] (RP), c/o Victor Spencer, PO Box 54, Ficksburg 9730 (+27-51-922700) (victor.spencer@cpsanet.co.za).

Boycott, Disinvestment and Sanctions Against Israel in South Africa [BDS SA] (HR RA), PO Box 2318, Houghton 2041, Johannesburg (+27-11 403 2097) (fax 86 650 4836) (administrator@bdssouthafrica.com) (www.bdssouthafrica.com).

Centre for the Study of Violence and Reconciliation (RE CR HR), PO Box 30778, Braamfontein, Johannesburg 2017 (+27-11 403 5650) (fax 11 339 6785) (info@csvr.org.za) (www.csvr.org.za). Also in Cape Town (+27-21 447 2470).

Earthlife Africa [ELA] (EL), PO Box 32131, Braamfontein 2107 (+27-11 339 3662) (fax 11 339 3270) (seccp@earthlife.org.za) (www.earthlife.org.za).

GroundWork / Friends of the Earth South Africa (FE), PO Box 2375, Pietermaritzburg 3200 (+27-33 342 5662) (fax 33 342 5665) (team@groundwork.org.za) (www.groundwork.org.za).

GunFree South Africa [GFSA] (AT PA RE), PO Box 12988, Mowbray 7705 (+27-72 544 0573) (fax 86 545 0094) (info@gfsa.org.za) (www.gunfree.org.za).

Institute for Healing of Memories (CR), PO Box 36069, Glosderry 7702 (+27-21 683 6231) (fax 21 683 5747) (info@healingofmemories.co.za) (www.healing-memories.org).

International Centre of Nonviolence [ICON] (RE HR), ML Sultan Campus, Durban University of Technology, PO Box 1334, Durban 4000 (+27-31 373 5499) (icon@dut.ac.za) (www.icon.org.za). Works for a culture of nonviolence.

Quaker Peace Centre (SF CR RE), 3 Rye Rd, Mowbray, Cape Town 7700 (+27-21 685 7800) (fax 21 686 8167) (qpc@qpc.org.za) (www.quaker.org/capetown).

Trauma Centre for Survivors of Violence and Torture (CR HR), Cowley House, 126 Chapel St, Woodstock, Cape Town 7925 (+27-21 465 7373) (info@trauma.org.za) (www.trauma.org.za).

SOUTH AFRICA

United Nations Association of South Africa [UNA-SA] (UN), c/o The Coachman's Cottage Museum, PO Box 1256, Somerset West 7129 (+27-21 850 0509) (fax 800 981771) (admin@unasa.org.za) (www.unasa.org.za).

SOUTH SUDAN

Organisation for Nonviolence and Development [ONAD] (WR CR HR), PO Box 508, Juba (+211-921-352592) (onadjuba2011@gmail.com) (www.onadev.org).

SPAIN

Alternativa Antimilitarista – Movimiento de Objeción de Conciencia [AA-MOC] (WR RA TR), C/San Cosme y San Damián 24-2º, 28012 Madrid (+34-91 475 3782) (moc.lavapies@nodo50.org) (www.antimilitaristas.org).

Amnistía Internacional España (AI), C/ Fernando VI – 8 – 1º Izda, 28004 Madrid (+34-91 310 1277) (fax 91 319 5334) (info@madrid.es.amnesty.org) (www.es.amnesty.org).

Antimilitaristes – MOC València (WR RA TR), C/ Roger de Flor 8 – baix-dta, 46001 València (+34-96 391 6702) (retirada@pangea.org) (mocvalencia.org).

Brigadas Internacionales de Paz – Estado Español [PBI] (CR HR TW), C/ Ballesta 9 – 3º E, Madrid (www.pbi-ee.org).

Centre d'Estudis per la Pau JM Delàs (WR RE AT RP IB), Rivadeneyra 6 – 10è, 08002 Barcelona, Catalunya (+34-93 317 6177) (fax 93 412 5384) (info@centredelas.org) (www.centredelas.org). *Materiales de Trabajo.*

Centro de Investigación para la Paz (RE), Duque de Sesto 40, 28009 Madrid (+34-91 576 3299) (fax 91 577 4726) (cip@fuhem.es) (www.cip-ecosocial.fuhem.es). *Papeles de Relaciones Ecosociales y Cambio Global.*

Ekologistak Martxan Bizkaia (ND EL TW), c/ Pelota 5 – Behea, 48005 Bilbo, Euskadi (+34-94 479 0119) (fax) (bizkaia@ekologistakmartxan.org) (www.ekologistakmartxan.org). *Eco Boletin.*

Escola de Cultura de Pau (RE), Plaça del Coneixement – Edifici MRA (Mòdul Recerca A), UAB, 08193 Bellaterra (+34-93 586 8848) (fax 93 581 3294) (escolapau@uab.cat) (escolapau.uab.cat).

Fundación Cultura de Paz [FCP] (IB WP RE), Calle Velázquez 14 – 3º dcha, 28001 Madrid (+34-91 426 1555) (fax 91 431 6387) (info@fund-culturadepaz.org) (www.fund-culturadepaz.org).

Fundación Seminario de Investigación para la Paz [SIP] (RE), Centro Pignatelli, Pº de la Constitución 6, 50008 Zaragoza (+34-976 217215) (fax 976 230113) (sipp@seipaz.org) (www.seipaz.org).

Gernika Gogoratuz – Peace Research Centre [GGG] (IB RE), Artekale 1-1, 48300 Gernika-Lumo, Bizkaia (+34-94 625 3558) (fax 94 625 6765) (gernikag@gernikagogoratuz.org) (www.gernikagogoratuz.org).

Gesto por la Paz de Euskal Herria – Euskal Herriko Bakearen Aldeko (PA HR RE), Apdo 10152, 48080 Bilbao (+34-94 416 3929) (fax 94 415 3285) (gesto@gesto.org) (www.gesto.org). Association for peace in the Basque Country.

Grup Antimilitarista Tortuga (PA), C/ Ametler 26 – 7ª, 03203 Elx, Alacant (tortuga@nodo50.org) (www.grupotortuga.com). Part of network Alternativa Antimilitarista – MOC.

Instituto de la Paz y los Conflictos (RE), C/ Rector López Argüeta, 18071 Granada (+34-958 244142) (fax 958 248974) (eirene@ugr.es). *Eirene.*

Justicia y Paz – España [CGJP] (RP), Rafael de Riego 16 – 3º dcha, 28045 Madrid (+34-91 506 1828) (juspax@juspax-es.org) (www.juspax-es.org).

Kontzientzi Eragozpen Mugimendua / MOC Euskal Herria [KEM-MOC] (WR AL RA TR), Calle Fika Nº 4 – lonja derecha, 48006 Bilbao, Euskadi (+34-94-415 3772) (mocbilbao@gmail.com) (www.sinkuartel.org). Part of network Alternativa Antimilitarista – MOC.

Liga Internacional de Mujeres por la Paz y la Libertad (WL), 26-28 bajo – Almería, Zaragoza (wilpf.espanya@gmail.com) (wilpf.es).

Moviment per la Pau (PA RE AT), C/ Providència 42, 08024 Barcelona (+34-93 219 3371) (fax 93 213 0890) (movpau@pangea.org). *Lletres de Pau.*

Paz y Cooperación / Peace and Co-operation (IB RE TW), Meléndez Valdés 68 – 4º izq, 28015 Madrid (+34-91 549 6156) (fax 91 543 5282) (pazycooperacion@hotmail.com) (www.peaceandcooperation.org). *Premio Escolar Paz y Cooperación.*

Servas España (SE), Calle de la Roca 5, 08319 Dosrius (servas.spain@gmail.com) (www.servas.es).

Servei Civil Internacional – Catalunya [SCI] (SC PA), c/ Carme 95 – baixos 2a, 08001 Barcelona, Catalunya (+34-93 441 7079) (comunicacio@sci-cat.org) (www.sci-cat.org).

Servicio Civil Internacional [SCI] (SC), c/Ronda de Segovia 55 – oficina 2, 28005 Madrid (+34-91 366 3259) (fax 91 366 2203) (oficina@ongsci.org) (www.ongsci.org).

Survival International (España) [SI] (HR), C/Príncipe 12 – 3º, 28012 Madrid (+34-91 521 7283) (fax 91 523 1420) (info@survival.es) (www.survival.es). *Boletín de Acción Urgente.*

SRI LANKA
Lanka Jathika Sarvodaya Shramadana Sangamaya [Sarvodaya] (HR TW), Damsak Mandira, 98 Rawatawatte Rd, Moratuwa (+94-11-264 7159) (fax 265 6512) (ed@sarvodaya.org) (www.sarvodaya.org).
Mahatma Gandhi Centre (PO PA RE), 22/17 Kalyani Rd, Colombo 00600 (+94-11-250 1825) (fax) (power2people@gandhiswaraj.com) (gandhiswaraj.con).
National Peace Council of Sri Lanka [NPC] (CR RE CD), 12/14 Purana Vihara Rd, Colombo 6 (+94-11-281 8344) (fax 281 9064) (npc@sltnet.lk) (www.peace-srilanka.org). *Paths to Peace.*
Nonviolent Direct Action Group [NVDAG] (FR WR IB), PO Box 2, 29 Kandy Rd, Kaithady-Nunavil, Chavakachcheri (del-smskr@eureka.lk). *NVDAG Report.*

SUDAN
Life & Peace Institute (RE RP), PO Box 13119, Khartoum (+249-18-348 0627) (jody.henderson@life-peace.org) (www.life-peace.org).
Peace Desk of New Sudan Council of Churches (RP CD CR HR), see under Kenya.
Sudanese Women's Voice for Peace, see under Kenya.

SWEDEN
Göteborgs Ickevåldsnätverk / Nonviolence Network of Gothenburg (AL PA CR RA), c/o Elisabet Ahlin, Norra Krokslättsgatan 17A, 41264 Göteborg (+46-31-832187) (elisabet.ahlin@gmail.com).
Greenpeace (GP), Rosenlundsgatan 29 B, 11863 Stockholm (+46-8-702 7070) (info.se@greenpeace.org) (www.greenpeace.se).
Internationella Kvinnoförbundet för Fred och Frihet [IKFF] (WL), Norrtullsgatan 45 – 1 tr, 11345 Stockholm (+46-8-702 9810) (info@ikff.se) (www.ikff.se).
Jordens Vänner / Friends of the Earth Sweden (FE TW), Box 7048, 40231 Göteborg (+46-31-121808) (fax 121817) (info@jordensvanner.se) (www.jordensvanner.se).
Kristna Fredsrörelsen (FR), Ekumeniska Centret, Box 14038, 16714 Bromma (+46-8-453 6840) (fax 453 6829) (info@krf.se) (krf.se). *Fredsnytt.*
Kvinnor för Fred / Women for Peace [KFF] (IB ND EL CR), Hammarby Allé 93 – 4tr, 12063 Stockholm (+46-8-667 9727) (kff@telia.com) (www.kvinnorforfred.se).
Life & Peace Institute [LPI] (RP AT RE TW CR), Säbygatan 4, 75323 Uppsala (+46-18-660130) (info@life-peace.org) (www.life-peace.org). *Horn of Africa Bulletin.* Projects in East Africa and Central Africa.
Ofog (WR RA AT ND AL), c/o Göteborgs Fredskommitté, Linnégatan 21, 41304 Göteborg (+46-733-815361) (info@ofog.org) (www.ofog.org).
PBI-Sverige (HR CR), Blixtåsvägen 6, 42437 Angered (+46-31-330 7509) (info@pbi-sweden.org) (www.pbi-sweden.org).
PeaceQuest International (CD CR RE), Box 55913, 10216 Stockholm (+46-8-5592 1180) (info@peacequest.eu) (www.peacequest.eu).
Servas Sverige (SE), c/o Eva Hartman-Juhlin, Svankärrsvägen 3B, 75653 Upsalla (sweden@servas.se) (www.servas.se).
Svenska FN-Förbundet (UN), Box 15115, 10465 Stockholm (+46-8-462 2540) (fax 641 8876) (info@fn.se) (www.fn.se). *Världshorisont.*
Svenska Fredskommittén / Swedish Peace Committee [SFK] (DA ND), Tegelviksgatan 40, 11641 Stockholm (info@svenskafredskommitten.nu) (www.svenskafredskommitten.nu).
Sveriges Fredsråd / Swedish Peace Council (IB), Tegelviksgatan 40, 11641 Stockholm (info@FredNu.se) (frednu.se). National federation.
Swedish Peace and Arbitration Society / Svenska Freds- och Skiljedomsföreningen [SPAS] (WR IB AT), Polhemsgatan 4, 11236 Stockholm (+46-8-5580 3180) (info@svenskafreds.se) (www.svenskafreds.se). *Pax.*
Vännernas Samfund (Kväkarna) (SF), Box 9166, 10272 Stockholm (+46-8-668 6816) (fax) (info@kvakare.se).

SWITZERLAND
Action des Chrétiens pour l'Abolition de la Torture / Aktion der Christen für die Abschaffung der Folter [ACAT-Suisse] (HR), CP 5011, 3001 Berne (+41-31 312 2044) (fax 31 312 5811) (info@acat.ch) (www.acat.ch).
Amnesty International (AI), Speichergasse 33, 3011 Bern (+41-31 307 2222) (fax 31 307 2233) (info@amnesty.ch) (www.amnesty.ch). *Amnesty Magazin(e).*
APRED – Participative Institute for the Progress of Peace (RE PO PA), Route des Siernes Picaz 46, 1659 Flendruz (+41-79 524 3574) (info@demilitarisation.org) (www.apred.ch).
Ärzte/Ärztinnen für Soziale Verantwortung / Médecins pour une Résponsibilité Sociale [PSR/IPPNW] (IP), Bireggstr 36, 6003 Luzern (+41-41 240 6349) (fax) (sekretariat@ippnw.ch) (www.ippnw.ch).
Basel Peace Office (RE ND), Universität Basel, Petersgraben 27, 4051 Basel (info@baselpeaceoffice.org) (www.baselpeaceoffice.org).

For explanation of codes and abbreviations, see introduction

SWITZERLAND

Brethren Service (RP), PO Box 2100, 150 route de Ferney, 1211 Genève 2 (+41-22 791 6330) (brethrenservice@worldcom.ch) (www.brethrenvolunteerservice.org).
Centre pour l'Action Non-Violente [CENAC] (WR RP IB), 52 rue de Genève, 1004 Lausanne (+41-21 661 2434) (fax 21 661 2436) (info@non-violence.ch) (www.non-violence.ch).
cfd – the feminist peace organisation (PA CR), Postfach 5761, 3001 Berne (+41-31 300 5060) (info@cfd-ch.ch) (www.cfd-ch.ch). *cfd-Zeitung.*
Eirene Suisse (RP TW EL CR), 9 Rue du Valais, 1202 Genève (+41-22 321 8556) (fax) (info@eirenesuisse.ch) (eirenesuisse.ch).
Gesellschaft für bedrohte Völker / Société pour les Peuples menacés (HR), Schermenweg 154, 3072 Ostermunigen (+41-31 939 0000) (fax 31 939 0019) (info@gfbv.ch) (www.gfbv.ch).
Grüne Partei der Schweiz / Parti écologiste suisse / Partito ecologista svizzero (EL IB), Waisenhausplatz 21, 3011 Bern (+41-31 326 6660) (fax 31 326 6662) (gruene@gruene.ch) (www.gruene.ch). *Greenfo.*
Green party. Grüne / Les Verts / I Verdi.
Greenpeace (GP), Badenerstr 171, Postfach 9320, 8036 Zürich (+41-44 447 4141) (fax 44 447 4199) (gp@greenpeace.ch) (www.greenpeace.org/switzerland).
Gruppe für eine Schweiz ohne Armee / Groupe pour une Suisse sans Armée [GSoA/GSsA] (WR), Postfach, 8031 Zürich (+41-44 273 0100) (gsoa@gsoa.ch) (www.gsoa.ch).
Institute for Peace and Dialogue [IPD] (CR CD RE), Hegenheimerstr 175, 4055 Basel (+41-76 431 6170) (fhuseynli@ipdinstitute.ch) (www.idpinstitute.ch).
MIR Suisse / IFOR Schweiz (FR), Brue 4, 2613 Villeret (+41-32 940 7237) (secretariat@ifor-mir.ch) (ifor-mir.ch).
Neuer Israel Fonds Schweiz – NIF Switzerland (HR), Winkelriedplatz 4, 4053 Basel (+41-61 272 1455) (fax 61 361 2972) (info@nif.ch) (www.nif.ch).
Peace Brigades International – Schweiz/Suisse [PBI] (CD HR CR RE), Gutenbergstr 35, 3011 Bern (+41-31 372 4444) (info@peacebrigades.ch) (www.peacebrigades.ch).
Pro Natura (FE), Postfach, 4018 Basel (+41-61-317 9191) (fax 317 9266) (mailbox@pronatura.ch) (www.pronatura.ch).
Schweizerische Friedensbewegung (WP), Postfach 2113, 4001 Basel (+41-61 681 0363) (fax 61 681 7632) (mail@friedensbewegung.ch) (www.friedensbewegung.ch).
Schweizerische Friedensstiftung [swisspeace] (RE CR), Sonnenbergstr 17, PO Box, 3001 Bern (+41-31 330 1212) (info@swisspeace.ch) (www.swisspeace.ch).
Schweizerischer Friedensrat / Consiglio Svizzera per pa Pace / Conseil Suisse pour la Paix [SFR] (IB AT EL), Gartenhofstr 7, 8004 Zürich (+41-44 242 9321) (info@friedensrat.ch) (www.friedensrat.ch). *FriZ.*
Swiss Peace Council.
Service Civil International – Schweizer Zweig / Branche suisse / Sede svizzera [SCI] (SC), Monbijoustr 32, Postfach 7855, 3001 Bern (+41-31 381 4620) (info@scich.org) (www.scich.org).
Service Civil International.
Société Religieuse des Amis, Assemblée de Suisse (Quaker) [SYM] (SF), c/o Maison Quaker, 13 Av du Mervelet, 1209 Genève (+41-22 748 4800) (fax 22 748 4819) (symclerk@swiss-quakers.ch) (www.swiss-quakers.ch). *Entre Amis.*
Société Suisse – Nations Unies / Schweizerisches Versicherungsverband (UN), Postfach 762, 6431 Schwyz (info@schweiz-uno.ch) (www.schweiz-uno.ch).
umverkehR (EL), Kalkbreitestrasse 2, Postfach 8214, 8036 Zürich (+41-44 242 7276) (info@umverkehr.ch) (www.umverkehr.ch).
Working especially to cut car use.
Weltföderalisten Schweiz / Fédéralistes mondiaux Suisse (WF), c/o Hexagon AG, Graben 5, 6300 Zug (info@weltfoederalisten.ch) (www.weltfoederalisten.ch).
Member of World Federalist Movement (WFM).
Women's International League for Peace and Freedom (WL), Postfach 923, 3000 Bern 9 (wilpfschweiz.ch).

SYRIA

Syrian Human Rights Committee [SHRC] (HR), see under Britain. Syrian human rights group in exile in Britain.

TAIWAN

Chinese Association for Human Rights [CAHR] (HR), 4F-3 – No 23 – Sec 1 – Hangchow S Rd, Taipei 10053 (+886-2-3393 6900) (fax 2395 7399) (humanright@cahr.org.tw) (www.cahr.org.tw).
Greenpeace East Asia – Taipei Office (GP), No 10, Lane 83, Section 1, Roosevelt Rd, Zhongzheng District, Taipei City 10093 (+886-2-2321 5006) (fax 2321 3209) (inquiry.tw@greenpeace.org) (www.greenpeace.org/eastasia).

For explanation of codes and abbreviations, see introduction

John Paul II Peace Institute / Fujen Peace Centre (RP), Fujen Catholic University, 24205 Hsinchuang, Taipei County (+886-2-2905 3111) (fax 2905 2170) (peace@mail.fju.edu.tw) (peace.fjac.fju.edu.tw). *Peace Papers.*

TANZANIA
United Nations Association of Tanzania (UN), PO Box 9182, Dar es Salaam (+255-22-219 9200) (fax 266 8749) (info@una.or.tz) (una.or.tz).

THAILAND
Asian Institute for Human Rights [AIHR] (HR), 109 Soi Sithicon, Suthisarnwinichai Road, Samsennok, Huaykwang, Bangkok 10310 (+66-2 277 6882) (fax) (kalpalatad@aihr.info) (aihr.info).

Greenway Thailand (WC), 40/1 Moo 4 Ban Vihan, Kaow Tambon Vihan, Kaow, Tha Chang district, Singburi 16140 (+66-36 521619) (info@greenwaythailand.org) (www.greenwaythailand.org).

TIBET
Tibetan Centre for Human Rights and Democracy (FR HR), see under India. Works for human rights of Tibetans in Tibet.

TOGO
Amis de la Terre – Togo [ADT] (FE), BP 20190, Lomé (+228-2222 1731) (fax 2222 1732) (adt-togo@amiterre.tg) (www.amiterre.tg).

Amnesty International Togo (AI), 2 BP 20013, Lomé 2 (+228-2222 5820) (fax) (contact@amnesty.tg) (www.amnesty.tg). *Echos d'Al; Miafé Dzena.*

TRINIDAD AND TOBAGO
United Nations Association of Trinidad & Tobago [UNATT] (UN), 106 Woodford Street, Newtown, Port of Spain (+1 868-221 7645) (info@unassociationtt.org) (unassociationtt.org).

TUNISIA
Coalition Nationale Tunisienne contre la Peine de Mort (HR), 56 Avenue de la Liberté, 1002 Tunis (+216-2168 7533) (abolitionpm@gmail.com). National Coalition Against the Death Penalty.

TURKEY
Greenpeace Mediterranean (GP), İstiklal Caddesi Kallavi Sok – No 1 Kat 2, Beyoğlu, İstanbul (+90-212-292 7619) (fax 292 7622) (bilgi.tr@greenpeace.org) (www.greenpeace.org/turkey). See also Israel, Lebanon.

İnsan Hakları Derneği / Human Rights Association [İHD] (HR), Necatibey Cad 82/11-12, Kizilay, çankaya, 06430 Ankara (+90-312-230 3567) (fax 230 1707) (posta@ihd.org.tr) (www.ihd.org.tr).

Şiddetsizlik Eğitim ve Araştırma Denerği / Nonviolent Education and Research Association (RE WR), Kuloğlu Mah Güllabici sok no 16 – Daire 2, 34433 Cihangir, İstanbul (+90-212-244 1269) (merhaba@siddetsizlikmerkezi.org) (www.siddetsizlikmerkezi.org).

Türkiye İnsan Hakları Vakfı / Human Rights Foundation of Turkey [TIHV/HRFT] (HR), Mithatpaşa Cad – No 49/11 – 6 Kat, 06420 Kızılay / Ankara (+90-312-310 6636) (fax 310 6463) (tihv@tihv.org.tr) (www.tihv.org.tr). In Istanbul: +90-212-249 3092.

Türkiye çevre Vafki / Environment Foundation of Turkey [TçV] (EL), Tunalı Hilmi Cd 50/20, Kavaklidere, 06660 Ankara (+90-312-425 5508) (fax 418 5118) (cevre@cevre.org.tr) (www.cevre.org.tr). *çevre.*

Vicdani Ret Derneği / Conscientious Objector Association [VR-DER] (WR HR), Osmanağa Mah Söğütlüçeşme Cad – Sevil Pasajı No 74 – Kat 5 – Ofis 108, Kadıköy, İstanbul (+90-216-345 0100) (fax) (vicdaniretdernegi@gmail.com) (vicdaniret.org). For legalising conscientious objection.

UGANDA
International Friendship League – Uganda [IFL] (CD), c/o Ismael Nyonyintono, PO Box 37692, Kampala (ismaeluk@yahoo.com).

Jamii Ya Kupatanisha [JYAK] (FR WR CR), PO Box 198, Kampala (+256-41-427 1435) (fax 434 7389) (jyak.peace@gmail.com).

Justice & Peace Commission of Gulu Archdiocese (PC HR), PO Box 200, Gulu (+256-471-32026) (fax 432860) (jpcgulu@infocom.co.ug).

UKRAINE
Mama-86 (EL), Bul Chapaeva 14 – Of 1, 01030 Kiyiv (+380-44-234 6929) (fax) (info@mama-86.org.ua) (www.mama-86.org.ua). Includes anti-nuclear campaigning.

Zeleniy Svit – Druzi Zemli (FE PA), A/C 61, 49000 Dnipropetrovsk +380-56-370 9572) (fax 370 9573) (foeukraine@gmail.com) (www.zsfoe.org). Green World – Friends of the Earth.

UNITED STATES OF AMERICA
350.org (EL), 20 Jay St – Suite 732, Brooklyn, NY 11201 (+1-646-801 0759) (feedback@350.org) (350.org). Campaign on climate change. Formerly Step It Up.

A Rocha USA (EL), PO Box 1338, Fredricksburg, TX 78624 (+1-830-522 5319) (usa@arocha.org) (arocha.us). Christian.

USA

Action Reconciliation Service for Peace – US [ARSP] (CD RE), 1501 Cherry St, Philadelphia, PA 19102 (+1-215-241 7249) (fax 241 7252) (info@actionreconcilation.org) (actionreconciliation.org).

AJ Muste Memorial Institute (IB RE WR), 168 Canal St – 6th Flr, New York, NY 10013 (+1-212-533 4335) (info@ajmuste.org) (www.ajmuste.org).
Muste Notes.

Al-Awda – The Palestine Right to Return Coalition (HR), PO Box 8812, Coral Springs, FL 33075 (+1-760-918 9441) (fax 918 9442) (info@al-awda.org) (al-awda.org).

Albert Einstein Institution (RE SD), PO Box 455, East Boston, MA 02128 (+1-617-247 4882) (fax 247 4035) (einstein@igc.org) (www.aeinstein.org).

Alliance for Global Justice (HR RA EL), 225 E 26th St – Suite 1, Tucson, AZ 85713 (+1-202-540 8336) (afgj@afgj.org) (afgj.org). Focus on changing US policy towards Latin America.

Alliance for Humane Biotehcnology (EL HR), 155 21st Ave, San Francisco, CA 94121 (info@humanebiotech.org) (www.humanebiotech.com).

Alliance for Middle East Peace [ALLMEP] (CD), 2550 M St NW, Washington, DC 20037 (+1-202-618 4600) (fax 888-784 4530) (info@allmep.org) (www.allmep.org). Promoting people-to-people coexistence.

Alliance for Nuclear Accountability [ANA] (ND DA EL), 322 4th St NE, Washington, DC 20002 (+1-202-544 0217) (sgordon@ananuclear.org) (www.ananuclear.org).

Alternatives to Violence Project – USA [AVP/USA] (CR PO), 1050 Selby Ave, St Paul, MN 55104 (+1-888-278 7820) (info@avpusa.org) (avpusa.org).

American Civil Liberties Union [ACLU] (HR), 125 Broad St – 18th Floor, New York, NY 10004 (aclu@aclu.org) (www.aclu.org).

American Friends of Neve Shalom / Wahat al-Salam (CD HR PA RE), 229 N Central Ave – Suite 401, Glendale, CA 91203-3541 (+1-818-662 8883) (afnswas@oasisofpeace.org) (www.oasisofpeace.org). Support mixed (Jewish-Palestinian) Israeli village.

American Friends Service Committee [AFSC] (SF RE CR), 1501 Cherry St, Philadelphia, PA 19102 (+1-215-241 7000) (fax 241 7275) (afscinfo@afsc.org) (www.afsc.org).
Quaker Action.

American Jews for a Just Peace [AJJP] (RA), PO Box 1032, Arlington, MA 02474 (www.ajjp.org).

Amnesty International USA [AIUSA] (AI), 5 Penn Plaza – 16th floor, New York, NY 10001 (+1-212-807 8400) (admin-us@aiusa.org) (www.amnestyusa.org).

Anglican Pacifist Fellowship – US [APF] (RP), c/o Nathaniel W Pierce, 3864 Rumsey Dr, Trappe, MD 21673-1722 (+1-410-476 4556) (nwpierce@verizon.net).

Arkansas Coalition for Peace and Justice (DA HR), PO Box 250398, Little Rock, AR 72225 (+1-501-952 8181) (acpj@arpeaceandjustice.org) (arpeaceandjustice.org).

Arms Control Association [ACA] (AT ND RE), 1200 18th St – Ste 1175, Washington, DC 20036 (+1-202-463 8270) (fax 463 8273) (aca@armscontrol.org) (www.armscontrol.org).

Asian Pacific Environmental Network [APEN] (EL), 426 17th St – Suite 500, Oakland, CA 94612 (+1-510-834 8920) (fax 834 8926) (apen@apen4ej.org) (apen4ej.org).

Association of Christians for the Abolition of Torture [ACAT] (HR), PO Box 314, Pleasant Hill, TN 38578-0314 (revhdsmith@starpower.net).

Baptist Peace Fellowship of North America – Bautistas por la Paz [BPFNA] (RP), 300 Hawthorne Lane – Ste 205, Charlotte, NC 28204 (+1-704-521 6051) (fax 521 6053) (bpfna@bpfna.org) (www.bpfna.org).
Baptist Peacemaker.

Beyond Nuclear (EL ND), 6930 Carroll Ave – Suite 400, Takoma Park, MD 20912 (+1-301-270 2209) (fax 270 4000) (info@beyondnuclear.org) (www.beyondnuclear.org).

Brady Campaign to Prevent Gun Violence (RE HR DA PO), 840 First St NE – Suite 400, Washington, DC 20002 (+1-202-370 8100) (policy@bradymail.org) (www.bradycampaign.org).

Brethren Volunteer Service (PA CD RP), Church of the Brethren, 1451 Dundee Ave, Elgin, IL 60120 (+1-847-742 5100) (fax 429 4394) (bvs@brethren.org) (www.brethrenvolunteerservice.org).

Bruderhof Communities (RP), 101 Woodcrest Dr, Rifton, NY 12471 (+1-845-658 7700) (info@bruderhof.com) (www.bruderhof.com). Also known as Church Communities International.

Buddhist Peace Fellowship [BPF] (FR IB), PO Box 3470, Berkeley, CA 94703 (+1-510-239 3764) (info@bpf.org) (www.buddhistpeacefellowship.org).

Campaign for Peace & Democracy [CPD] (IB HR RE), 2808 Broadway – No 12, New York, NY 10025 (+1-212-666 5924) (cpd@igc.org) (www.cpdweb.org).

Campaign to Establish a US Department of Peace (RE PO CR CD), c/o The Peace Alliance, 2108 Military Rd, Arlington, VA 22207 (1-202-684 2553) (www.thepeacealliance.org).

Cat Lovers Against the Bomb [CLAB] (ND AT HR), c/o Nebraskans for Peace, PO Box 83466, Lincoln, NE 68501-3466 (+1-402-475 4620) (fax 483 4108) (catcal@aol.com) (www.catloversagainstthebomb.com). *Calendar*.

Catholic Mobilizing Network to End the Use of the Death Penalty [CMN] (RP), 415 Michigan Ave NE – Suite 210, Washington, DC 20017 (+1-202-541 5290) (info@catholicsmobilizing.org) (catholicsmobilizing.org). Formerly Catholics Against Capital Punishment.

Catholic Peace Fellowship (RP PA), PO Box 4232, South Bend, IN 46634 (+1-574-232 2811) (staff@catholicpeacefellowship.org) (www.catholicpeacefellowship.org). Promotes conscientious objection.

Catholic Worker Movement (AL RP PA), 36 E 1st St, New York, NY 10003 (+1-212-777 9617). *The Catholic Worker*.

Center for Applied Conflict Management [CACM] (RE CR), Kent State University, PO Box 5190, Kent, OH 44242-0001 (+1-330-672 3143) (fax 672 3362) (cacm@kent.edu) (www.kent.edu/cacm).

Center for Citizen Initiatives [CCI] (CD), 820 N Delaware St – Ste 405, San Mateo, CA 94401 (+1-650-458 8115) (info@ccisf.org) (ccisf.org). Organise US-Russia citizen exchanges.

Center for Energy Research (EL CR ND), 104 Commercial St NE, Salem, OR 97301 (pbergel@igc.org). Dedicated to breaking the nuclear chain.

Center for Genetics and Society [CGS] (EL HR), 1936 University Ave – Suite 350, Berrkeley, CA 94794 (+1-510-625 0819) (fax 665 8760) (info@geneticsandsociety.org) (www.geneticsandsociety.org).

Center for Jewish Nonviolence [CJNV] (PA DA HR), c/o T'ruah – The Rabbinic Call for Human Rights, 266 West 37th St – Suite 803, New York, NY 10018 (CJNV.campaigns@gmail.com) (centerforjewishnonviolence.org). Organises visits to Israel for nonviolent action.

Center for Nonviolence and Peace Studies [CNPS] (RE CR PO), University of Rhode Island, 74 Lower College Rd – MCC 202, Kingston, RI 02881 (+1-401-874 2875) (fax 874 9108) (nonviolence@etal.uri.edu) (www.uri.edu/nonviolence). Become the Change.

Center for Nonviolent Solutions (RE CR), 901 Pleasant St, Worcester, MA 01602 (+1-774-641 1566) (inquiry@nonviolentsolution.org) (www.nonviolentsolution.org).

Center for Religious Tolerance [CRT] (RP CR), 520 Ralph St, Sarasota, FL 34242 (+1-941-312 9795) (info@c-r-t.org) (www.c-r-t.org). Supports international interfaith initiatives.

Center for Restorative Justice & Peacemaking (CR RE), University of Minnesota, 105 Peters Hall, 1404 Gortner Ave, Saint Paul, MN 55108 (+1-612-625 1220) (fax 624 3744) (www.cehd.umn.edu/ssw/rjp). For community-based response to crime and violence.

Center for the Study and Promotion of Zones of Peace (RE), 139 Kuulei Rd, Kailua, HI 96734 (+1-808-263 4015) (fax) (lop-rey.zop-hi@worldnet.att.net).

Center for Victims of Torture (HR RE), 2356 University Ave W – Suite 430, Saint Paul, MN 55114 (+1-612-436 4800) (cvt@cvt.org) (www.cvt.org).

Center on Conscience & War [CCW] (PA HR), 1830 Connecticut Ave NW, Washington, DC 20009-5706 (+1-202-483 2220) (fax 483 1246) (ccw@CenteronConscience.org) (www.centeronconscience.org). *The Reporter for Conscience' sake*.

Christian Peacemaker Teams [CPT] (RP PA RA), PO Box 6508, Chicago, IL 60680-6508 (+1-773-376 0550) (fax 376 0549) (peacemakers@cpt.org) (www.cpt.org).

Citizens for Peaceful Resolutions [CPR] (ND PA PO), PO Box 364, Ventura, CA 93002-0364 (www.c-p-r.net). Committed to interconnectedess of all life.

Co-operation Ireland (USA) (CD), 1501 Broadway – Suite 2600 (Attn Richard Pino), NY 10036 (www.cooperationireland.org).

Coalition to Stop Gun Violence (DA AT), 1424 L Street NW – Suite 2-1, Washington, DC 20005 (+1-202-408 0061) (csgv@csgv.org) (www.csgv.org).

CODEPINK: Women for Peace (PA), 2010 Linden Ave, Venice, CA 90291 (+1-310-827 4320) (fax 827 4547) (info@codepink.org) (www.codepink.org). A women-initiated grassroots peace campaign.

Colgate University Peace & Conflict Studies Program (RE CR), 13 Oak Dr, Hamilton, NY 13346-1398 (+1-315-228 7806) (fax 228 7121) (peace@colgate.edu) (www.colgate.edu/departments/peacestudies/).

Colombia Support Network (TW HR CD), PO Box 1505, Madison, WI 53701-1505 (+1-608-257 8753) (fax 255 6621) (csn@igc.org) (www.colombiasupport.net). *Action on Columbia*.

Committee Opposed to Militarism & the Draft [COMD] (PA), PO Box 15195, San Diego, CA 92175 (+1-760-753 7518) (comd@comdsd.org) (www.comdsd.org). *Draft NOtices*.

Common Defense Campaign [CDC] (RE), c/o William Goodfellow, Centre for International Policy, 2000 M St NW – Suite 720, Washington, DC 20036-3327 (+1-202-232 3317) (wcg@ciponline.org) (www.ciponline.org). Previously the Project on Defense Alternatives.

USA

Community of Christ Peace and Justice Ministries (RP CR TW HR), 1001 W Walnut, Independence, MO 64050-3562 (+1-816-833 1000) (fax 521 3082) (shalom@CofChrist.org) (www.CofChrist.org/peacejustice). *Herald.*

Council for Responsible Genetics [CRG] (EL HR), 5 Upland Rd – Suite 3, Cambridge, MA 02140 (+1-617-868 0870) (fax 491 5344) (crg@gene-watch.org) (www.councilforresponsiblegenetics.org). *GeneWatch.*

Courage to Resist (WR HR), 484 Lake Park Ave – No 41, Oakland, CA 94610 (+1-510-488 3559) (www.couragetoresist.org). Supports public military refusers facing court.

Creative Response to Conflict [CRC] (FR CR PO), PO Box 271, Nyack, NY 10960-0271 (+1-845-353 1796) (fax 358 4924) (inquiries@crc-global.org) (crc-global.org).

Creativity for Peace (CD), 369 Montezuma Ave – No 566, Santa Fe, NM 87501 (+1-505-982 3765) (dottie@creativityforpeace.com) (www.creativityforpeace.com).

Cultural Survival [CS] (HR), 2067 Massachusetts Ave, Cambridge, MA 02140 (+1-617-441 5400) (fax 441 5417) (culturalsurvival@cs.org) (www.cs.org).

Culture Change (EL AL PO), PO Box 3387, Santa Cruz, CA 95063 (+1-215-243 3144) (fax) (info@culturechange.org) (www.culturechange.org). 4 yrly. Supports immediate cut in petrol cosumption.

Cumberland Center for Justice and Peace [CCJP] (CR HR RE EL), PO Box 307, Sewanee, TN 37375 (+1-931-636 7527) (contact@ccjp.org) (www.ccjp.org). *Local Action and Beyond.*

Death Penalty Information Center (HR RE), 1015 18th St NW – Suite 704, Washington, DC 20036 (+1-202-289 2275) (dpic@deathpenaltyinfo.org) (www.deathpenaltyinfo.org).

Democratic World Federalists (WF), 55 New Montgomery St – Suite 55, San Francisco, CA 94105 (+1-415-227 4880) (dwfed@dwfed.org) (www.dwfed.org).

Earthworks (EL HR), 1612 K St NW – Suite 904, Washington, DC 20006 (+1-202-887 1872) (fax 887 1875) (info@earthworksaction.org) (www.earthworksaction.org). Protecting communities from mining etc.

Ecumenical Accompaniment Programme in Palestine and Israel – USA [EAPPI-USA] (RP HR), c/o Steve Weaver, Church World Service, 475 Riverside Dr – Suite 700, New York, NY 10115 (info@eappi-us.org) (www.eappi-us.org).

Ecumenical Peace Institute / Clergy and Laity Concerned [EPI/CALC] (RP HR TW), PO Box 9334, Berkeley, CA 94709 (+1-510-990 0374) (epicalc@gmail.com) (www.epicalc.org).

Education for Peace in Iraq Center [EPIC] (CD HR RE), 1140 3rd St NE – Space 2138, Washington, DC 20002 (+1-202-747 6454) (info@epic-usa.org) (www.epic-usa.org). Founded by war veterans.

Educators for Peaceful Classrooms and Communities [EPCC] (RE), 520 Calabasas Rd, Watsonville, CA 95076 (www.educators-forpeacefulclassroomsandcommunities.org).

Environmentalists Against War (EL DA ND PA AT), PO Box 27, Berkeley, CA 94701 (+1-510-843 3343) (info@envirosagainstwar.org) (www.envirosagainstwar.org).

Episcopal Peace Fellowship [EPF] (FR CD), PO Box 15, Claysburg, PA 16625 (+1-312-922 8628) (epf@epfnational.org) (epfnational.org).

Equal Justice USA (HR), 20 Jay St – Suite 808, Brooklyn, NYC, NY 11201 (+1-718-801 8940) (fax 801 8947) (info@ejusa.org) (www.ejusa.org). Against executions.

Everytown for Gun Safety (DA), PO Box 4184, New York, NY 10163 (+1-646-324 8250) (info@everytown.org) (everytown.org). Working to end gun violence.

Farms Not Arms – Peace Roots Alliance [PRA] (DA EL), 425 Farm Rd – Suite 5, Summertown, TN 38483 (+1-931-964 2119) (fna_info@farmsnotarms.org) (www.farmsnotarms.org). Also West Coast office (+1-707-765 0196).

Fellowship for Intentional Community [FIC] (PO CR AL), 23 Dancing Rabbit Lane, Rutledge, MO 63563 (+1-660-883 5545) (fic@ic.org) (www.ic.org). *Communities.*

Fellowship of Reconciliation [FOR] (FR WR), 521 N Broaday, Nyack, NY 10960-0271 (+1-845-358 4601) (fax 358 4924) (communications@forusa.org) (www.forusa.org). *Fellowship.*

Food Not Bombs [FnB-US] (PA PO RA), PO Box 424, Arroyo Seco, NM 87514 (+1-575-770 3377) (menu@foodnotbombs.net) (www.foodnotbombs.net).

Footprints for Peace (ND EL), 1225 North Bend Rd, Cincinnati, OH 45224 (jim@footprintsforpeace.org) (www.footprintsforpeace.org).

Franciscan Action Network (RP EL HR), PO Box 29106, Washington, DC 20017 (+1-202-527 7575) (fax 527 7576) (info@franciscanaction.org) (franciscanaction.org).

Free Palestine Movement (HR), 405 Vista Heights Rd, El Cerrito, CA 94530 (+1-510-232 2500) (info@freepalestinemovement.org) (www.freepalestinemovement.org). Formerly Free Gaza Movement.

Fresno Center for Nonviolence (PA PO), 1584 N Van Ness Ave, Fresno, CA 93728 (+1-559-237 3223) (info@centerfornonviolence.org) (centerfornonviolence.org).

Friends for a Nonviolent World (PA PO CR), 1050 Selby Ave, Saint Paul, MN 55104 (+1-651-917 0383) (info@fnvw.org) (www.fnvw.org).

Friends of Peace Pilgrim (PO CR), PO Box 2207, Shelton, CT 06484-1841 (+1-203-926 1581) (friends@peacepilgrim.org) (www.peacepilgrim.org).

Friends of the Earth (FE), 1100 15th St NW – 11th Floor, Washington, DC 20005 (+1-202-783 7400) (fax 783 0444) (foe@foe.org) (www.foe.org).

Friends Peace Teams [FPT] (SF CR), 1001 Park Ave, St Louis, MO 63104 (+1-314-588 1122) (Office@FriendsPeaceTeams.org) (friendspeaceteams.org). *PeaceWays*.

Genocide Watch (HR RE), 3351 N Fairfax Dr – MS4D3, Arlington, VA 22201 (+1-202-643 1405) (fax 703-993 1302) (communications@genocidewatch.org) (www.genocidewatch.com).

Global Exchange (HR RE CD TW), 2017 Mission St – 2nd floor, San Francisco, CA 94110 (+1-415-255 7296) (fax 255 7498) (www.globalexchange.org). *Global Exchange*.

Global Family (CD WF RP), 17738 Minnow Way, Penn Valley, CA 95946 (www.globalfamily.org).

Global Green USA (EL AT CR), 1617 Broadway – 2nd floor, Santa Monica, CA 90404 (+1-310-581 2700) (fax 581 2702) (social@globalgreen.org) (www.globalgreen.org).

Global Majority (CR RE), 411 Pacific St – Suite 318, Monterey, CA 93940 (+1-831-372 5518) (fax 372 5519) (info@globalmajority.net) (globalmajority.org). Promoting peace through dialogue.

Global Meditations Network (CR PO), c/o Barbara Wolf, 218 Dartmouth St, Rochester, NY 14607 (bjwolf@globalmeditations.com) (www.globalmeditations.com).

Global Peace Foundation [GPF] (RP), 9320 Annapolis Rd – Suite 100, Lanham, MD 20706 (+1-202-643 4733) (fax -240-667 1709) (info@globalpeace.org) (www.globalpeace.org).

Global Security Institute [GSI] (ND RE WF), 220 East 49th St – Suite 1B, New York, NY 10017 (+1-646-289 5170) (fax 289 5171) (info@gsinstitute.org) (gsinstitute.org).

Global Witness (EL HR TW CR), 1100 17th St NW – Suite 501, Washington, DC 20036 (+1-202-827 8673) (www.globalwitness.org). Also in Britain.

GMO Free USA (EL), PO Box 458, Unionville, CT 06085 (info@gmofreeusa.org) (www.gmofreeusa.org).

Green Party of the United States (EL HR CD), PO Box 75075, Washington, DC 20013 (+1-202-319 7191) (info@gp.org) (www.gp.org).

Greenpeace USA (GP), 702 H St NW – Suite 300, Washington, DC 20001 (+1-202-462 1177) (fax 462 4507) (info@wdc.greenpeace.org) (www.greenpeace.org/usa). *Greenpeace*.

Ground Zero Center for Nonviolent Action (ND PA RA), 16159 Clear Creek Rd NW, Poulsbo, WA 98370 (+1-360-930 8697) (info@gzcenter.org) (gzcenter.org). *Ground Zero*.

Guatemala Human Rights Commission USA [GHRC] (HR), 3321 12th St NE, Washington, DC 20017 (+1-202-529 6599) (fax 526 4611) (ghrc-usa@ghrc-usa.org) (www.ghrc-usa.org). *El Quetzal*.

Hand in Hand (PO CD RE), PO Box 80102, Portland, OR 97280 (+1-503-892 2962) (info@handinhandk12.org) (www.handinhandk12.org). Supports integrated education in Israel.

Harmony for Peace Foundation (PO CD ND), PO Box 2165, Southeastern, PA 19399 (+1-484-885 8539) (info@harmonyforpeace.org) (harmonyforpeace.org). Music for peace. Works with group in Japan.

Historians for Peace and Democracy [H-PAD] (DA HR CR), c/o Van Gosse, Department of History, PO Box 3003, Franklin & Marshall College, Lancaster, PA 17604-3003 (www.historiansforpeace.org). Formerly Historians Against the War.

ICAHD-USA (HR), PO Box 81252, Pittsburgh, PA 15217 (info@icahdusa.org) (www.icahdusa.org).

Institute for Food and Development Policy / Food First (RE TW EL), 398 60th St, Oakland, CA 94618 (+1-510-654 4400) (fax 654 4551) (info@foodfirst.org) (www.foodfirst.org).

Institute for Inclusive Security (RE CR), 1615 M St NW – Suite 850, Washington, DC 20036 (+1-202-403 2000) (fax 808 7070) (info@inclusivesecurity.org) (www.inclusivesecurity.org). Promotes women's contributions to peacebuilding.

Institute for Middle East Understanding [IMEU] (RE CD), 2913 El Camino Real – No 436, Tustin, CA 92782 (+1-718-514 9662) (info@imeu.org) (imeu.org). Provides research and experts about Palestine.

Institute for Social Ecology (EL AL PO), PO Box 48, Plainfield, VT 05667 (info@social-ecology.org) (www.social-ecology.org).

Interfaith Peace-Builders (RP CD CR), 1628 16th St NW, Washington, DC 20009 (+1-202-244 0821) (fax -866-936 1650) (office@ifpb.org) (www.ifpb.org). Send delegations to Israel/Palestine.

USA

International Center for Transitional Justice [ICTJ] (CR HR), 50 Broadway – 23rd Floor, New York, NY 10004 (+1-917-637 3800) (fax 637 3900) (info@ictj.org) (www.ictj.org). Offices in Europe, Asia, Africa, South America.

International Center on Nonviolent Conflict [ICNC] (RE SD), 1775 Pennsylvania Ave NW – Ste 1200, Washington, DC 20006 (+1-202-416 4720) (fax 466 5918) (icnc@nonviolent-conflict.org) (www.nonviolent-conflict.org).

International Rivers (FE HR), 2150 Allston Way – Suite 300, Berkeley, CA 94704-1378 (+1-510-848 1155) (fax 848 1008) (info@internationalrivers.org) (www.internationalrivers.org). *World Rivers Review.*

Israeli-Palestinian Confederation Committee (CD CR), 15915 Ventura Blvd – No 302, Encino, CA 91436 (+1-818-317 7110) (mail@aboutipc.org) (www.aboutipc.org).

Jewish Peace Fellowship [JPF] (FR), PO Box 271, Nyack, NY 10960-0271 (+1-845-358 4601) (fax 358 4924) (jpf@forusa.org) (www.jewishpeacefellowship.org). *Shalom.*

Jewish Voice for Peace [JVP] (HR RA), 1611 Telegraph Ave – Suite 1020, Oakland, CA 94612 (+1-510-465 1777) (fax 465 1616) (info@jvp.org) (jewishvoiceforpeace.org). Promotes US policy based on human rights.

JustPeace – Center for Mediation and Conflict Transformation (CR RE RP), 100 Maryland Ave NE, Washington, DC 20002 (+1-202-488 5647) (justpeace@justpeaceumc.org) (justpeaceumc.org).

Kansas Institute for Peace and Conflict Resolution [KIPCOR] (RE CR), Bethel College, 300 E 27th St, North Newton, KS 67117 (+1-316-284 5217) (fax 284 5379) (kipcor@bethelks.edu) (www.kipcor.org). Formerly Kansas Peace Institute.

Karuna Center for Peacebuilding [KCP] (CR HR RE), 447 West St, Amherst, MA 01002 (+1-413-256 3800) (fax 256 3802) (info@karunacenter.org) (www.karunacenter.org).

Law Center to Prevent Gun Violence (DA), 268 Bush St – No 555, San Francisco, CA 94104 (+1-415-433 2062) (fax 433 3357) (smartgunlaws.org).

Lawyers' Committee on Nuclear Policy [LCNP] (ND AT DA), 866 UN Plaza – Suite 4050, New York, NY 10017-1830 (+1-212-818 1861) (fax 818 1857) (contact@lcnp.org) (www.lcnp.org).

Los Angeles Peace Council [LAPC] (WP), PO Box 741104, Los Angeles, CA 90004 (+1-323-498 0973) (lapeacecouncil@outlook.com) (www.lapeacecouncil.org).

Lutheran Peace Fellowship [LPF] (RP), 1710 11th Ave, Seattle, WA 98122-2420 (+1-206-349 2501) (lpf@ecunet.org) (www.lutheranpeace.org).

Mahatma Gandhi Center for Global Nonviolence (RE), James Madison University, MSC 2604, The Annex, 725 S Mason St, Harrisonburg, VA 22807 (+1-540-568 4060) (fax 568 7251) (GandhiCenter@jmu.edu) (www.jmu.edu/gandhicenter).

Mahatma Gandhi Library (RE), c/o Atul Kothari, 4526 Bermuda Dr, Sugar Land, TX 77479 (+1-281-531 1977) (fax 713-785 6252) (info@gandhilibrary.org) (www.gandhilibrary.org).

Maryknoll Office for Global Concerns (PC EL RE), 200 New York Ave NW, Washington, DC 20001 (+1-202-832 1780) (fax 832 5195) (ogc@maryknoll.org) (www.maryknoll.org).

Maryland United for Peace and Justice [MUPJ] (DA HR CR), c/o Tony Langbehn, 327 E 25th St, Baltimore, MD 21218 (+1-301-390 9684) (tonylang4peace@gmail.com) (www.mupj.org).

Matsunaga Institute for Peace and Conflict Resolution (RE CR), University of Hawaii, 2424 Maile Way – Saunders 723, Honolulu, HI 96822 (+1-808-956 4237) (fax 956 0950) (uhip@hawaii.edu) (peaceinstitute.hawaii.edu).

Metta Center for Nonviolence (RE), 205 Keller St – Suite 202D, Petaluma, CA 94952 (+1-707-774 6299) (info@mettacenter.org) (mettacenter.org).

Mid-South Peace & Justice Center (IB ND EL), 3573 Southern Ave, Memphis, TN 38111 (+1-901-725 4990) (centre@midsouthpeace.org) (midsouthpeace.org).

Middle East Research & Information Project [MERIP] (TW HR AT), 1344 T St NW – No 1, Washington, DC 20009 (+1-202-223 3677) (fax 223 3604) (www.merip.org). *Middle East Report.*

Minds of Peace (CR), PO Box 11494, St Louis, MO 63105-9998 (peace.public@gmail.com) (mindsofpeace.org). Helps discussions in divided communities.

Minnesota Alliance of Peacemakers (FR UN WL PC), PO Box 19573, Minneapolis, MN 55419 (info@mapm.org) (www.mapm.org). Umbrella group of many local organisations.

MK Gandhi Institute for Nonviolence (RE), 929 S Plymouth Ave, Rochester, NY 14608 (+1-585-463 3266) (fax 276 0203) (kmiller@admin.rochester.edu) (www.gandhiinstitute.org).

Murder Victims' Families for Human Rights (HR CR RE PO), 2161 Massachusetts Ave, Cambridge, MA 02140 (+1-617-491 9600) (info@murdervictimsfamilies.org) (www.mvfhr.org). Oppose death penalty.

Musicians and Fine Artists for World Peace [MFAWP] (PO CD), 3274 Andrea St – Apt C, Las Vegas, NV 89102 (+1-415-424 7238) (bflyspirit8@aol.com) (www.reverbnation.com/musiciansforpeace).

National Campaign for a Peace Tax Fund [NCPTF] (TR), 2121 Decatur Pl NW, Washington, DC 20008 (+1-202-483 3751) (info@peacetaxfund.org) (www.peacetaxfund.org). *Peace Tax Fund Update.*

National Campaign for Nonviolent Resistance (RA), 325 E 25th St, Baltimore, MD 21218 (+1-410-366 1637) (mobuszewski@verizon.net). Co-ordinates anti-war trainings and actions.

National Coalition Against Censorship [NCAC] (HR), 19 Fulton St – Suite 407, New York, NY 10038 (+1-212-807 6222) (fax 807 6245) (ncac@ncac.org) (ncac.org). Alliance of over 50 national organisations.

National Coalition to Abolish the Death Penalty [NCADP] (HR), 1620 L St NW – Suite 250, Washington, DC 20036 (+1-202-331 4090) (info@ncadp.org) (www.ncadp.org).

National Network Opposing the Militarization of Youth [NNOMY] (DA PO), c/o AFSC Wage Peace Program, 65 Ninth St, San Francisco, CA 94103 (+1-760-634 3604) (admin@nnomy.org) (www.nnomy.org).

National Peace Academy [NPA] (RE), PO Box 2024, San Mateo, CA 94401 (+1-650-918 6901) (nationalpeaceacademy.us).

National War Tax Resistance Coordinating Committee [NWTRCC] (TR RA PA), PO Box 150553, Brooklyn, NY 11215 (+1-718-768 3420) (nwtrcc@nwtrcc.org) (www.nwtrcc.org). *More Than a Paycheck.*

Natural Resources Defense Council [NRDC] (EL), 40 West 20th St, New York, NY 10011 (+1-212-727 2700) (fax 727 1773) (nrdcinfo@nrdc.org) (www.nrdc.org). Works to protect planet's wildlife and wild places.

Network of Spiritual Progressives [NSP] (RP PO), 2342 Shattuck Av – Suite 1200, Berkeley, CA 94704 (+1-510-644 1200) (fax 644 1255) (www.tikkun.org). *Tikkun.*

Nevada Desert Experience [NDE] (RP ND DA RA), 1420 West Bartlett Ave, Las Vegas, NV 89106-2226 (+1-702-646 4814) (info@nevadadesertexperience.org) (www.nevadadesertexperience.org). *Desert Voices.*

New Israel Fund (HR), 6 East 39th St, New York, NY 10016-0112 (+1-212-613 4400) (fax 714 2153) (info@nif.org) (www.nif.org). Supports progressive civil society in Israel.

Nicaragua Solidarity Network (TW HR), PO Box 10587, Tompkins Square Station, New York, NY 10009 (weeklynewsupdate.blogspot.com). *Weekly News Update on the Americas.*

Nobel Peace Laureate Project (RE), PO Box 21201, Eugene, OR 97402 (+1-541-485 1604) (info@nobelpeacelaureates.org) (www.nobelpeacelaureates.org). Promote peace by honouring peacemakers.

North American Congress on Latin America [NACLA] (TW HR), c/o NYU CLACS, 53 Washington Sq South – Fl 4W, New York, NY 10012 (+1-646-535 9085) (nacla.org). *Report on the Americas.*

North American Vegetarian Society (EL PO), PO Box 72, Dolgeville, NY 13329 (+1-518-568 7970) (fax 568 7979) (navs@telenet.net). *Vegetarian Voice.*

Nuclear Age Peace Foundation [NAPF] (PA ND IB RE), PMB 121, 1187 Coast Village Rd – Suite 1, Santa Barbara, CA 93108-2794 (+1-805-965 3443) (fax 568 0466) (wagingpeace@napf.org) (www.wagingpeace.org). *The Sunflower.*

Nuclear Ban – Treaty Compliance Campaign (ND), 59 Gleason Rd, Northampton, MA 01060 (+1-413-329 3778) (info@nuclearban.us) (www.nuclearban.us). Supporting 2018 UN nuclear weapons ban treaty.

Nuclear Energy Information Service [NEIS] (EL RA), 3411 W Diversey Ave – No 13, Chicago, IL 60647 (+1-773-342 7650) (neis@neis.org) (neis.org). Educates about and campaigns against nuclear power.

Nuclear Information and Resource Service [NIRS] (EL ND), 6930 Carroll Ave – Suite 340, Takoma Park, MD 20912 (+1-301-270 6477) (fax 270 4291) (timj@nirs.org) (www.nirs.org). *WISE/NIRS Nuclear Monitor.* Works with WISE, Amsterdam, to provide information.

Nuclear Resister (ND RA TR PA), PO Box 43383, Tucson, AZ 85733 (+1-520-323 8697) (fax) (nukeresister@igc.org) (www.nukeresister.org). 4 yrly, $25 ($35 abroad) pa.

Nuclear Threat Initiative [NTI] (ND), 1776 Eye St NW – Suite 600, Washington, DC 20006 (+1-202-296 4810) (fax 296 4811) (contact@nti.org) (www.nti.org).

Nuclear Watch South (EL ND), PO Box 8574, Atlanta, GA 31106 (+1-404-378 4263) (info@nonukesyall.org) (www.nonukesyall.org). *Nuclear Watch Tower.*

Nukewatch (EL ND RA PA RE), 740A Round Lake Rd, Luck, WI 54853 (+1-715-472 4185) (nukewatch1@lakeland.ws) (www.nukewatchinfo.org). *Nukewatch Quarterly.*

Oak Ridge Environmental Peace Alliance (ND RA), PO Box 5743, Oak Ridge, TN 37831 (+1-865-483 8202) (orep@earthlink.net) (www.orepa.org).

On Earth Peace (RP), PO Box 188, 500 Main St, New Windsor, MD 21776 (+1-410-635 8704) (onearthpeace.org). Linked to Church of the Brethren.

USA

OneVoice Movement – USA (CD CR), PO Box 1577-OCS, New York, NY 10113 (+1-212-897 3985) (info@OneVoiceMovement.org) (www.onevoicemovement.org). See also under Israel, Palestine, and Britain.

Orthodox Peace Fellowship [OPF] (RP), PO Box 76609, Washingtgon, DC 20013 (opfnorthamerica@gmail.com) (incommunion.org).

Pace e Bene (RP PA), PO Box 2460, Athens, OH 45701-5260 (+1-510-268 8765) (fax 702-648 2281) (info@paceebene.org) (www.paceebene.org). For nonviolence and cultural transformation.

Pathways to Peace (CD RE), PO Box 1057, Larkspur, CA 94977 (+1-415-461 0500) (fax 925 0330) (info@pathwaystopeace.org) (www.pathwaystopeace.org).

Pax Christi USA (PC CD EL), 415 Michigan Ave NE – Suite 240, Washington, DC 20017-4503 (+1-202-635 2741) (info@paxchristiusa.org) (www.paxchristiusa.org).

Peace & Justice Program of the United Methodist Church (RP), c/o General Board of Global Ministries, 475 Riverside Drive, New York, NY 10115 (info@gbgm-umc.org) (new.gbgm-umc.org).

Peace Abbey Foundation (RP PA RE), 16 Lavender St, Millis, MA 02054 (+1-508-655 2143) (administration@peaceabbey.org) (www.peaceabbey.org). Includes Pacifist Living History Museum.

Peace Action (IB ND AT), Montgomery Center, 8630 Fenton St – Suite 524, Silver Spring, MD 20910 (+1-301-565 4050) (fax 562 7305) (kmartin@peace-action.org) (peace-action.org).

Peace Action West (ND DA), 2201 Broadway – Suite 321, Oakland, CA 94612 (+1-510-849 2272) (www.peaceactionwest.org).

Peace and Justice Studies Association [PJSA] (RE), 1421 37th St NW – Suite 130, Poulton Hall, Georgetown University, Washington, DC 20057 (+1-202-681 2057) (info@peacejusticestudies.org) (www.peacejusticestudies.org).

Peace Brigades International [PBI-USA] (PA RA CR), PO Box 75880, Washington, DC 20013 (+1-202-232 0142) (fax 232 0143) (info@pbiusa.org) (pbiusa.org).

Peace Development Fund [PDF] (HR EL PA), PO Box 40250, San Francisco, CA 94140-0250 (+1-415-642 0900) (peacedevfund@gmail.com) (www.peacedevelopmentfund.org). *Peace Developments.* Also PDF Center for Peace and Justice, Amherst, MA.

Peace Education and Action Centre of Eastern Iowa (RE DA), Old Brick, 26 East Market St, Iowa City, IA 52245 (+1-319-354 1925) (information@PEACEIowa.net) (peaceiowa.org).

Peace Educators Allied for Children Everywhere [PEACE] (WR RE EL), 55 Frost St, Cambridge, MA 02140 (+1-617-661 8374) (1peaceeducators@gmail.com) (www.peaceeducators.org). Network of parents, teachers and others.

PeaceJam Foundation (RE CR HR), 11200 Ralston Rd, Arvada, CO 80004 (+1-303-455 2099) (rockymoutain@peacejam.org) (peacejam.org). Also in Maine (maine@peacejam.org).

Peaceworkers (CR CD PA RA SD), 721 Shrader St, San Francisco, CA 94117 (+1-415-751 0302) (fax) (davidrhartsough@gmail.com) (www.peaceworkersus.org). Promote international peace teams.

Physicians Committee for Responsible Medicine [PCRM] (PO), 5100 Wisconsin Av NW – Suite 400, Washington, DC 20016 (+1-202-686 2210) (fax 686 2216) (pcrm@pcrm.org) (www.pcrm.org). *Good Medicine.*

Physicians for Human Rights [PHR] (HR), 256 W 38th St – 9th Floor, New York, NY 10018 (+1-646-564 3720) (fax 564 3750) (communications@phrusa.org) (physiciansforhumanrights.org). Also offices in Washington DC amd Boston.

Physicians for Social Responsibility [PSR] (IP), 1111 14th St NW – Suite 700, Washington, DC 20005 (+1-202-667 4260) (fax 667 4201) (psrnatl@psr.org) (www.psr.org).

Ploughshares Fund (ND), 1808 Wedemeyer St – Suite 200, The Presidio of San Francisco, San Francisco, CA 94129 (+1-415-668 2244) (fax 668 2214) (ploughshares@ploughshares.org) (www.ploughshares.org). Promoting elimination of nuclear weapons.

Plowshares Network (RP RA ND PA), c/o Jonah House, 1301 Moreland Av, Baltimore, MD 21216 (+1-410-233 6238) (disarmnow@verizon.net) (www.jonahhouse.org).

Popular Resistance (RA HR EL), c/o Alliance for Global Justice, 225 E 26th St – Suite 1, Tucson, AZ 85713 (info@popularresistance.org) (popularresistance.org). Against corporate takeover of government.

Positive Futures Network, 284 Madrona Way NE – Suite 116, Bainbridge Island, WA 98110-2870 (+1-206-842 0216) (fax 842 5208) (info@yesmagazine.org) (www.yesmagazine.org). *Yes!.*

Presbyterian Peace Fellowship [PPF] (FR), 17 Cricketown Rd, Stony Point, NY 10980 (+1-845-786 6743) (info@presbypeacefellowship.org) (www.presbypeacefellowship.org).

Project on Youth and Non-Military Opportunities [Project YANO] (RE PA), PO Box 230157, Encinitas, CA 92023 (+1-760-634 3604) (projyano@aol.com) (www.projectyano.org).

Promoting Enduring Peace [PEP] (DA EL PA), 323 Temple St, New Haven, CT 06511-6602 (+1-202-573 7322) (coordinator@pepeace.org) (www.pepeace.org).

Proposition One Campaign (ND AT), 401 Wilcox Rd, Tryon, NC 28782 (+1-202-210 3886) (et@prop1.org) (prop1.org). For nuclear weapons abolition.

Psychologists for Social Responsibility [PsySR] (ND RE CR), c/o Brad Olsen, 122 S Michigan Ave, National Louis University, Chicago, IL 60603 (+1-917-626 7571) (fax 312-261 3464) (info@psysr.org) (psysr.org).

Quaker House (SF RE), 223 Hillside Ave, Fayetteville, NC 28301 (+1-910-323 3912) (qpr@quaker.org) (www.quakerhouse.org). Work includes counselling disaffected soldiers.

Rainforest Action Network [RAN] (FE RA HR), 425 Bush St – Ste 300, San Francisco, CA 94108 (+1-415-398 4404) (fax 398 2732) (answers@ran.org) (www.ran.org).

Random Acts of Kindness Foundation [RAK] (CD CR PO), 1727 Tremont Pl, Denver, CO 80202 (+1-303-297 1964) (fax 297 2919) (info@randomactsofkindness.org) (www.randomactsofkindness.org).

Refuser Solidarity Network (PA HR), PO Box 75392, Washington, DC 20013 (+1-202-232 1100) (info@refusersolidarity.net) (www.refusersolidarity.net). Supports Israeli COs and resisters.

Religions for Peace USA (RE RP CR HR), 777 UN Plaza – 9th floor, New York, NY 10017 (+1-212-338 9140) (fax 983 0098) (rfpusa@rfpusa.org) (www.rfpusa.org).

Renounce War Projects (RP PA), 8001 Geary Blvd, San Francisco, CA 94121 (+1-415-307 1213) (peacematters@renouncewarprojects.org) (renouncewarprojects.org). Promotes Gandhian ideals.

Reprieve US (HR), PO Box 3627, New York, NY 10163 (+1-917-855 8064) (info@reprieve.org) (www.reprieve.org). Supports people facing death penalty.

Resistance Studies Initiative – Critical Support of People Power and Social Change (RE RA WR), University of Massachusetts Department of Sociology, 200 Hicks Way – Thompson Hall, Amherst, MA 01003-9277 (+1-413-545 5957) (fax 545 3204) (resist@umass.edu) (www.umass.edu/resistancestudies).

Resource Center for Nonviolence [RCNV] (WR FR HR), 612 Ocean St, Santa Cruz, CA (+1-831-423 1626) (rcnvinfo@gmail.com) (rcnv.org).

Rising Tide North America [RTA] (EL RA), 268 Bush St – Box 3717, San Francisco, CA 94101 (+1-503-438 4697) (networking@risingtidenorthamerica.org) (risingtidenorthamerica.org). Network of groups working on climate change.

Rocky Mountain Peace and Justice Centre (ND PA RE), PO Box 1156, Boulder, CO 80306 (+1-303-444 6981) (fax 720-565 9755) (www.rmpjc.org).

Ruckus Society (RA), PO Box 28741, Oakland, CA 94604 (+1-510-931 6339) (fax 866-778 6374) (ruckus@ruckus.org) (www.ruckus.org). Tools and training for direct action.

Salam Institute for Peace & Justice (RE RP CR HR), 1628 16th St NW, Washington, DC 20009 (+1-202-360 4955) (info@salaminstitute.org) (salaminstitute.org).

San José Peace & Justice Center, 48 South 7th St, San Jose, CA 95112 (+1-408-297 2299) (sjpjc@sanjosepeace.org) (www.sanjosepeace.org).

Satyagraha Institute (RP PA PO), c/o Carl Kline, 825 Fourth St, Brookings, SD 57006 (www.satyagrahainstitute.org). Promotes understanding of satyagraha.

School of the Americas Watch [SOA Watch] (HR), 5525 Illinois Ave NW, Washington, DC 20011 (+1-202-234 3440) (info@soaw.org) (www.soaw.org).

Secular Coalition for America (HR), 1012 14th St NW – No 205, Washington, DC 20005 (+1-202-299 1091) (www.secular.org).

Seeds of Peace (CD CR PO), 370 Lexington Ave – Suite 1201, New York, NY 10017 (+1-212-573 8040) (fax 573 8047) (info@seedsofpeace.org) (www.seedsofpeace.org). Brings together teenagers from conflict areas.

September 11th Families for Peaceful Tomorrows [PT] (CD CR RE), PO Box 20145, Park West Finance Station, New York, NY 10025 (+1-212-598 0970) (info@peacefultomorrows.org) (peacefultomorrows.org). Promote nonviolent resolution of conflict.

Service Civil International / International Voluntary Service [SCI-IVS USA] (SC), PO Box 1082, Great Barrington, MA 01230 (+1-413-591 8050) (fax 434-366 3545) (sciivs.usa.ltv@gmail.com) (www.volunteersciusa.org).

Sikh Human Rights Group (HR CR), 103 Omar Ave, Evenel, NJ 07001 (shrgusa@shrg.net) (shrg.net).

States United to Prevent Gun Violence (DA RE), PO Box 1359, New York, NY 10276-1359 (info@supgv.org) (www.ceasefireusa.org). 30 affiliates.

For explanation of codes and abbreviations, see introduction

USA

Swarthmore College Peace Collection (RE), 500 College Ave, Swarthmore, PA 19081 (+1-610-328 8557) (fax 328 8544) (wchmiel1@swarthmore.edu) (www.swarthmore.edu/Library/peace). Also houses Global Nonviolent Action Database.

Syracuse Cultural Workers (HR PA EL PO), PO Box 6367, Syracuse, NY 13217 (+1-315-474 1132) (fax 234 0930) (scw@syracuseculturalworkers.com) (www.syracuseculturalworkers.com). *Peace Calendar, Women Artists Datebook.* Also posters, cards, T-shirts, books.

Syracuse Peace Council (PA EL RA), 2013 East Genesee St, Syracuse, NY 13210 (+1-315-472 5478) (spc@peacecouncil.net) (www.peacecouncil.net).

Teachers Resisting Unhealthy Children's Entertainment [TRUCE] (RE PO), 160 Lakeview Ave, Cambridge, MA 02138 (truce@truceteachers.org) (www.truceteachers.org).

The Progressive (HR), 30 W Mifflin St – Suite 703, Madison, WI 53703 (+1-608-257 4626) (editorial@progressive.org) (www.progressive.org). Mthly, $32 ($80 abroad) pa.

Torture Abolition and Survivor Support Coalition [TASSC] (HR AT CR), 4121 Harewood Rd NE – Suite B, Washington, DC 20017 (+1-202-529 2991) (fax 529 8334) (info@tassc.org) (www.tassc.org).

Training for Change (RA RE PO), PO Box 30914, Philadelphia, PA 19104 (+1-267-289 2288) (info@trainingforchange.org) (www.trainingforchange.org).

Tri-Valley CAREs (ND EL), 2582 Old First St, Livermore, CA 94550 (+1-925-443 7148) (fax 443 0177) (marylia@earthlink.net) (www.trivalleycares.org). *Citizen's Watch.* Communities Against a Radioactive Environment.

United for Peace and Justice [UFPJ] (DA), 244 Fifth Ave – Suite D55, New York, NY 10001 (+1-917-410 0119) (info.ufpj@gmail.com) (www.unitedforpeace.org). Major coalition.

United National Antiwar Coalition [UNAC] (DA), PO Box 123, Delmar, NY 12054 (+1-518-227 6947) (UNACpeace@gmail.com) (www.UNACpeace.org).

United Nations Association of the USA [UNA-USA] (UN RE), 801 Second Avenue, New York, NY 10017-4706 (fax +1-212-697 3316) (membership@unausa.org) (www.unausa.org). Also in Washington DC (+1-202-854 2360).

United States Institute of Peace [USIP] (RE), 2301 Constitution Ave NW, Washington, DC 20037 (+1-202-457 1700) (fax 429 6063) (www.usip.org). *Peace Watch.* Officially funded.

US Campaign for Burma (HR), PO Box 34126, Washington, DC 20043 (+1-202-702 1161) (fax 234 8044) (info@uscampaignforburma.org) (www.uscampaignforburma.org).

US Campaign for Palestinian Rights [USCPR] (HR), PO Box 3609, Washington, DC 20027 (uscpr.org). Formerly US Campaign to End the Israeli Occupation.

US Climate Action Network (EL RA), 50 F St NW – 8th floor, Washington, DC 20001 (+1-202-495 3046) (fax 547 6009) (www.usclimatenetwork.org).

US Peace Memorial Foundation (RE PA), 334 East Lake Rd – Unit 136, Palm Harbor, FL 34685-2427 (+1-202-455 8776) (info@USPeaceMemorial.org) (www.uspeacememorial.org). Produces US Peace Registry.

US Servas (SE), 1125 16th St – Suite 201, Arcata, CA 95521-5585 (+1-707-825 1714) (fax 825 1762) (info@usservas.org) (usservas.org). *Open Doors.*

Veterans For Peace [VFP] (DA PA RA), 1404 North Broadway, St Louis, MO 63102 (+1-314-725 6005) (fax 227 1981) (vfp@veteransforpeace.org) (www.veteransforpeace.org).

Voices for Creative Nonviolence (PA), 1249 W Argyle St – No 2, Chicago, IL 60640 (+1-773-878 3815) (info@vcnv.org) (vcnv.org).

Volunteers for Peace [VFP] (WC HR PO CD EL), 7 Kilburn St – Ste 316, Burlington, VT 05410 (+1-802-540 3040) (info@vfp.org) (www.vfp.org).

Waging Nonviolence, PO Box 180369, Brooklyn, New York, NY 11218 (contact@wagingnonviolence.org) (wagingnonviolence.org). Internet-based resource.

War Resisters League [WRL] (WR IB TR AT), 168 Canal St – 6th Floor, New York, NY 10013 (+1-212-228 0450) (fax 228 6193) (wrl@warresisters.org) (www.warresisters.org).

War Resisters League – New England Regional Office (WR), PO Box 1093, Norwich, CT 06360 (+1-860-639 8834) (joanne@warresisters.org) (www.warresisters.org/new-england-office).

Washington Peace Center (HR PA RE), 1525 Newton St NW, Washington, DC 20010 (+1-202-234 2000) (fax 558 5685) (info@washingtonpeacecenter.org) (washingtonpeacecenter.net).

Win Without War, 2000 M St NW – Suite 720, Washington, DC 20036 (+1-202-232 3317) (info@winwithoutwar.org) (winwithoutwar.org). Coalition engaging mainstream who want a safe USA.

Witness Against Torture (RP HR), c/o New York Catholic Worker, 55 East 3rd St, New York, NY 10003 (www.witnessagainsttorture.com). Campaign to close Guantanamo and end torture.

Witness for Peace [WfP] (RP HR TW), 1616 P St NW – Suite 100, Washington, DC 20036 (+1-202-547 6112) (fax 536 4708) (witness@witnessforpeace.org) (www.witnessforpeace.org)

Women for Genuine Security (CD PA), 965 62nd St, Oakland, CA 94608 (+1-415-312 5583) (info@genuinesecurity.org) (www.genuinesecurity.org).

Women's Environment and Development Organization [WEDO] (TW EL HR), 355 Lexington Av – 3rd floor, New York, NY 10017 (+1-212-973 0325) (wedo@wedo.org) (www.wedo.org).

Women's International League for Peace and Freedom – US Section [WILPF US] (WL HR), AFSC House, PO Box 13075, Des Moines, IA 50310 (+1-617-266 0999) (info@wilpf.org) (wilpfus.org). *Peace and Freedom*.

Working Group for Peace and Demilitarization in Asia & the Pacific (DA RE), 2161 Massachusetts Ave, Cambridge, MA 02141 (+1-617-661 6130) (info@asiapacificinitiative.org) (www.asiapacificinitiative.org).

World Beyond War (PA DA), PO Box 1484, Charlottesville, VA 22902 (research@worldbeyondwar.org) (worldbeyondwar.org).

World Can't Wait (DA HR), 305 West Broadway – No 185, New York, NY 10013 (1-866-973 4463) (info@worldcantwait.org) (www.worldcantwait.net). "Putting humanity and the planet first".

World Future Society (PO), 333 N LaSalle St, Chicago, IL 60654 (info@wfs.org) (wfs.site-ym.com). Clearinghouse for ideas about the future.

World Peace Now (CD ND DA), PO Box 275, Point Arena, CA 95468 (ellen.rosser@gmail.com). Formerly Friendship and Peace Society.

Worldwatch Institute (EL TW, 1400 16th St NW – Suite 430, Washington, DC 20036 (+1-202-745 8092) (fax 478 2534) (worldwatch@worldwatch.org) (www.worldwatch.org). Europe office in Copenhagen (+45-2087 1933).

URUGUAY

Amnistía Internacional Uruguay (AI), Wilson Ferreira Aldunate 1220, Montevideo 11100 (+598-2-900 7939) (fax 900 9851) (oficina@amnistia.org.uy) (www.amnistia.org.uy).

SERPAJ-Uruguay (FR RE HR), Joaquín Requena 1642, 11200 Montevideo (+598-2-408 5301) (fax 408 5701) (serpajuy@serpaj.org.uy) (www.serpaj.org.uy).

UZBEKISTAN

"Esperanto" Xalqaro Do'stlik Klubi / International Friendship Club "Esperanto" (CD), c/o PO Box 76, 703000 Samarkand (+998-66-233 1753).

Servas (SE), c/o PO Box 76, 140100 Samarkand (+998-66-233 1753) (imps86@yahoo.com).

Xalqaro Tinchlik va Birdamlik Muzei / Internacia Muzeo de Paco kaj Solidaro (IB RE CD), PO Box 76, 140100 Samarkand (+998-66-233 1753) (fax) (imps86@yahoo.com) (peace.museum.com). International Museum of Peace and Solidarity.

VENEZUELA

Programa Venezolnao de Educación-Acción en Derechos Humanos [PROVEA] (HR), Apdo Postal 5156, Carmelitas 1010-A, Caracas (+58-212-862 1011) (fax) (www.derechos.org.ve).

VIETNAM

Vietnam Peace Committee [VPC] (WP), 105a Quan Thanh, Ba Dinh, Ha Noi (+84-4-3945 4272) (fax 3733 0201) (vietpeacecom@gmail.com).

ZAMBIA

International Friendship League – Zambia [IFL] (CD), c/o G Siluyele, PO Box 234, Chongwe.

OneWorld Africa [OWA] (TW), PO Box 37011, Lusaka (+260-21-129 2740) (fax 129 4188) (priscilla.jere@oneworld.net) (africa.oneworld.net). Part of OneWorld Network, in 11 countries.

Zambian Health Workers for Social Responsibility [ZHSR] (IP), c/o Department of Medicine, School of Medicine, PO Box 50110, Lusaka (bobmtonga@hotmail.com).

ZIMBABWE

Gays and Lesbians of Zimbabwe [GALZ] (WR HR), Private Bag A6131, Avondale, Harare (+263-4-741736) (fax 778165) (director@galz.co.zw). *Galzette*.

Practical Action Southern Africa (EL TW PO), 4 Ludlow Road, off Enterprise Road, Newlands, Harare (+263-4-776631) (fax 788157) (info@practicalaction.org.zw) (practicalaction.org/southern-africa). Formerly Intermediate Technology Development Group.

Society of Friends (SF), 3 Vincent Ave, Belvedere, Harare (+263-4-778028) (rknottenbelt621@gmail.com).

Women of Zimbabwe Arise [WOZA] (HR), PO Box FM701, Famona, Bulawayo (info@wozazimbabwe.org) (wozazimbabwe.org).

Zimbabwe Human Rights NGO Forum (HR), PO Box 9077, 8th Floor, Bluebridge, Eastgate, Harare (+263-4-250511) (fax 250494) (admin@hrforum.co.zw) (www.hrforumzim.com).

Zimbabwe Lawyers for Human Rights [ZLHR] (HR), Box CY 1393, Causeway, Harare (+263-4-764085) (fax 705641) (info@zlhr.org.zw) (www.zlhr.org.zw).

Notes

Notes

Notes

Notes

Notes

PEACE DIARY 2020

The 2020 Peace Diary should be available from the organisation or bookshop where you bought this Diary, or can be ordered direct from Housmans Bookshop in September 2019. For information about 2020 prices, and other details, contact Housmans in the summer of 2019, or see www.housmans.com/diary.php.